CONVERSATIONS WITH
MAJOR DICK WINTERS

Also by Cole C. Kingseed

CONVERSATIONS WITH
MAJOR DICK WINTERS

★ ★ ★

Life Lessons from the Commander of the Band of Brothers

Colonel Cole C. Kingseed

BERKLEY CALIBER, NEW YORK

THE BERKLEY PUBLISHING GROUP
Published by the Penguin Group
Penguin Group (USA) LLC
375 Hudson Street, New York, New York 10014

USA • Canada • UK • Ireland • Australia • New Zealand • India • South Africa • China

penguin.com

A Penguin Random House Company

This book is an original publication of The Berkley Publishing Group.

CONVERSATIONS WITH MAJOR DICK WINTERS

Grateful acknowledgement is made to Harold Mohn for permission to reprint the poem "Edelweiss."

BERKLEY CALIBER and its logos are registered trademarks of Penguin Group (USA) LLC

An application to register this book for cataloging has been submitted to the Library of Congress.

ISBN: 978-0-425-27153-7

First edition: November 2014

PRINTED IN THE UNITED STATES OF AMERICA

10 9 8 7 6 5 4

While the author has made every effort to provide accurate telephone numbers and Internet
addresses at the time of publication, neither the author nor the publisher is responsible for errors,
or for changes that occur after publication. Further, the publisher does not have any control over
and does not assume any responsibility for author or third-party websites or their content.

Penguin is committed to publishing works of quality and integrity.
In that spirit, we are proud to offer this book to our readers;
however, the story, the experiences, and the words are the author's alone.

To the memory of

Chief Commissaryman William B. Kingseed, Jr., U.S. Navy (Ret.)
and
Lieutenant General Hal Moore, U.S. Army (Ret.),
the finest sailor and the best soldier I have ever known.

Now, as I look back,
they loom larger than ever.

CONTENTS

Contents

PART FOUR Winter

AUTHOR'S NOTE

I am generally skeptical of any author who puts within quotation marks conversations he never heard or who pretends to recollect with absolute fidelity conversations he heard many years ago. I, too, am guilty of some reconstruction, but the conversations with Major Dick Winters that appear in this book are as I best remember them. There are a few conversations in which I did not participate and others that I heard firsthand more than fifteen years ago. The former conversations are based on the memory of mutual friends who shared their recollections with me to provide the reader with a fuller understanding of Major Winters. In the latter conversations, the key phrases appear as I meticulously recorded them in my journal within days of my visits with the major. Additionally, the candid conversations outlined in the forthcoming pages follow a more thematic than chronological order; hence within each chapter the dialogue quoted often transpired over repeated sessions with Dick Winters and was not confined to a single visit. Consequently, I urge the reader to exercise some discretion in accepting with absolute certainty every word that is recorded and to take my recollections with the necessary grain of salt.

FOREWORD

Aside from an occasional short wrap-up on the national network news stations and an Associated Press release that appeared in the obituary section of Harrisburg, Pennsylvania's *Patriot-News* on January 10, 2011, I suspect few Americans noticed the passing of Major Dick Winters of Hershey, Pennsylvania. Winters was a most remarkable man whose story was chronicled by historian Stephen E. Ambrose in *Band of Brothers*. In the wake of the 2001 Emmy Award–winning HBO miniseries of the same title, Winters published his own memoirs in an effort to set the record straight and to record the accomplishments of an airborne company in combat during World War II. *Beyond Band of Brothers* rapidly climbed on the *New York Times* bestseller list for nonfiction, peaking at number ten within two months of publication. As for Winters, one reviewer stated that he "was too humble for a genre that requires a little bit of conceit." The American public disagreed.

I suppose the obituary would have attracted greater attention had it read, "Died January 2, 2011, the commanding officer of the Band of Brothers," for it was by that title that Dick Winters was more widely known. I had every reason to know him, for not only had he asked me to coauthor his memoirs in November 2003, but our personal and professional association also predated his death by well over a decade. In his declining years, when public access to this aging veteran was extremely limited, I was privileged to visit Winters on a monthly basis. At first, our discussions revolved around his role in the twentieth century's bloodiest conflict. Ironically, after I mailed the memoir manuscript to our publisher in April 2005, we never again addressed the war in detail. Winters had finally left it behind him. "It is finished," he stated emphatically when we submitted the manuscript. In his final years, we spoke only of more pleasant issues, nothing more than two old soldiers sharing memories of time long past. What struck me most was his undying loyalty to the soldiers whom he led in the most cataclysmic war in history. In the twilight of his own memory, his thoughts always returned to Easy Company, to happier times when a group of young men joined together to fight for freedom and to liberate a world from tyranny. Especially treasured were the memories of experiences he shared with family, friends, and the men of Easy Company. None was ever forgotten by the old soldier who resided in the white house along picturesque Elm Avenue in Hershey, Pennsylvania.

I first met Dick Winters on April 6, 1998, when he traveled to the U.S. Military Academy to address the Corps of Cadets on the topic of frontline leadership during World War II. As chief of military history in the Department of History at West Point, I routinely encouraged my officers to ask veterans to speak to their respective classes. Few members of the military faculty took me up on my suggestion, for no other reason than that ambitious young officers preferred to teach the cadets themselves and seemed reluctant to turn over control of their classes to outside teachers. On that particular afternoon, however, Major Matt Dawson entered my office to inform me that he had invited Major Dick Winters to address his class on the Battle of the Bulge.

"You know who Dick Winters is, don't you, sir?"

I had never heard of Winters, although I had read Ambrose's

Band of Brothers six years earlier. His name simply did not register. Fortunately, I did not have to reveal my ignorance because Dawson added, "You know, the guy from *Band of Brothers*."

"Yes, Matt, Dick Winters from *Band of Brothers*."

"Would you like to join us for dinner tonight?"

Seldom did I "pull rank" on one of my subordinates, but on this occasion I made an exception to my long-standing policy. As with most of the leaders who spoke at West Point on the subject of leadership in combat, I wanted the opportunity to explore how leadership among the ground troops is essentially different from any other situation—even air forces and navies, where the violence is indirect and depersonalized. This reflects the fact that armies are *sui generis*: Their primary function involves the direct employment and the direct experience of human-generated violence. Consequently, I graciously thanked Major Dawson for the invitation, but added that I preferred to host Winters alone for a quiet dinner at the Hotel Thayer on the grounds of West Point. It was one of the best decisions that I ever made as an army officer. And so it began.

I remember him as if it were yesterday. The old soldier emerged from the elevator in the hotel lobby at the U.S. Military Academy at West Point, dapperly attired in a dark blazer with the crest of the 101st Airborne Division on his pocket. His neatly cropped gray hair reflected a military man far younger than his current seventy-nine-plus years. I am not sure what I had expected to see. At the time of our initial encounter, most veterans of World War II were in their late seventies or early eighties. Most veterans who visited West Point to share their reminiscences with the cadets walked with the aid of canes or walkers. In Winters's case, there was a noticeable spring in his step that belied his age.

This shy, quiet gentleman who introduced himself simply as "Dick Winters" immediately made an indelible impression on me. From the beginning, I was "Cole," he was "Dick." Never once for the next thirteen years did we ever address each other by rank or surname. Over dinner Dick and I discussed a myriad of topics, all associated with his wartime experience and his thoughts on leadership in war. Why were some commanders more effective than others in inspiring their men? How did you identify the best soldiers in your company? Had he relieved any commander in combat? To what did he attribute his success in Easy Company? Were his leadership principles applicable to the civilian and the corporate worlds? Minutes evolved into hours as we discussed leadership under a number of circumstances. Before we finished dinner, I had already decided that I would include Dick Winters in the book I was writing about combat leadership during World War II. To my great satisfaction, he invited me to spend a few days on his farm outside Fredericksburg, Pennsylvania. By the time that the evening was over, I had received the best primer on leadership than I had obtained in twenty-five years of commissioned service.

No man, with the exception of my own father, exerted a greater influence on my life. For the next decade, Dick's and my lives were mutually intertwined. I am honored that he considered me his friend. For some inexplicable reason, he chose to share his memories with me. He seemed comfortable communicating with me in a way he never could or would with popular historian Ambrose. Little could I have realized that henceforth my professional life would revolve around the heart of the company town founded by Dick's boyhood hero, Milton S. Hershey. In the decade of our association, I remained a frequent guest, never missing an opportunity to visit the man who not only captured the imagination of veterans of the Greatest Generation, but had also bequeathed a legacy of selfless service to a younger generation in search of heroes and heroines. Now that he is gone, it seems appropriate to share the story of our friendship, how it began and how it matured over time. And if the readers will be patient, surely they will understand the manner by which this citizen-soldier touched thousands of lives with his favorite aphorism, "Hang Tough!"

CONVERSATIONS WITH
MAJOR DICK WINTERS

PART ONE

★ ★ ★

Spring

CHAPTER I

Incidents at War

We have shared the incommunicable experience of war. We have felt, we still feel, the passion of life to its top. . . . In our youths, our hearts were touched by fire.

—OLIVER WENDELL HOLMES, JR.

It was nearly two years from our initial meeting and less than six months from my visit to the farm outside Fredericksburg, Pennsylvania, before Dick extended an invitation to join him in Hershey to answer any "questions that you have." We had corresponded regularly during that interval, but a number of things had precluded a visit. First, on Easter Sunday in 1998, Dick had experienced a bad fall that resulted in him landing on the back of his neck and suffering a mild concussion. "In the past," he wrote, "following a fall or injury, all I needed was a good night's sleep and I would wake up feeling good as new. Not this time. I am feeling much better, but progress is slow. It's like taking two steps forward, then going back one step." I later learned that the concussion was severe enough that Dick cancelled all his speaking engagements for the remainder of the summer.

Then in mid-September, I received another letter from Dick in which he begged off once again and asked my understanding of his position. What generated this second postponement was a letter from actor Tom Hanks. What Dick related in his missive was that Hanks had called to inform him that Steven Spielberg had purchased the rights of Stephen Ambrose's *Band of Brothers* and he intended to produce a miniseries about combat in western Europe during World War II as a sequel to *Saving Private Ryan*. As Dick wrote, "You can, I am sure, read between the lines what they would like me to contribute. Let me get back to you after the dust settles on this latest development." Dick signed his letter with his signature closing, "Hang Tough!"

Now, driving past the beautiful rolling hills where Dick Winters made his home near Hershey, I was struck by the fact that everyone remembers one's own past in color, but all too often we make the mistake today of seeing the historical past in black-and-white. Just as anyone alive today remembers childhood, youth, events from when he or she was twenty-five years old, all in color and fresh, so too did those now long gone, those of the Greatest Generation who fought in World War II, or those who saw battle in the Civil War, the Revolution, any era—this is how they remembered their lives and experiences. Seeing the stunning green hills of Dick Winters's life, it was hard to imagine them as he remembered them from years past, but the reality is that to him they were just as green and just as beautiful then as they were to me that day. This is the challenge of remembering the past—it is not black-and-white, dull and faded, but rather vibrant and rich, in vivid color regardless of the era.

An hour later, I pulled up to a white house on spacious Elm Avenue in Hershey. Dick greeted me at the door and immediately escorted me to his upstairs office. "Cole, this is my den where I retreat to share my memories. Here, my maps, my decorations, and my memorabilia surround me. This is my personal refuge." On the walls were maps, photographs, the Easy Company guidon or pennant, and the escape map that he carried when he jumped into Normandy on D-Day. Next to his chair were his spit-shined Corcoran jump boots that he wore on that historic day of days. Even in today's U.S. Army, Corcoran jump boots and bloused trousers are the mark of distinction of the airborne soldiers and distinguish paratroopers from the "straight-legged" infantry. Dick called those boots his "good luck charm." The bullet hole in one of the boots dated from Carentan in mid-June 1944. When he returned to England that July, he put new soles on the boots, and he kept them every step of the way through the remainder of the war.

Looking at all the memorabilia, I could not help but ask what he considered his most prized possession. I was surprised by his response. Every military officer who commands a company in combat treasures the company flag—we call it a guidon in the military—that bears the designation of the unit and crossed rifles if you are an infantry commander. Different branches of the service have various insignia, and their guidons bear different colors. Infantry guidons are always blue. As a fellow infantry officer, I naturally assumed Easy Company's guidon would occupy the highest place in Dick's affection. "I know you think it is the guidon," he said, "but you're wrong." Pointing to a flower mounted under a glass frame, Dick replied, "As I look at these mementos from the war, what I treasure most is this edelweiss. After the loss of so many soldiers and after witnessing untold suffering during the war, the edelweiss symbolizes freedom to me. It represents renewed life and hope for a better world. Edelweiss is one of the few flowers that grow in the snow, above the tree line, in the Alps.

I personally climbed a mountain in the Austrian Alps to pick this edelweiss, and I have cherished it ever since."

We spoke for the better part of an hour, and then Dick suggested we get down to business. "I know you have lots of questions. Last year when I spoke to the cadets at West Point, I noticed you took pages of notes. That impressed me. As I recall, we were discussing D-Day and the fighting outside Brecourt Manor. Why don't we start there?"

A word of explanation—Brecourt is a small farm outside of Ste. Marie-du-Mont, just two miles inland from Utah Beach. On June 6, 1944, the mission of the 101st Airborne Division, to which then Lieutenant Dick Winters was assigned as a member of Easy Company, 2nd Battalion, 506th Parachute Infantry Regiment, was to secure four causeways behind the beach to facilitate movement of the amphibious forces into the interior of the countryside. The causeways were actually elevated roadways over which wheeled traffic could pass since Field Marshal Erwin Rommel had flooded the surrounding countryside to preclude amphibious and airborne forces from landing behind the beaches of Normandy. Easy Company operated as part of 2nd Battalion whose specific mission was to seize causeway number two, leading directly from Utah Beach to Ste. Marie-du-Mont.

And perhaps here is the place to remind readers that an infantry squad in World War II consisted of twelve soldiers armed with rifles and led by a sergeant. Three squads formed a platoon led by a lieutenant, and a company consisted of four platoons, one of which was a heavy weapons platoon with machine guns and mortars for indirect fire. A captain usually commanded a company, although the British units were commanded by the next higher grade of major. When Ambrose wrote *Band of Brothers*, he was describing one such company, Easy Company, an airborne company that jumped into Normandy on D-Day and fought throughout the campaign to liberate Europe. Three companies then formed a numbered battalion and three such battalions formed a regiment, such as the 506th Parachute Infantry Regiment. In today's U.S. Army, most infantry battalions are affiliated with a numbered brigade, but air or ground cavalry units still maintain their regimental designation.

Going back to D-Day, senior Allied planners had decided that the paratroop drop would be conducted at night in order to achieve an element of surprise preceding the amphibious landings scheduled shortly after dawn. A night drop is the most dangerous of all airborne operations, and as a result, the paratroopers were scattered across the Norman countryside. Unbeknownst to Lieutenant Winters at the time, Easy Company's commanding officer, First Lieutenant Thomas Meehan, had perished when his plane was struck by anti-aircraft fire.

"Tell me about D-Day, Dick."

"It was a special day for every soldier who participated in what General Eisenhower called 'the great crusade.' In one of his first books on D-Day, Stephen Ambrose said, 'Sometimes a single day's combat reveals more about the character of a nation than a generation of peace.' That's how I feel about June 6, 1944."

"What was it like that night as you prepared for your first combat jump? I know that you lost your weapon and most of the gear when you jumped into Normandy shortly after midnight."

"Our division was experimenting with what we called leg-bags, cloth bags strapped to your leg. The bags contained our weapons, extra ammunition, and other equipment. Why we decided to use these bags when we had never used them before was beyond me. When you jump from an airplane that is traveling at excessive speed, the propeller blast literally tears away everything not securely tied down. So I jumped around one o'clock in the morning and landed in a field outside Ste. Mère-Eglise at the base of the Cotentin Peninsula. When I landed, the only weapon I had in my possession was a trench knife that I had placed in my boot. I stuck the knife in the ground before I went to work cutting the risers from my chute. Here I was in the middle of enemy country, alone, no weapon, and not exactly aware of where I was. This was a hell of a way to begin a war."

"What happened next?"

"Fortunately, I encountered a few men from Easy Company and we were able to identify our exact location. As the ranking officer, I took charge and began the slow trek toward our battalion objective that I reasoned was approximately seven kilometers away. We later ran into more paratroopers, and around dawn we reached our battalion command post outside a small village named Le Grand Chemin. When I say village, I am being generous. Le Grand Chemin was a collection of houses and that was about all. By this time the amphibious forces were already landing at Utah Beach. H-Hour at Utah Beach was 0630 hours."

As dawn broke on D-Day, only ten soldiers from Easy Company were in the vicinity when Winters received orders to destroy four German 105mm guns firing on Utah Beach. The Germans had placed a battery of self-propelled guns in the area in February 1944. Around April, they had taken the motorized battery and moved it toward Cherbourg at the tip of the Cotentin Peninsula. They then replaced the self-propelled guns with a battery of horse-drawn artillery guns, but Allied aerial photography failed to detect the concealed gun position. The artillery pieces were located along a shallow ditch in a pasture outside a fourteenth-century manor house called Brecourt. A former French colonel named Michel de Vallavieille, who lived in the manor house with his wife and two children, owned the farm. Colonel de Vallavieille was a decorated veteran who had served his country gallantly during the Great War of 1914–1918. During the subsequent battle, Lieutenant Winters inflicted fifty casualties and destroyed three of the enemy cannons. Lieutenant Ronald Speirs from Dog Company destroyed the final gun. Regrettably, Winters lost two soldiers killed in action and several wounded. Considering that the Americans were heavily outnumbered and outgunned, Easy Company's battle serves as a classic case of fire and maneuver.

"Brecourt holds a special place in your heart, doesn't it, Dick?"

"It does indeed. I have returned many times to pay my respects to the family who still farms the land. D-Day was my first time in combat. I was mentally prepared and felt that I had done everything necessary to prepare myself for this precise moment. And yet you never know if you will measure up as a leader until the minute arrives when you face the enemy for the first time. Baptism by fire is a soldier's sacrament. There is always doubt. Hopefully, in combat, you perform as you train." Having taken out a piece of loose-leaf paper, Dick then sketched the position of the four artillery guns that had been firing on Utah Beach that morning. "My mission was to silence the guns. I only had two officers, including myself, and eleven men for the job. I viewed it as a 'high-risk opportunity.' When confronted with unexpected and ambiguous circumstances, you can either see opportunity or obstacles. I believe that opportunity is present even in chaotic situations. Brecourt was such an opportunity. In retrospect, D-Day served as one of the defining moments in my life as well as one of the defining moments in my development as a leader."

Such moments often occur but once in a leader's life. History is replete with such examples: Washington risking the fate of the Continental Army by crossing the Delaware to attack the Hessians at Trenton, Colonel William Barrett Travis accepting only "Victory or Death" for the besieged defenders of the Alamo, General Dwight D. Eisenhower selecting June 6, 1944, as D-Day. In describing Robert E. Lee's decision to resign his commission as an officer in the U.S. Army at the outset of the Civil War, historian Douglas S. Freeman entitles the chapter "The Answer He Was Born to Make." I place Dick's decision in how to employ his force at Brecourt in the same category.

I continued, "Last year, you mentioned how you divided your soldiers in two teams and how you laid a base of fire to cover your team as you made the assault on the first gun. Tell me again how you selected which men for each team."

"If you recall at West Point, I mentioned my 'killers.' On D-Day I had to work with the team that I had since most of the company was so widely dispersed after the night jump. Fortunately, several of my noncommissioned officers and key leaders were present. All I had to do was put them into a position where I could use them most effectively. I hate to use the term 'killers' because I don't want to give the wrong impression. Soldiers are trained to fight. As a leader, you obtain a sense of the better soldiers during training. They have a quiet confidence about them and a swagger that sets them apart. They are people who want to win in combat, just as those who desire to win in sports competition. With soldiers, a leader develops a sense about which soldiers you can trust. You look for the soldiers who perform consistently. That is generally no more than fifteen percent of an organization. Solid leadership and association with your top performers can influence another seventy percent of your unit. The final fifteen percent will never perform up to standard. Concentrate on the seventy percent and you can't help but be successful. That's what I did on D-Day. One of war's tragedies is that the best men are lost early. You can replace the men easier than you can replace their spiritual worth. The problem is that your killers sustain the highest rate of casualties since they are always in the action. By the time we reached Bastogne, most of the 'killers' were gone."

"As I remember, in addition to destroying the artillery battery, you also discovered a critical map that saved countless American lives."

Dick responded, "At the third gun, I found several maps, very important. I'm looking at these maps and realize that they contain the entire defense of Utah Beach, machine guns, minefields, and concertina wire. Only later did I come to understand what I had done, but at the time, it was another job. It was just another job that had to be done."

Because I was familiar with Dick's fight on D-Day, I saw little need to get into the details of how he destroyed each gun in rapid succession. I was far more interested in the leadership that he had exhibited. So I asked, "This was also the first time you fired your weapon in combat. How did that affect you?"

"Last year a young cadet asked if killing made me happy. No, it did not. It was not so much a feeling of happiness as it was satisfaction, satisfaction that I got the job done and that I had proved myself to my men. Satisfaction led to self-confidence that I hoped would be felt by others. Once you perform once, twice, or even three times, soldiers develop confidence in your leadership. You can only hope that this confidence will be passed to other leaders within the company. Brecourt gave me confidence in my ability to lead. That's why it remains so special to me."

"I remember that Eisenhower's historian S. L. A. Marshall once claimed that to destroy the enemy battery, you hiked to Utah Beach, borrowed four Sherman tanks from the 4th Infantry Division, and sicced them on the enemy guns."

"I don't know what war Marshall was describing. If I had that many men, I could have taken Berlin," Dick replied.

Of the battles in which Dick fought in World War II, Brecourt remained preeminent in his mind. Perhaps because it was his initial combat, but I suspect more because the fighting there reinforced his conviction that he had "measured up" to his own standard of what was expected of an officer. Dick returned to Europe only once more after our initial meeting at West Point in 1998. The occasion was the world premiere of *Band of Brothers*. Before consenting to participate in the festivities, Dick informed executive producers Steven Spielberg and Tom Hanks that he would forgo the activities scheduled for Paris. In lieu of those events, Dick preferred to visit friends in Normandy, but he promised to be present for the actual premiere ceremonies at Utah Beach. While other veterans wined and dined in the City of Light, Dick and his wife Ethel returned to Brecourt Manor outside Ste. Marie-du-Mont. Charles de Vallavieille, the grandson of the farmer who owned Brecourt on D-Day, hosted Mr. and Mrs. Winters. Charles's father, Michel de Vallavieille, had been a twenty-three-year-old man in 1944 when Dick destroyed the

German battery. Michel had been seriously wounded on D-Day and was evacuated to England. After convalescence there, Michel returned to his home, and he was elected mayor of Ste. Marie-du-Mont in 1949. He served honorably as mayor until 1991. During his tenure and against tremendous opposition from the local citizens who preferred to put memories of the war aside, Michel established the Utah Beach Museum as "a living expression of the town's appreciation and gratitude toward the Allies and their sacrifices." Michel's son Charles currently serves as city councilman and deputy mayor of the village and has carried on the work that his father had so nobly initiated. Having received Dick on a number of his visits to Normandy, Charles was delighted to once again host him and Ethel on what he assumed would be their final visit to Brecourt.

While Ethel stayed in the manor house, Dick walked alone across the pasture where he had led a small band of intrepid warriors on "the Day of Days." "I spent hours along that hedgerow where the cannons were placed, just thinking of Carwood Lipton, Bill Guarnere, Joe Toye, and the others," he confided to me. "I couldn't put them out of my mind. I knew I would never again walk this field."

Charles, too, became emotional when I asked him about Dick's last visit. Touching his heart with his fingertips, he said, "I consider Dick Winters a close member of my family. He has been an absolute gentleman. I have always admired and respected the manner in which Dick conducted himself."

Charles spoke not of Dick Winters, the soldier, but rather of Dick Winters, the man. Said Charles, "Dick's remarkable attributes were his calmness, serenity, integrity, and his courage. I miss him greatly, but I will always remember the remarkable man he was. I have four children of my own: a daughter who is a doctor, a son who is a teacher in an agricultural college, and two sons who work with me on the farm. I sincerely hope that the bonds that bound me to Dick Winters will not be broken and our children will continue the friendship that has transcended two continents."

Today a monument commemorating Easy Company stands at the corner of the main road east of Le Grand Chemin and the dirt road that leads directly to Brecourt Manor. The monument lists the names of Easy Company's fatalities on D-Day, including Lieutenant Meehan and his plane of paratroopers, who perished in one of the invasion's first actions. There were no survivors. As the next ranking officer, Winters assumed temporary command of Easy Company on D-Day and was promoted shortly thereafter to acting command.

Not far from Brecourt Manor also stands a new statue symbolizing the fighting spirit of the junior leaders who spearheaded the invasion on D-Day. The placement of the statue attracted worldwide attention when it was announced in 2011 that a memorial was being placed near Utah Beach and would be dedicated the following year on the anniversary of D-Day. An eleven-year-old South Lebanon Elementary School student named Jordan Brown raised much of the money for the statue. When Brown first read a newspaper story about the effort to establish a monument near where Lieutenant Dick Winters parachuted into France, he decided that he would help raise money by selling olive-green bracelets embossed with the words "Hang Tough." Documentary filmmaker Tim Gray oversaw the fund-raising effort to raise $400,000 for the project and was present for the dedication on June 6, 2012. At his side was Jordan Brown. The monument stands on the three-mile-long thoroughfare—old causeway number two—between Ste. Marie-du-Mont and Utah Beach. Sculptor Stephen Spears selected Dick Winters as the epitome of the airborne leader and used Dick's likeness to represent the American fighting man. Inscribed on the side of the statue is Dick's personal message to future generations, "Wars do not make men great, but wars sometimes bring out the greatness in good men." I wish my friend had been alive long enough to view the unveiling of the statue. I know he would have been very humbled, but also extremely proud.

As Dick and I continued our conversation, I asked how combat changed him and what differences he noticed in his men following D-Day.

Dick responded, "Now that they had experienced combat firsthand, I could sense a new jubilation that came over the troops. They exhibited a confidence that I had not witnessed before. We felt we were now combat veterans, although we realized the war would go on and on and that greater adversity lay ahead. Brecourt was merely the initial step in what proved a long road to victory."

Before leaving Normandy, on June 12 Dick led Easy Company in the attack on Carentan, a town of four thousand inhabitants located at the base of the Cotentin Peninsula. He later recalled that the German counterattack on Carentan the following day was the toughest fight of the war for the 506th Parachute Infantry Regiment (PIR). That day the German attackers pushed back the 506th and nearly overran the American paratroopers. Describing the action in a letter written in June 1945, Dick wrote, "So what happened in the biggest and toughest fight I was ever in? I am so pooped I can hardly walk after three nights and four days of no rest, and I am running through an actual hail of bullets, two or three times an hour, and I am not kidding, it was a hail. This one time I am halfway through and a machine gun opens up on me, down I go, and the enemy thinks he has me. I am playing dead, and what do I do? I get up and lead Easy Company to capture the intersection. Here I am today—a lucky fellow. For that day's work and several others, they recommended me for the Medal of Honor. I received the Distinguished Service Cross [DSC] instead." Pointing to his jump boots next to his desk, Dick added, "I received my Purple Heart at Carentan."

Winters ignored his wound, writing weeks later to a friend in the States, "Is being wounded supposed to be something interesting? Now, if I'd been killed or something, that would be something to write home about. But being 'pinked' in the leg is about as interesting as cutting yourself while shaving. The only difference is that you get a little purple heart."

Yet Lieutenant Winters had demonstrated unusual composure under fire during the enemy counterattack, and his men recognized that he was an exceptional officer. Years later one of his officers informed Dick, "God, I was glad to see you." Sergeant Floyd Talbert wrote years later as well, saying, "I'll never forget seeing you in the middle of the road. You were my total inspiration. All my boys felt the same way." Dick, too, considered the fight around Carentan as critical in his evolution as a leader and was extremely pleased by Easy Company's performance. As to the adulation that he received from his men, Dick said, "I'm proud that my men feel that way."

No sooner had E Company returned to England than the Army Signal Corps took a "head and shoulders shot" of the recent recipient of the Distinguished Service Cross. "I was told not to smile," Dick recalled, "in order to project the proper warrior image." Reflecting on the photograph, he wrote a platonic friend, "Honestly I didn't know I looked that mean and tough. I am actually afraid to send the photo to my mother for I know she'll worry and wonder what this army's doing to her son. Her son, the boy who could never even get mad enough to raise his voice. However, I don't feel quite so hard inside as I did in Normandy, but I guess I still look the part."

Dick Winters commanded Easy Company for only three months following his promotion to the grade of captain in early July. The company remained in Normandy until mid-summer when they redeployed to England to prepare for the next airborne operation. Higher headquarters scrubbed several subsequent drops, but on September 17, 1944, Dick commanded the company in Operation Market Garden, the aerial invasion of Holland. At the time, Holland had been under Nazi occupation since May 1940. Easy Company's mission was to seize a bridge outside Zon, Holland, and to conduct additional operations as directed. Market Garden proved a colossal failure, but the 101st Airborne Division remained in the country until early November.

If Brecourt Manor marked Dick's baptism by fire as a company commander, Holland proved an even more severe challenge of his leadership abilities. In continuous combat for six weeks, Easy Company found itself on "the Island," a long, narrow corridor north of Nijmegen between the Lower Rhine and the Waal Rivers, on October 2, 1944. The ground between the dikes of the two rivers was flat farmland, dotted with small villages and towns. The dikes along the waterways were twenty feet high, and the fields were crisscrossed with drainage ditches that were covered with heavy vegetation. On top of the dikes were narrow roadways that ran through the adjoining fields. It was along one of these dikes that newly promoted Captain Winters faced his toughest challenge as a company commander.

Easy Company had been in position for only two days when one of its patrols encountered a small body of German soldiers occupying a listening post at a crossroads a mile and a half east of Winters's command post. Due to the gravity of the situation, Dick personally assembled a squad of soldiers and quickly eliminated the enemy threat by employing all the weapons at his disposal. By dawn of the following morning, October 5, he remained concerned that the enemy might conduct another attack and replace the observation post that he had destroyed the previous evening. Consequently, he ordered the remainder of his reserve platoon forward. His options were limited. He could stay where he was and attempt to withdraw under fire. Or he could attack. To surrender the initiative was indefensible, so Dick ordered his men to fix bayonets and charge the enemy.

Bayonet attacks against a numerically superior force bordered the fine line between sheer audacity and complete lunacy. Fortunately for Easy Company, Dick's unorthodox assault caught the enemy by complete surprise. His attack carried him to the top of the dike, where he unexpectedly encountered an entire Waffen SS company, in excess of one hundred soldiers. As he and his men took the first company under fire, a second SS company appeared on the horizon. Without missing a beat, Dick called for reinforcements and peppered the enemy with artillery fire. By late morning October 5, Easy Company had inflicted well over one hundred casualties, before Dick was compelled to retreat under intense artillery fire from the far bank.

In an uncensored letter at the end of the war, Dick summarized this action as his greatest thrill of the entire war because he "had taken a squad [12 men] and beat the devil out of a machine-gun crew, then brought up two more squads [40 men in all], and attacked two companies of SS troops across 175 yards of open field and cut them all to pieces. During our assault, I was running faster than I had ever run in my life. Nor have I ever run that fast again. Everyone else was moving so slowly—my men, as well as the Germans. And I couldn't understand it. I'm normal, but they aren't."

I asked him why that day was so significant.

"At the time our strength was low and our front wide. In my estimation, the actions by Easy Company on that memorable day constituted Easy Company's crowning achievement of the war and my apogee as a company commander. The destruction of the German artillery battery at Brecourt Manor on D-Day was extremely important to the successful landing at Utah Beach, but this action demonstrated Easy Company's overall superiority, of every soldier, of every phase of infantry tactics: patrol, defense, attack using a base of fire, withdrawal, and, above all, superior marksmanship with rifles, machine guns, and mortar fire. All this was accomplished against numerically superior forces that had an advantage of ten to one in manpower and excellent observation for artillery and mortar support. By late October 5, we had sustained twenty-two casualties of the forty or so soldiers engaged under my personal command. All but a few casualties resulted from artillery fire after we had destroyed the two SS companies. My friend Lieutenant Lewis Nixon and I estimated the enemy casualties as fifty killed, eleven captured, and countless wounded. Colonel Robert Sink, commanding officer of the 506th PIR, ordered me to prepare a written summary of the battle since no senior officer witnessed the engagement. I purposely avoided the use of the first personal pronoun 'I' because I wanted each soldier to receive credit for what he had done. Later Sink issued a citation to the 1st Platoon that shouldered the principal burden of the fight."

"To what do you attribute your success?" I inquired.

"Not my success, Easy Company's success. As a company, we had suffered multiple casualties in Normandy and during the fighting around Eindhoven a few weeks earlier, but the core of Easy Company remained intact throughout Holland. The paratroopers who had trained together at Camp Toombs outside Toccoa, Georgia, in 1942 constituted the heart and soul of E Company. They formed the company's core. The loss of a single core soldier, however, dealt a crippling blow to the paratroopers who had worked together for two years. At the crossroads fight, Corporal William Dukeman was killed. 'Duke' was a Toccoa man who was beloved by everyone in the company. All of us deeply felt his loss."

"I completely understand, but do you agree that the action on October 5 constituted your moment of truth as a battlefield commander?"

"I guess so, but I really don't think of it that way. I had commanded E Company for only four months. During that time, we had fought outside Brecourt Manor, Carentan, Eindhoven, and on the Island. I felt extraordinarily confident in my ability to manage a battlefield and to lead paratroopers. Call it a sixth sense if you will. On the dike, I was faced with a couple situations that required my immediate attention. I knew I was backed by a truly first-rate team of solid noncommissioned officers and great paratroopers. I made my decisions on what I knew was best for Easy Company. Fortunately, these decisions proved to be right."

As I listened to Dick relate this story, I could picture Captain

Winters, having made the decision to attack, leading the assault across that open field on October 5, 1944. Totally oblivious as to if his men were matching him stride for stride, his combat instincts kicking in, and his adrenaline pumping to a feverish pitch, he crosses the dike and before him stand a company of Waffen SS soldiers as surprised to see him as he is to encounter them. Winters is no longer a leader; for a second, he surveys the field and regresses to being a pure warrior, a modern Achilles who as in Homeric legend stands high over the battlefield, all grim with dust, all horrible in blood. An instant frozen in time. As Easy Company's paratroopers join their captain, the enemy puts up stubborn resistance before attempting to flee to the safety of the Lower Rhine, only to be pelted by murderous artillery fire. For the SS, there is no refuge within the walls of Ilium. They resign themselves to their fate, leaving scores of dead and wounded on that ghastly field.

Dick then added a footnote. "Interestingly, Cole, that was the last time I fired my weapon in combat."

"You fought the rest of the war and you never fired your rifle again?"

"Never did. I saw no reason why I should. At battalion, I was no longer a troop commander and I couldn't afford to act like one. I had other responsibilities, not the least of which was providing support for the three rifle companies in the battalion."

"You fought the Battle of the Bulge, the largest battle in the history of the U.S. Army, and you didn't fire a shot? I find that hard to believe."

"You have to remember that at Bastogne, I served as acting battalion commander because Lieutenant Colonel Robert Strayer spent most of his time at regimental headquarters. At that level of command, my job was no longer to fight, but to direct others to fight. I almost crossed the line when my 2nd Battalion's attack on the village of Foy stalled because Easy Company's commander froze. Before I could act, Colonel Sink intervened and reminded me that I needed to command the battalion and not get bogged down in the weeds with Easy Company. He was correct of course, so I relieved the company commander and ordered Lieutenant Ronald Speirs to assume command of Easy."

Following the session in which he reminisced about the fighting in Holland, I sensed that Dick needed a breather. He agreed. "Let's take a break," he said. "We can talk about Bastogne later this afternoon."

When we resumed our discussions, I could see that some memories still troubled Dick, so I turned my focus from battlefields and inquired about his relationship with Captain Lewis Nixon. "You seem to have been polar opposites. You didn't drink, nor did you swear. Nixon did both and in huge quantities. He would have been the last man whom I think you would have befriended. What was the foundation of your friendship with Nixon?"

Dick's eyes shone as he recalled his old friend. "It is hard to explain. I had first met Nix when we were at Fort Benning, Georgia, in officer candidate school. Later we served as platoon leaders under Sobel's command. A special bond always exists among the platoon commanders in any military company, particularly when they perceive their own commander as 'the enemy.' I stayed in Easy Company, but Nix was transferred to higher headquarters. He drank too much, but he was also very conscientious. He was conscientious in his own way, on a man-to-man basis, and he always looked at what would best benefit the battalion. His contribution cannot truly be measured. There is no question in my mind that Nixon was the best combat soldier in 2nd Battalion. By the time we jumped into Holland, I was so lonely that I needed someone in whom I could confide my inner thoughts. That someone was Nix. Whenever the bullets began to fly, I could turn and there stood Nix. He always walked on my left side, one or two steps behind me. This was his token of respect for me as a commander."

Dick continued, "I also had the opportunity to observe how he handled himself under fire. The best way to illustrate this was in Holland when we encountered a German roadblock. As the 2nd Battalion peeled off to the left, Easy Company was placed on the extreme left flank, crossing a flat field in broad daylight. About two hundred yards before we encountered the roadblock, we came under intense machine gun fire. The Germans stopped us dead in our tracks. Nixon and I hit the ground simultaneously. When he did, he took off his helmet and saw that a bullet had pierced it. Nixon had a smile on his face. Here's a guy who came under enemy fire and laughed about it. Of course that night, Nix got roaring drunk. In hindsight, Nix probably needed me as much as I needed him. He was undoubtedly the coolest man under fire whom I ever encountered in combat."

"Any other leaders who struck you as unusually capable?"

"Ron Speirs, who took command of Easy Company during the Battle of the Bulge, was an incredibly capable commander. I respected him as a commander, but not as a man. He killed for the effect of killing. You probably know the stories about him in Normandy and what he did with some German prisoners. There was another whose company I enjoyed. I guess aside from Nixon, Harry Welsh was as close of a friend that I had during the war. He joined us shortly after Easy Company left Toccoa, but before we deployed overseas. Like Nixon, he was present on V-E Day. Easy Company also had very capable noncommissioned officers."

Though it was late in the afternoon, I wanted to address Bastogne, but Dick suggested that we go to dinner. "Enough talk of war. We'll reconvene tomorrow morning. Bastogne is a story in itself."

CHAPTER II

More War Stories

The pageant has passed. The day is over. But we linger,
loath to think we shall see them no more together—these
men, these horses, these colors afield.

—JOSHUA LAWRENCE CHAMBERLAIN

The following day we began our discussion of Bastogne. The
scope of what became known as the Battle of the Bulge was in-
comprehensible, even by the scale of most battles that the Western
Allies fought in World War II. In January 1945, the U.S. Army
suffered more battle casualties—more than thirty-nine thousand—
than in any other month of the campaign in northwest Europe.
The final reckoning of casualties totaled more than eighty thousand American soldiers killed, wounded, or missing. One-third of
the American casualties resulted from trench foot and frostbite.
Winters's 2nd Battalion was in the thick of the action. The battle
began in the foggy early morning of December 16, 1944, when
two massive German armies struck a thinly held portion of the
American line in the Ardennes. It was Hitler's last desperate gam-
ble to reverse the tide of the war in western Europe. Operating in
radio silence and inclement weather that denied the Allies aerial

observation, the Germans achieved total surprise. By the end of the first day, German forces had quickly penetrated the American defenses. After the initial shock that the enemy was still capable of assembling such a powerful force, General Dwight D. Eisenhower moved to contain the "bulge" that now existed in the Allied line. He directed General George S. Patton with his Third U.S. Army to strike the southern shoulder of the bulge as soon as possible. In the interim, Ike committed the Supreme Headquarters, Allied Expeditionary Force's strategic reserve, consisting of the 82nd Airborne and the 101st Airborne Divisions, to the vicinity of Bastogne to hold the line. Bastogne was a crossroads town in Belgium where a series of transportation networks came together. If the Germans captured Bastogne, they would be able to cross the Meuse River and perhaps reach the Belgium port of Antwerp. As the American reinforcements boarded hundreds of trucks, headquarters directed the 82nd Airborne to St. Vith on the northern shoulder of the bulge. The 101st trucked to Bastogne, right in the center of the German penetration.

Easy Company and 2nd Battalion marched through Bastogne the evening of December 19 and established positions along the Bastogne-Foy-Noville Road that ran northeast from Bastogne's city center. There they remained for the next thirty days, attacking, defending, and then attacking again. By the time that 2nd Battalion was pulled from the line on January 17, Easy Company was virtually unrecognizable. Most of the Toccoa corps had become casualties, and Winters had relieved Easy Company's commander. Even more so than D-Day, Bastogne formed the crucible that transformed Easy Company into a "band of brothers." As war correspondent Ernie Pyle wrote, "The common bond of death draws soldiers together over the artificial vestiges of rank." I could not imagine a more difficult leadership challenge, and I was anxious to ask Dick about it.

"Okay, let's talk about Bastogne. You were now serving as acting battalion commander, and Easy Company and its sister companies endured a month of excruciating combat in one of the most frigid winters in recent history."

Dick paused before responding, "Bastogne was the toughest campaign in which I ever participated. At night I still think about Bastogne. I've seen death. I've seen my friends, my men, getting killed. It doesn't take many days like this and you change dramatically. Some died and others lived and nobody knows why it is so. As casualties mounted in both Easy Company and the battalion, the rest of us had to go on. At the same time, I was supremely confident that we could endure against anything the Germans threw at us."

Brigadier General Jim Gavin, commander of Dick's sister airborne division, the 82nd, noted his own confidence following his initial combat in Sicily: "I want to come back from this one, much more than I have ever wanted to come back before. I am not as uneasy about going in as I have been before. Although it is certain to be a hell of a fight, those of us who have been there before are all a bit more certain of ourselves, and our ability to handle anything that develops. There are not as many unknowns this time. It is the unknowns that bother the new soldier." Gavin's assessment on the eve of D-Day matched Dick's own confidence in his ability to orchestrate the upcoming battles.

I asked Dick's reaction when his battalion reached Bastogne and witnessed American soldiers in full retreat.

"We had never seen this before, and would never see it again for the remainder of the war. Their faces told us this was 'panic,' pure and simple. We moved directly to the front lines. The first night was very confused as to just exactly what was our sector, what was going on in general, what was our responsibility. Fortunately, Captain Nixon made a special trip back to find regimental headquarters to ensure we had our orders correct. Nix made many of those trips back to regimental headquarters over the next few weeks to keep us informed and to make sure we had the exact and correct orders. That system worked. He kept the 2nd Battalion out of trouble. Nixon did a great job keeping me informed."

I interrupted Dick and asked him to comment more on that first evening in Bastogne. "Moving into a position at night, under fire, must have been confusing."

"You bet it was. Let me relate an incident that occurred during one of those first days that demonstrates the amount of confusion that existed. A heavy fog from the preceding night hung over the woods and fields at dawn on the second day that we were at Bastogne. I was standing in the edge of the woods, next to a field to the rear of our battalion command post. All was quiet and peaceful. Suddenly, to my left, out of the woods walked a German soldier in his long winter overcoat. He had no rifle, no pack, and he continued to walk slowly towards the middle of the field. A couple of men instinctively brought their rifles to their shoulders, but by a hand signal, I told them to hold their fire. We watched as the German soldier stopped, took off his overcoat, pulled down his pants, and relieved himself. After he was finished, I hollered to him in my best German, 'Kommen sie hier!' He then looked up, came towards me, and surrendered. All the poor fellow had in his pockets were a few pictures, trinkets, and the butt end of a loaf of black bread, which was very hard. Think of this. Here is a German soldier, in the light of early dawn, who went to take a crap, got turned around in the woods, walked through our front lines, past the company command post, and ended up behind my battalion command post. That sure was some line of defense we had that first night!"

"I can't imagine what those first few days must have been like," I added.

"Most of the soldiers in Easy Company also felt that Bastogne was the most challenging month of the war," continued Dick. "Staff Sergeant Bill Guarnere later claimed that he had been scared before, but he was absolutely petrified at Bastogne. From my perspective Bastogne was the most miserable place I've been in my life. I was wet through and through. And naturally, being a paratrooper, I didn't have a change of clothes along, no blanket, nothing. And it was cold as a son of a gun. Things were all snafued, walking around in the black of night, not knowing where we were exactly, where anybody else was, houses burning, civilians crying, wringing your hands, and behind every bush a prospective enemy. We took our greatest number of casualties during that campaign. Easy Company was never the same after Bastogne because we lost so many of the veterans who had fought in Normandy and Holland: Joe Toye, Bill Guarnere, Buck Compton, Don Hoobler, and many others. I operated the battalion command post that was situated approximately seventy-five yards from the main line of resistance."

"How important is it for a commander to be in the forward foxholes?"

"You might not think seventy-five yards is consequential, but it gave me the opportunity to think things through and divorce myself from the chaos surrounding the front line and to make calm, rational decisions under pressure. That is the toughest challenge for any leader."

Colonel Kevin Farrell, a recent combat veteran who just returned from commanding a battalion task force in the war in Iraq, echoed the importance that Dick attached to emotional calmness. Says Farrell, "I made a concerted effort never to let my soldiers see me lose emotional control. Composure in combat was something I viewed as essential. Day in and day out I strove to keep my emotions at bay. Late at night I would watch DVDs—mindless entertainment that was escapist and allowed me to get away in my own private way. I found I could not read serious history or delve deeply. I kept a journal, but did not engage in academic research. This was all I allowed myself, but outwardly my troops never saw me overly sad or emotional. They knew I listened and was compassionate, as if I could absorb it all but at the same time not become saddled by the burden. Aloof is not the term I would use, but rather externally tough and walled off, impenetrable on the one hand, but still able to listen, respond, and be flexible."

Farrell's experiences were so similar to those described by Dick in his discussion of the challenges associated with leading his men at Bastogne. Considering how the tactical situation changed so frequently and the weather conditions remained so deplorable in Belgium, I asked Dick if he had a regular routine that he followed during the Battle of the Bulge.

"I've been thinking about this for some time. I did have a routine, a routine that was instilled into me by Colonel Sink. At Toccoa, Colonel Sink insisted that officers always shave in the morning regardless of the situation. He would say, 'You shave every morning for the troops, and if you want to shave every evening for the women that is up to you.' I followed his orders because I realized that I had to set the proper example for the men. I needed to get their attention and let them know that I intended to be around for a while and that the situation was not as bad as they might think. I remember before 2nd Battalion attacked Foy, I had awakened early and shaved before I ate breakfast. I later discovered that I had cut my face in multiple places. When Sink came up to check on the battalion's readiness before the attack commenced, he took one look at me and smiled. I realized that he was laughing at me for shaving on that bitterly cold morning. In hindsight, shaving at zero-dark-thirty in freezing temperatures was pretty ridiculous."

"Other than the tactical challenges associated with combat around Bastogne, the Bois Jacques, and Foy, does anything about the Battle of the Bulge stand out that you haven't already mentioned?"

"Well, that covers a lot of territory. The Battle of the Bulge was not a single battle, but it consisted of a campaign or series of individual battles. During the attack on Foy in early January, I relieved Lieutenant Norman S. Dike as commander of Easy Company during the middle of an attack. This is highly unusual. First Sergeant Carwood Lipton had informed me that the soldiers in Easy Company had lost confidence in Dike to command the company. I listened to what Lipton had said, but there was little I could do at the time other than ensure that everything was in order for the next day's attack. I moved forward and observed the initial assault across an open field approximately two hundred yards wide. No sooner did our soldiers reach the edge of the village than they received direct fire from the Germans concealed in the village. All of a sudden the attack stopped. Dike had simply frozen and lost control. I tried to raise him on the radio and he wouldn't answer. In Lipton's eyes, Lieutenant Dike had 'fallen apart.' I only had two options, take control of the assault myself or find someone else to assume command. There were a number of officers standing behind me, and when I turned, there was Lieutenant Speirs from Dog Company. As acting battalion commander, I was aware of Speirs's reputation, but more importantly, I had seen him in action. I simply said, 'Speirs, take command of Easy Company and finish the attack.' That was all there was to it. He performed magnificently and we transported Dike to the rear."

That evening Colonel Sink convened a meeting at regimental headquarters to discuss the attack. As Dick recalled, "Lieutenant Colonel Strayer, my battalion commander, was present, but Sink turned to me and asked what I intended to do with Dike. That question should have been directed to Colonel Strayer as battalion commander, but I replied, 'Relieve Dike and put Lieutenant Speirs in command of Easy Company.' And that concluded the matter. Speirs commanded E Company for the remainder of the war."

He continued, "You mentioned Bastogne, the Bois Jacques, and Foy, but the battalion also attacked Recogne and Noville in mid-January. The last attack in mid-January really pissed me off because I could not believe that after what we had gone through and done, after all the casualties we had suffered, division headquarters had ordered us to conduct another attack. It just had the flavor of an ego trip for General Maxwell Taylor, a play to show Eisenhower that now that Taylor was back with his troops, he would ensure that we would get off our backsides and launch another attack."

For their stand at Bastogne, the 101st Airborne Division received the Presidential Unit Citation. General Eisenhower presented the award at Mourmelon, France, on March 15, 1945. This was the first time that an entire division of the U.S. Army was so recognized. Ike delivered his characteristic personal accolades, stating, "You met every test. . . . I am awfully proud of you." Then he added, "With this great honor goes also a certain responsibility. . . . You must realize, each of you, that from now on, the spotlight will beat on you with particular brilliance. Whenever you say you are a soldier of the 101st Division, everybody, whether it's on the street, in the city, or in the front line, will expect unusual conduct of you. I know that you will meet every test of the future like you met it at Bastogne. Good luck and God be with each of you."

I asked Dick if Bastogne reinforced his admiration of the American paratrooper.

"You repeatedly cite war correspondent Ernie Pyle. I've read most of his wartime dispatches. Take a look at what he says about the American infantryman and you will have the answer to your question."

That evening, I read Pyle's dispatches from North Africa and Sicily. I regretted that he never attached himself to one of the airborne companies, but Pyle felt more comfortable with the frontline infantrymen of the line divisions, particularly the 1st Infantry Division and the 1st Armored Division. In two of his more popular columns written before the Axis surrendered in North Africa, Pyle describes the infantryman. He could just as easily have been describing the American paratroopers at Bastogne. Pyle wrote:

"On their shoulders and backs, they carry heavy steel tripods, machine-gun handles, leaden boxes of ammunition. Their feet seem to sink into the ground from the overload they are bearing.

They don't slouch. It is the terrible deliberation of each step that spells out their appalling tiredness. Their faces are black and unshaven. They are young men, but the grime and whiskers and exhaustion make them look middle-aged."

Pyle continued:

"The god-damn infantry, as they like to call themselves. I love the infantry because they are the underdogs. They are the mud-rain-frost-and-wind boys. They have no comforts, and they learn to live without the necessities. And in the end, they are the guys that wars can't be won without."

Dick and I then briefly discussed the fighting in Alsace and into Germany. I had intended to ask him about the "last patrol" that Ambrose describes in *Band of Brothers*, but I decided to defer that discussion because it seemed more appropriate to address it as an example of leadership and character than as a narrative about the war. Instead, I directed our conversation about the work camp that Easy Company discovered once Dick's 2nd Battalion entered Germany. "Outside Munich, your men came across a concentration camp near Landsberg, where Hitler himself was once imprisoned after 'the Beer Hall Putsch' failed in 1923. I remember reading that your reaction was, 'Now I know why I am here!'"

"It was absolutely unbelievable. You cannot describe it; you cannot explain it; you cannot exaggerate it. To this day, the memory of starved, dazed men, who dropped their eyes and heads when we looked at them through the chain-link fence, in the same manner that a beaten, mistreated dog would cringe, leaves feelings that cannot be described and will never be forgotten. Later we discovered that there were several similar labor camps in the area. E Company had found a work camp, not an extermination camp like Treblinka and Auschwitz. When Eisenhower first viewed the death camps farther north, he ordered that all the local inhabitants of the neighboring towns walk through the camps and witness the Holocaust firsthand. I did the same thing. How one people can inflict so much evil and cruelty upon their fellow man was beyond comprehension. I knew then I must see the war to its successful conclusion. Because of what I had just witnessed, I saw no problem evicting German citizens from their private homes when we needed space to establish headquarters after we reached Berchtesgaden."

"As the war drew to a close, I imagine that maintaining discipline became more of a challenge."

"Not really, because the battalion was an experienced outfit. Still, you get the feeling that you are going to survive the war. Step carefully and you're going to make it home."

Dick continued, "Since I was now commanding 2nd Battalion, I ordered Easy Company to capture the Eagle's Nest, Hitler's mountain retreat overlooking Berchtesgaden. We entered Berchtesgaden shortly after noon on May 5, 1945. Our first order of business was to place a guard on the Berchtesgaden Hof because General Taylor wanted to make this his headquarters. As Lieutenant Harry Welsh, now serving as my intelligence officer, and I walked in the front door of the hotel, we could see the backs of the service personnel disappear around the corner. We walked into the main dining room, and there was one very brave waiter putting together a very large set of silverware in a velvet-lined case. Obviously, he was getting ready to hide this last set of silverware, but he was just a little late in getting the job done. Harry and I simply walked towards the man. There was no need for orders; he took off. Since there was so much silverware, I turned to Harry and said, 'Why don't we split the set?' He agreed, so we split the set right down the middle. Today, we are both still using this silver-ware from the Berchtesgaden Hof in our homes."

I interrupted, "Other divisions claim that they liberated Berchtesgaden and the Eagle's Nest."

Dick wasn't hearing any of it. "I know several divisions make similar claims, but all I can tell you is that we picked up our share of loot. My account is substantiated by my memory, my personal maps that I used at the time, one of my lieutenant's logbook that he kept at that time without my knowledge, and photographs taken by Sergeant Al Krochka, the division photographer who attached himself to my headquarters during those days. My version of the capture of Berchtesgaden is a first person account. My memory is quite positive on all points. My sources speak for themselves. If the 7th Infantry Regiment of the 3rd Division was first in Berchtesgaden, just where did they go? Berchtesgaden is a relatively small community. I walked into the Berchtesgaden Hof with Lieutenant Welsh and saw nobody other than some servants. Goering's Officers' Club and wine cellar certainly would have caught the attention of a French soldier from LeClerc's 2nd Armored Division, or a rifleman from the U.S. 3rd Division. I find it hard to imagine, if the 3rd Division were there first, why they left those beautiful Mercedes staff cars untouched for our men."

"You have convinced me," I replied. "Now, tell me where you were on V-E Day and how you felt when Supreme Allied Head-quarters notified everyone that Germany had surrendered uncon-ditionally on May 7, 1945."

"You know, I was just as glad as anyone that the war was over. Second Battalion had just entered Berchtesgaden when the news came down from Sink's headquarters on May 6. The mes-sage said in effect: 'Effective immediately all troops will stand fast on present positions. German Army Group G in this sector has surrendered. No firing on Germans unless fired upon.' The war was ending about as gloriously as I'd ever hoped. Berchtesgaden was really the heart of Germany, not Berlin, and it was quite an honor to be in on it. Goering, Kesselring, generals by the dozen, and Krauts by the thousands were all there. Never saw anything like it or could imagine it, that was really something. The Germans were backed up right into the mountains and no place to go. Then they threw in the towel and started coming from the hills. As we approached Munich at the end of April, there were more German soldiers with weapons going north than there were paratroopers [506] going south. We looked at each other with great curiosity. Every road we traveled was lined with German soldiers looking for someone to surrender to. They surrendered to American, French, and British soldiers. Anyone was preferential to the Russians. As you know, the Soviet Union did not release their German captives until the early 1950s. I am sure both armies shared one thought—just let me alone. All I want is to get this war over and go home. Days before the final surrender, the Germans knew it was over. It was not as chaotic as you might think. The German Army in defeat remained a disciplined force."

"I can't imagine what it was like when the final German surrender was announced the next day."

Dick smiled and said, "It was an incredible feeling. It was unimaginable the power we had. Whatever we wanted, we just took. As I said, I confiscated Hitler's personal silverware, and Alton More, a soldier in Easy Company, claimed the Führer's private scrapbook."

Handing me a photograph of 2nd Battalion officers drinking Hermann Goering's finest liquor at the Eagle's Nest, Dick added,

"This photograph says it all. This is how we felt on V-E Day. It was a holiday atmosphere. No more fighting, no more shooting. We were now at peace with the world. We had survived the war and would be going home. When we moved into Austria the night of V-E Day, the convoy moved out with the headlights of all the trucks on full beam. In the back of the trucks, my paratroopers were still in a party mood. For the past year, the normal mood of the troops when in a night convoy had been to get all the sleep they could because they never knew what the next day was going to demand from them. But, this night was a happy night, a night to celebrate, a night to remember."

"I imagine your final months in Europe following the German surrender brought a new series of challenges."

"Did they ever, particularly the first two months! While the war was going on, no one ever contemplated the difficulties associated with leading when the danger subsided."

"Can you describe what your duties consisted of once you entered Austria and the American Army essentially became an army of occupation?"

"Well, the situation was entirely different of course. Even Private David Webster, who hated officers and hated the U.S. Army, claimed that the only time he enjoyed in the army was when we were in Germany. Webster liked Germany, but he loved Austria. In his memoirs Webster called Austria a 'soldier's dream life.' He wrote that although the men were treated to great quantities of mountain rain and plenty of sunshine, the occupation forces had little work, excellent food, and soft beds. Yet even Webster anticipated problems as soon as prisoners returned home, because the German infrastructure had been destroyed. He was definitely right, but right now, I had to control the situation at hand. Consequently, the first thing I did was to contact the local German commander. My instructions to him were: First, I want all weapons collected and left at either the airport, the school, or the church; second, all officers can keep their sidearms, and you can keep weapons for your own military police; and third, tomorrow I will inspect your camps, your troops, and your kitchens. Let me point out that at this time, I was twenty-seven years old, a few years out of college, and like all the troops, I was wearing a dirty, well-worn combat fatigue jacket and pants, and had that bucket on my head for a helmet. I felt a little ridiculous giving orders to a professional Prussian colonel, about twenty years my senior, who was dressed in a clean field uniform with his medals all over his chest."

"And did they comply?"

"Of course they did. I already stated that the German Army in defeat remained highly disciplined. The next morning, with Nixon at my side, I took off in my jeep to inspect the sites where I had ordered the weapons to be deposited. I was shocked at the mountain of weapons that had been assembled at each location. Then I realized that I was looking at the result of that famous German reputation for efficiency. I had said yesterday 'all weapons.' They had not questioned my order. We found hunting rifles, target rifles, hunting knives, antiques, and, of course, all military weapons. I next inspected the camps and kitchens and I found everything organized. Some of the troops were lined up for review. They were clean, dressed in their best uniforms, and disciplined. The kitchens were in excellent order."

"Military inspections provide a commander critical information. What did you learn?"

"The inspection of a few camps and troops was nothing more than a means of establishing a line of communications and a relationship between our headquarters and their headquarters. After that, each day, the Germans would send a staff officer who could speak English to my headquarters in the morning. We left the German soldiers alone. They respected us and there was no trouble."

"Now that the war was over, did you become friendly with any of the Germans?"

"Friendly is too strong a word. After the German liaison officer got to know me, he told me stories about his tour of duty on the Eastern Front. He told me how in the winter, the tanks would be so cold that if your bare skin touched the metal of the tank, the skin would just stick and tear off as you pulled away. He mentioned that he had fought the 101st Airborne Division at Bastogne. He later suggested that 'our armies should join hands and wipe out the Russian Army.' I can also remember my answer to that invitation, 'No thanks, all I want to do is get out of the army and go home.'"

"I remember you telling the cadets at West Point about the German officer who surrendered his personal weapon to you in Austria."

Dick replied, "He was a German major from a panzer unit, a true German and one hell of a good soldier. We talked over tactics, soldiering in general, and were pleased to find that at Bastogne we had fought each other tooth and nail. He had been wounded six times during the war. Now that the war was over, I had directed that all enemy soldiers bring their individual weapons to Kaprun's town square, where we could collect them. This

German officer appeared in my battalion headquarters and handed me his personal luger as a formal surrender between the two of us, rather than place the pistol on a desk in some office of some unknown officer. Naturally, I accepted his surrender gracefully. It was the end of the war for his men; it was the end of the war for my men. Upon later examination, I noted that the pistol had never been fired. And to this day, the pistol still hasn't been fired. That's the way all wars should end, with no blood on the weapons and no blood on the surrender document."

"Going back to occupation duty, how long did you have to contend with the prisoners and displaced persons in your area?"

"Only about two weeks. There is a difference between German soldiers and displaced persons [DPs]. As soon as possible, in an orderly manner, truck convoys moved German prisoners from our area and to stockades in the Nuremberg area and around Munich. We had no idea how many German soldiers were still in those hillside forests. Some were in small groups; some were loners. Each day, we sent out jeeps to patrol secondary roads and trails trying to locate and direct these troops to our airport compound. To this day, I am amazed that we did not suffer any casualties resulting from these patrols, for we were all sitting targets for some die-hard German soldier who wasn't ready to surrender. In reviewing my notes, I estimate that approximately twenty-five thousand German soldiers and displaced persons had surrounded my 2nd Battalion of six hundred men when we moved into the area. The displaced persons were a more difficult problem with which to contend. The area was just jammed with the DPs, as we called them. Feeding all these people was a problem we were in no position to handle. As quickly as possible, we gathered these people in groups according to their nationality: Hungarians, Poles, and Czechoslovakians. Within ten days to two weeks, the area was cleared of prisoners and DPs."

"Now that the prisoners and DPs were out of your area, to what did you turn your attention?"

"The next job was to sort out and consolidate all the captured German equipment and the U.S. Army equipment we had that was no longer needed for combat. My job was to organize convoys and ship the consolidated equipment to depots in France. This consolidation of equipment got down to the point that one day they asked all officers who had received the silk escape map before the jump into Normandy to turn them in or be fined seventy-five dollars. I had my escape map sewn in the belt lining of my pants all through the war. That map had sentimental value to me after four campaigns. There are times that the army comes up with some rules and orders that defy logic. This time I took a stand and a punch line from General McAuliffe at Bastogne, and I said, 'Nuts!' Nor did I pay the fine. Memories of this type of efficiency made it easier for me to decide not to make the U.S. Army a career."

"Dick, how did you handle disciplinary problems now that the war was over?"

"Regardless of how disciplined an outfit is, too much time on your hands, too little activity, and too much alcohol make a volatile combination. The battalion was no longer a combat unit, but a garrison outfit. It was important to keep the troops gainfully employed to prevent boredom and monotony. That would lead to a breakdown in discipline, and when that occurs, soldiers get careless. Consequently, the first things we organized were calisthenics and athletic programs. I vividly recall watching the men stripped to their waist or wearing only shorts as they played base-ball. The sight of all those scars made me conscious of the fact that only a handful of men in the battalion had been lucky enough to make it through all four campaigns without at least one scar. Some men had two, three, or even four scars on their chest, back, arms, or legs. Keep in mind that this was after the war, so I was looking only at the men who were not seriously wounded. Next, we set up rifle ranges and sharpened up our marksmanship. Close order drills and troop reviews were once again back on the train-ing schedule. I also established a schedule where each of our pla-toons could rotate every seventy-two hours to a ski lodge in the Alps for rest and relaxation. The purpose of using this retreat was to let the men get away from the routine of a military schedule."

"Any particular challenges you remember concerning the welfare of your soldiers?"

"There were two things that were unavailable. First was sufficient food. Starvation ran rampant in most of Germany fol-lowing the war. At Kaprun, we were at the end of the pipeline in the distribution of food. Everybody from the ports of Cherbourg, Le Havre, and Antwerp right down the pipeline had a crack at the food for themselves, their girlfriends, and the black market before we were taken care of, way down in the Alps. We were hurting for about the first three weeks after the end of the war. Dried potatoes and dried tomatoes do not maintain body weight for a young soldier, so we all lost weight. Complaining to Colonel Sink didn't do much good either. After a month, the situation improved dra-matically.

"The second thing we needed was dental care. We had troops quartered in the home of a civilian dentist. I found that he had a problem with our troops occupying his nice home, so we struck a deal. He would take care of my personal dental care, and if I moved my troops from his home, he would take care of twelve of my men a day. From that day on, the dentist had a steady stream of customers each day, and this group included Lieutenant Colonel Robert Strayer from regimental headquarters. If you recall, Strayer was Easy Company's first battalion commander from Toccoa. Dental hygiene is one of those minor problems that can escalate to a major problem if not addressed early."

"You once mentioned that the battalion suffered more casualties in Bavaria and Austria than you did during the last four months of the war."

"Unfortunately, we did. It seemed a tragedy that men survived several campaigns only to die in a car wreck or be shot by a drunken soldier. That's what happened to Sergeant Grant when he came across a soldier from higher headquarters who was intoxicated and who had killed an officer. Grant survived, but he nearly died before a German surgeon saved his life. That's the effect of excessive liquor, captured vehicles, and too many weapons at one's disposal."

"How long did your battalion remain in Austria?"

"The 506th left the Zell am See, Kaprun, Bruck area by the end of July. We went by train to Joigny, France. Joigny was an old town of cobblestoned, narrow streets. Memories of Joigny are few. I was mostly passing time until I could return home. I would go for a run daily, play football or baseball. Bored out of my mind, I took a two-week leave and returned to Aldbourne. When Japan surrendered, everyone, including me, wanted to go home as quickly as possible. I had enough points to be in the initial group, but Colonel Sink deemed me 'mission-essential.' On October 1, I finally received orders to make my way home via Marseille, France. In late November, the 101st Airborne Division was deactivated."

"Any final thoughts on your wartime service?"

As we concluded our discussion of the war, Dick sighed and said, "On a national front, the United States went to war not to conquer territory or to subject their fellow man, but merely to liberate a conquered people from the chains of tyranny. There is a certain nobility in all that. Today we are bombarded in the news media about how everyone hates America and how this country is deployed around the world. World War II wasn't like that, and I am proud to be part of it."

"Dick, last month I visited the museum on Utah Beach. On one of the placards inside the museum is the 'Letter to an American,' from Antoine de Saint-Exupéry, who was returning to his native land aboard an American convoy in April 1943 to do his part in the war. Saint-Exupéry was a French aviator and novelist. His most famous book was *The Little Prince*. In his letter, Saint-Exupéry spoke of his pride in the United States for its sacrifice. He wrote, 'I know—and will later tell my countrymen—that it was a spiritual crusade that led you into the war. . . . The fifty-thousand soldiers in my convoy went to war not to save American citizens, but rather for Man himself, respect for Mankind, liberty for all men, and the greatness of Man.' To me, Saint-Exupéry has captured the essence of the American character."

Dick asked, "Did he survive the war?"

"Unfortunately, he did not. His specially configured Lockheed P-38 Lightning reconnaissance aircraft disappeared in a cloud off shore, south of Marseille on July 31, 1944. Saint-Exupéry was presumed killed in action. The remnants of the plane were later discovered, in May 2000, and recovered in October 2003. Sorry for digressing, Dick. I didn't mean to cut you off. Before we adjourn, anything else you want to add?"

"Just this. Leadership's defining quality is honesty. To honesty, add fairness and consistency. I was able to develop a sixth sense during the war that allowed me to size up a situation rapidly. I could look at terrain and be able to see opportunities instead of challenges. By leading from the front, I believe I achieved a high degree of success."

CHAPTER III

Band of Brothers

From this day to the ending of the World
. . . we in it shall be remembered
. . . we band of brothers.

—*HENRY V*

WILLIAM SHAKESPEARE

Life in an infantry company at war is difficult to describe to someone who has not experienced the rigors of combat. The associations that characterize soldiers in war form a far more intimate relationship than that between a man and his wife. Survival literally rests on the individual soldier to one's left and to one's right. Soldiers will give the most basic forms of human sustenance to their comrades rather than see them suffer. A soldier will share the last drops of water from his canteen or divide his K ration equally with his foxhole mate. He will risk his own life to pull a wounded soldier to safety. This intimacy of life between soldiers in combat does not exist in any other form of human endeavor. As Pyle wrote, "The ties that grow up between men who live savagely and die relentlessly are ties of great strength. There is a sense of fidelity to each other who have endured so long and whose hope in the end can be so small." It is this powerful fraternity in the ghastly brotherhood of war, to use correspondent Pyle's terminology, that formed the backbone of Easy Company that historian Stephen Ambrose later chronicled in *Band of Brothers*.

When Ambrose wrote *Band of Brothers* in 1992, he claimed that Easy Company was "Dick Winters's company." Over the course of the war, this specific airborne company would have a number of commanders, including Herbert Sobel, Winters, Fred Heyliger, Norman Dike, and Ron Speirs. All made an indelible impact on Easy Company, but Winters was the only officer associated with the company from Day 1 to Day 1,095, when Easy Company and the 101st Airborne Division were inactivated, on November 30, 1945. At war's end, no commander matched Dick Winters in terms of adulation and esteem. He was the type of leader who was not only idolized, but also respected. He was destined for high places. Ninety percent of morale is pride in your outfit and confidence in your leaders and fellow fighters. Dick Winters earned that confidence. In my own military experience that spanned three decades, I can truthfully say that I have never known any man prouder of his company than Dick Winters.

Easy Company was formed at Camp Toombs outside Toccoa, Georgia, in August 1942. Airborne warfare was a relatively new concept in the American Army in World War II, and army chief of staff General George C. Marshall ordered the formation of several provisional parachute regiments to conduct airborne training. One of those regiments was the 506th Parachute Infantry Regiment (PIR) under the command of West Point graduate Colonel Robert Sink. All paratroopers were volunteers, many of whom had been enamored of *Life* magazine's May 12, 1941, cover that featured U.S. Army parachutist Hugh Randall. Under Sink's command was Easy Company, 2nd Battalion, whose commander was

First Lieutenant Herbert Sobel, a National Guard officer from Chicago, Illinois. Most of the platoon leaders were recent graduates from Officer Candidate School (OCS) at Fort Benning, Georgia. OCS was another one of Marshall's innovations designed to supply junior officers to the rapidly expanding land forces. The vast majority of OCS candidates were either college graduates or soldiers selected by their commanding officers for commissions to 2nd lieutenant, the normal rank of an infantry platoon leader.

As new soldiers joined Easy Company, Sobel received a promotion from lieutenant to captain, the traditional rank associated with an infantry company commander. It was to Easy Company that Second Lieutenant Dick Winters reported for duty in August 1942.

"Dick, let's start at the beginning. Why did you join the paratroopers?"

"I joined the army in 1941. As a college graduate I was not challenged as a private or a corporal, so I applied to OCS. I debated whether I should apply to armor candidate school at Fort Knox, Kentucky, or stick with the infantry at Fort Benning, Georgia. I decided to go with infantry since I was already familiar with infantry tactics based on my training at Camp Croft, South Carolina. I first encountered airborne soldiers while I was at Fort Benning, where the paratroopers were going though their pre-jump training. They looked impressive, were physically fit, and demonstrated what I could only call a tolerant scorn for any soldier who was not airborne qualified. I wanted to be with the best, and paratroopers were the cream of the crop. I volunteered immediately to become a paratrooper as soon as I received my commission as second lieutenant."

To those who are familiar with Stephen E. Ambrose's *Band of*

Brothers or the HBO miniseries of the same name, the daily routine at Camp Toombs began with a six-mile forced march conducted at an "airborne shuffle" up and down Mount Currahee, a towering peak that overlooked the training camp. "Three miles up and three miles down" became the badge of honor for the paratroopers who trained at Toccoa. Sobel drove his company hard, always finding fault with Lieutenant Winters and the other platoon leaders and sergeants. Inspections were impossible to pass because Sobel found any excuse to withhold a three-day pass or to place a soldier on additional duty, often fabricating minor deficiencies to justify his actions. That said, Sobel also imposed iron discipline on Easy Company, trained them to the highest degree of proficiency, and infused an *esprit de corps* that separated Easy Company from the other companies in Sink's command. Sobel's major shortcoming as a leader was simply that the soldiers lacked confidence in his ability to lead.

I wanted to know Dick's opinion of what made this particular airborne company such a tightly knit military organization, so I asked him directly, "What made E Company so special?"

"That's easy. I think we were special, but every soldier thinks his outfit is special. I'm sure you can say the same thing about Companies Able, Baker, Charlie, Dog, and Fox that you say about Easy Company, so take what I say with a grain of salt. One thing Easy Company had that the other outfits did not was Herbert Sobel. You know what happened in training. Sobel forced us to run up Currahee every day, and every paratrooper shared this experience equally. That hill was just as tough on each and every man, each and every officer. Currahee showed no favorites. It was a tough assignment. Then officers and men worked together later in the afternoons, conducted long marches, and then participated in countless hours of night training. All the while, Sobel was constantly screaming at the men and trying to force each soldier to stand on his own. The name Currahee itself derives from a Cherokee word that means 'We stand alone, together.' No one was allowed to help a comrade. If you attempted to assist a fellow soldier, Sobel had the authority to kick you out of the company. Naturally, the men resented his harsh discipline that served no purpose in their eyes. What struck me, however, was that as time went on, when the men started receiving packages from home, they shared within their squad, within their platoon. And later, of course, when Easy Company engaged the enemy in combat, they shared the good and the bad, the tough and easy times. As I look back from the perspective of sixty years, the shared stress and hardship created a bond that still exists today. Even at our reunions this bond is still apparent. The original members who trained at Camp Toombs still sit together because we comprise the core element of Easy Company. The replacements sit at a different table."

"Going back to the training outside Toccoa, what was your first impression when you saw Currahee?"

"You could see Currahee as soon as you got off the train. Having grown up in Pennsylvania, I thought Currahee resembled a high hill more than a mountain. Our base camp lay at the foot of Currahee, cut from the north Georgian forests. I knew from the start that sooner or later we were going to climb that hill. Running up that mountain was one of the most important bonding experiences we had."

Even though I knew the answer, I inquired about Dick's assessment of Sobel as a leader. No one liked Sobel, but many officers who served at the battalion and regimental levels credited him with preparing the company to meet the rigors of combat. Dick was not as easily impressed. He told me that long after the war, one of his children discovered a photograph of Sobel taken in 1942. Someone had drawn a "Hitler mustache" on the thirty-year-old company commander. When asked who had done such a thing, Dick proudly owned up to his crime. "I did. That's exactly how we felt about him."

He continued, "Captain Sobel commanded through fear and intimidation. That is not how a leader should conduct himself. Sobel was not just unfair; he was mean-spirited. His attitude created a special bond within Easy Company that allowed the men to identify with their platoons more so than with the company, which is more normal in most military units. Second lieutenants by their nature are a clannish group. Some are more serious than others, but for the most part, they wander around a military post as General Eisenhower once said 'in a rather aimless search for excitement.' E Company's platoon leaders, of which I was one, did our best to take care of our soldiers to soften Sobel's dictatorial behavior. I lost all respect for our commander the day he announced to the officers, 'In Easy Company we will lead through fear, not by example.' It made such an impression on me that I recorded his words in my diary. Under ordinary circumstances a junior company officer attempts to reflect his company commander's leadership style, but Easy Company's lieutenants found that they simply could not emulate the image of Sobel and still live with themselves. Sobel had no friends within the company and few within the regiment. At the end of each day, he went one way and we lieutenants went another, hoping not to run into him at the officers' club. So traumatic was my personal relationship with

Sobel is that it's still painful remembering my initial meeting with him."

I asked if Sobel had any redeeming qualities.

"Not many in my opinion. Aside from what I said in response to your last question, he lacked confidence in his own ability as an infantry commander. He was completely honest, but he couldn't read a map to save his neck. His knowledge of tactics and of fire and maneuver was extremely poor. Captain Clarence Hester, who served as the battalion operations officer on D-Day, gives him higher marks. Hester said that in one sense Sobel made E Company and that he was the catalyst that bound all the men together as a unit. Every soldier in the company became so obsessed to prove Sobel was not capable of serving as company commander. Hester later wrote me that he firmly believed that Sobel was incapable of leading the company in combat, but by his harsh disciplinary measures in training, he bound the company into a cohesive fighting unit which was led later by more understanding and capable officers. I suppose Hester is correct on that point. He's certainly entitled to his own opinion."

I next asked Dick to comment on how his association with Easy Company at Toccoa contributed to his development as a leader.

"By the time that I joined Easy Company, I had already served in the army for eleven months. I had graduated from Officer Candidate School in July 1942, so my initial assignment as a commissioned officer was Easy Company. By the job's nature, a platoon commander is in daily contact with the soldiers under his command, so I developed a close bond both with my men and my fellow platoon leaders. Things moved fast in those days. At Camp

Toccoa—we referred to our training camp now as Toccoa rather than Toombs—we learned how to be soldiers. By the time we left Toccoa in December 1942, I detected camaraderie within the command that I had not seen at my former duty station in South Carolina. That was what was so special about Toccoa. The entire experience forged the brotherhood that paid such rich dividends in Europe."

As close as were the paratroopers in Easy Company, internal command problems threatened the cohesion within the company. By the time Easy Company deployed to England in September 1943, Captain Sobel had become so ineffective that the noncommissioned officers mutinied because their fear of going into battle with him was so strong. When Sobel attempted to court-martial Winters, the senior sergeants rebelled and threatened to turn in their stripes. Their actions were based on true fear of what lay ahead. Colonel Sink, the regimental commander, intervened and dealt with the mutiny severely. He transferred the ringleaders from the regiment and reduced several sergeants in rank. Having lost confidence in Sobel's ability to command Easy Company, Sink next transferred Sobel to a training command where his talents as a training officer might be better put to use. As Winters later recalled, "Sobel just disappeared. I later saw him at Mourmelon, later in the war, an event featured in the miniseries, but the timing was off." To protect Winters, 2nd Battalion commander Lieutenant Colonel Robert Strayer moved him to Headquarters Company until a new company commander had reestablished order.

"Let's get back to Easy Company," I suggested, "and the central core of officers and noncommissioned officers that led the paratroopers from Toccoa to Adolf Hitler's Eagle's Nest. What values did this core share?"

"Shared hardship and stress. Hardship and stress bring a family together. Easy Company became a family. Officers aren't family. The family belongs to the men, not the officers."

Dick served in Easy Company from July 1942 through October 1944 before being transferred to battalion headquarters as battalion executive officer. By this point in the war, Easy Company had already suffered nearly thirty soldiers killed in action and in excess of seventy-five wounded. As losses mounted with each successive operation, Dick doubled his efforts to improve himself for the task ahead.

Reflecting on his time with E Company and his time as battalion executive officer, Dick summarized the combat that he had witnessed since D-Day. "We went to Normandy, landing just on the outskirts of a little town called Ste. Mère-Eglise, the hottest place in the world at that time. Then we fought on down to the beachheads and our objectives and later into Carentan. Three months later, I led Easy to Holland, where we hit near Zon and the next day marched into Eindhoven. I led that one personally. There I fought east of the town, and then up to Nuenen and Veghel. Then at Uden, my company was surrounded and cut off after we'd been in Holland for about four days. Next we moved to Nijmegen and the Island, where we sat and fought off counterattacks from the north and east," he recalled. "Our time in Holland extended to seventy-three days of continuous war without relief . . . and in mid-December we received a twelve-hour notice at midnight the seventeenth of December that we were moving out. We did. Our commanding officer caught us on the way to Bastogne. Not all the men had weapons; we had little rifle ammo. Some soldiers had no ammunition at all and many had no winter clothes to speak of. We drove into Bastogne, got off the trucks and into one of the most confused fights I've ever been in outside of Normandy. After three weeks we went on the offense and took Noville and Rachamps. At the time, we were half our authorized strength. Then the prospects of a second bulge took form down around Haguenau in Alsace-Lorraine, so what do they do? Zip, down we go and hold that line." In Dick's words, the entire experience "was hell on my nerves."

"Did you experience problems with desertion or absent without leave [AWOL] in Easy Company?"

"In our outfit, never! Quite the opposite. We had soldiers who had been wounded and had been reassigned to medical holding companies in the rear areas, who went AWOL to rejoin E Company because if you remained in the rear for ninety days, you were subject to reassignment to a different command when you returned to the front lines. No one wanted to leave his buddies in Easy Company. Joe Toye was wounded three times prior to Bastogne, and he came back to E Company rather than be transferred from the company after he had recovered from his wounds. Two days later, he suffered his fourth wound and lost a leg in the Bois Jacques."

In late January 1945, just after 2nd Battalion was pulled from the line at Bastogne, Dick addressed the pressure he was under to ensure his men remained safe. "Since I am in the army, I daydream of fights, fighting Jerries, outmaneuvering, outthinking, outshooting, and outfighting them," he wrote. "But they're tense, cruel, hard, and bitter. They consist of about 80 percent of my dreams, but they pay off. You'd be surprised. Sometimes when you dream about a problem over and over, you get the solution, and by gosh, crazy as it may seem in the cold morning light, it usually works. In fact, to date, they've always worked."

I inquired if Dick had experienced a problem disassociating himself from Easy Company after he had been reassigned as executive officer of 2nd Battalion, 506th PIR. There are few positions in the army that provide greater joy and sorrow than the command of frontline troops—joy and sorrow because it is a privilege to be associated with soldiers in their success, and gut-wrenching sorrow when the gods of war snuff them away. Having commanded an infantry company myself, I recalled my chagrin at leaving the soldiers with whom I had trained for eighteen months. I knew every soldier in the company intimately and I truly enjoyed their company. On one training exercise, I joined my scout platoon after a hard day's march. Rain was falling in torrents and the platoon was in a defensive perimeter as night fell. As temperatures dipped, I unrolled my poncho and couldn't help but think, It doesn't get any better than this. I lost that camaraderie when I received orders to report to brigade staff. At battalion or brigade headquarters, an officer is no longer considered a troop leader, but now is a staff officer. Dick had been a member of Easy Company twenty-six months when he was reassigned. I knew exactly what Dick would say.

"Of course I had a problem leaving Easy Company," Dick replied. "Every officer I have known always remembers his first company command. That's why command is such a memorable experience and why commanders cherish the company guidon, such as the one you see hanging on my wall. When I was transferred to battalion, I no longer felt part of anything. I was simply the battalion executive officer. I no longer felt creative. I felt as if I had 'lost my men.' I knew every soldier in Easy Company personally. I had been their commander and their leader. I had served with them since they had joined the army. I felt a 'deep personal loss.' At battalion you really do not know the men. Staff officers interact with officers and noncommissioned officers at the company level, but not the soldiers. In Easy Company, we had shared our lives as soon as we joined the army. It was that shared experience that created the 'Band of Brothers.'"

I asked, "Did you maintain contact with Easy Company after you moved to battalion headquarters?"

"To a degree, but my responsibilities were now far different. I now had to be concerned with Dog and Fox Companies in addition to Easy Company. And I had complete confidence in my successor, Moose Heyliger. Whenever there was a tough assignment, however, I picked Easy Company for the mission because I knew I could count on them. The natural tendency for a leader is to assign key missions to the outfit that the commander knows will get the job done. In retrospect I probably should have been more balanced. Subconsciously, any leader wants to think that he or she is instrumental in the success of the team. That's a natural reaction, but the new leadership lies in self-denial and self-sacrifice. I never wanted Easy Company to fail because I was no longer in command. I was more intent that they succeed. If anything, I devoted more of my resources to ensure that Easy Company, led first by Heyliger, and later by Ron Speirs, was successful. If you never concern yourself with who receives credit, you always achieve greater results."

"What about contact with your soldiers after the war was over?"

Dick pointed to a file cabinet next to his desk and said, "As soon as the war ended, each soldier returned home and began his adjustment to civilian life in an America at peace. The adjustment was easier for some than it was others. Some, like Floyd Talbert, literally dropped from sight for nearly thirty years. Most veterans planned for a future together with a wife or girlfriend. A few years went by before we held our first reunion, but we have met regularly since then. These reunions are joyous events. Our memories revolve around old battle experiences and what we did when we were young, when we were united in a just cause and our lives depended upon each other. These conversations are reminiscent to what I observed in the week following V-E Day, when we talked about old battles, transferring to another outfit in the South Pacific, and about bad officers we knew and had known, or put on some flashy review with pigeons being released as the colors passed the reviewing stand and buglers blasted out from the top of one of those Alps and the music bounced around in the valleys. Sixty years later, the talks are the same. Doesn't matter what the conversation starts out about, it isn't long until it turns to combat. Funny thing, you'd think the conversations would become boring, but not to us. We talk the same battles over and over. By the mid-1980s, I decided to maintain a file on every soldier from Easy Company. Each paratrooper now has an individual file that contains copies of every letter that I sent or that I received. These men are members of my family."

"Recently, I read a book about Paul Tibbets," I said, "the pilot who dropped the atomic bomb on Hiroshima. The author, Bob Greene, asked Tibbets why he was so proud of the bomber command that he had formed for the atomic mission. He echoed similar sentiments that you have expressed about Easy Company."

"No need to go on," Dick replied. "Tibbets probably said that, as with Easy Company, he served in an outfit where you depended on the man to your left and to your right. You made decisions and risked your life every day for your buddies. You formed friendships that nothing and no one in your entire life will ever match. If there is something good that comes from war, this is it. When we returned from the war, we lost that closeness. But inside you, it is always there."

"That's exactly what he said, Dick. Is that closeness still there?"

"Of course it is. I look at the soldiers of Easy Company with great respect, a respect that I cannot describe in words. They were the best men I have ever known. If I had done a better job, perhaps more would have come home. During the war, I fell into a routine in organizing my platoons for an attack. In an assault, I routinely placed first platoon on the left, my second platoon on the right, and the third platoon in reserve. You continue on with that through the war, and on reflection, you realize that may be why today there are two men remaining from first platoon, three from second platoon, and twenty-five from third platoon. This bothers me a lot. That was a mistake, and I should have lined up the troops differently and with different formations."

Dick next shared two letters from Easy Company veterans that he felt summarized the bond that exists to this day. Sergeant Robert "Burr" Smith stayed with the paratroopers, where he later received a commission and eventually commanded a Special Forces Reserve unit. In December 1979, he wrote his former commander and said, "Funny thing about 'The Modern Army,' Dick. I am assigned to what is reputed to be the best unit in the U.S. Army, the Delta Force, and I believe that it is. Still, on a man-to-man basis, I'd choose my wartime paratroop company *anytime*! We had something there for three years that will never be equaled."

Sergeant Mike Ranney earned a journalism degree from the University of North Dakota after the war and then enjoyed a successful career as a reporter, newspaper editor, and public relations consultant. His assessment of Easy Company is the best known from any veteran, and it served as the fitting conclusion of the miniseries, as Dick quotes, "Do you remember the letter Mike Ranney wrote? You do. He said, 'I'm thinking back on the days of Easy Company, I'm treasuring my remark to my grandson who asked, 'Grandpa, were you a hero in the war?' 'No,' I answered, 'but I served in a company of heroes.'"

"When Ambrose finished *Band of Brothers*, he stated that 'Easy Company was Dick Winters's company.' How does that make you feel?"

"I don't disagree with Steve Ambrose on many points, but I do here. Easy Company didn't belong to me. It belonged to the soldiers. I was privileged to be a small part of its history. Officers, and commanders in particular, are merely caretakers. That the paratroopers respected me is more than enough reward."

"Well said. Dick, the last question I usually ask veterans from World War II is how do you want to be remembered?"

Without hesitation, he replied, "As company commander of Company E."

"Why?"

"Because I think of Easy Company every day. We sustained 150 percent casualties between the night that we jumped into Normandy and V-E Day. The result of sharing all the stress throughout training and combat has created a bond between the men of Easy Company that will last forever. In a sense, I don't think I ever left Company E. I may never again see the type of men in this outfit, but to me, Easy Company will always be 'my' company, not in the sense that Ambrose claimed, but in that I will always remain part of it. To this day they remain my second family. I still look at these men with great respect, respect I can't describe in words. That's the reason why I never joined the Veterans of Foreign Wars or the American Legion. I'm a strong supporter of veterans' organizations, but the brotherhood that I cherish revolves around Easy Company. My office serves as a testament to my love for these men. My life would have been very different without Company E. I am the man I am today because of Easy Company. Easy Company made me. As I reflect upon my life since the war, I can honestly say that it has been a lifetime search for men like those I knew in Easy Company. I haven't found too many. I don't think I know braver soldiers than Joe Toye, Bill Guarnere, or Floyd Talbert. I live with these guys every day. I mourn when they pass. Carwood Lipton died in December 2001. His death struck me particularly hard. So did Bull Randleman's. Lipton didn't live to see the acclaim Easy Company received when the miniseries was released. I try not to think of the bad times anymore. I think mostly of the good times. The emotion will always be there."

PART TWO

★ ★ ★

Summer

CHAPTER IV

Leadership

Our chief want is someone who will inspire us to be what we know we could be.

—RALPH WALDO EMERSON

During the first decade of our association, leadership became our favorite topic of discussion whenever the major and I were together. Not surprisingly, Dick maintained strong views on what made a man a strong or a weak leader. One day I asked him for his definition of leadership, and he replied, "Leadership is difficult to define. They talk about leadership at West Point every day. Leadership starts with honesty, dedication, and having a man who is dependable and fair. If you never deviate from the standards that you established, men have faith in you and you'll be out front to set the example. Sergeant Talbert once told me, 'Sir, I'd follow you into hell!' I take a great deal of pride in his remark."

Dick echoed similar sentiments when his *alma mater*, Franklin & Marshall College, recognized him as one of its most distinguished alumni in 2003. In a column titled "How Richard D. Winters '41 Kept the Story of Easy Company Alive for Future

Generations," *Franklin & Marshall Magazine* recorded Dick's definition of leadership: "It's something you have within you that gets the job done. You start with a cornerstone—honesty—and from there you build character, you build knowledge. With honesty goes being fair, making decisions, and being right, most of the time." Sounds like a good definition to me.

"Dick, let's talk about leadership today. Since I've known you, leadership has been the major component of our discussions. What's your take on the age-old question as to if leaders are born or made?"

"I believe that some men and women are born with the inherent qualities that make them good leaders. Writing to his son John who was a cadet at West Point in 1943, General Eisenhower once said, 'The one quality that can be developed by studious reflection and practice is the leadership of men.' I agree with Ike. Leaders are not born. Leaders are made, and they are made by solid effort and hard work."

I added, "Let me tell you a story about one of my heroes, Chuck Yeager. Yeager was a fighter ace in World War II before he received acclaim as the first man to break the sound barrier in October 1947. In his autobiography, he says—and I'm paraphrasing here—that the question that he most often fields from audiences is the same question I just asked you: 'Are leaders born or are they made?' His standard response is 'I was born with unusually good eyes and coordination. I was mechanically oriented and I understood machines easily. My nature was to stay cool in tight spots. But I also worked my tail off to learn how to fly, and worked hard at it all the way. I spent hundreds more hours in the cockpit than any other pilot I know. That experience made me better than the average pilot. I don't deny I was damn good. I may not have been the best pilot, but I at least was one of the title contenders.'"

"I'm very familiar with Chuck Yeager. Hard work and determination," Dick commented, "made Yeager the exceptional pilot that he became. He was the best of the best. Personally, I think I would have been effective in any airborne outfit, but Easy Company allowed me to excel. If you had anything good in you, E Company brought it out. One more thing about your question on whether leaders can be trained or whether they are born: If your response is that leaders are born and not made, then there is little reason why we should have West Point and the various service academies. You might be out of a job."

I laughed and returned to the subject of leadership. "Do you recall the conversation you had with Steve Ambrose about how you ought to spend the remainder of your life?"

"I sure do. Not long ago, Ambrose looked at me and said, 'From now on, Winters, if you are going to talk about anything, talk about leadership.' I've always prided myself on being a good leader. If you look at my journal and my wartime letters to DeEtta Almon, you'll see that leadership dominated my thoughts and, more importantly, my actions. I also attended a dinner with Ambrose after we walked the battlefields as he prepared to write *Band of Brothers*. He opened his comments that evening with this statement on leadership: 'If you aren't in good physical shape, forget it. You are not going to be a good leader.' That remark has stuck with me over the years. There is a lot of truth in it."

I asked Dick when he first realized that he had the qualities of leadership that he demonstrated during the war.

"That's difficult to determine. I can tell you about my first leadership position. When I was young, I lived for several years with my grandmother in Ephrata, Pennsylvania. I was a shy kid who had no brothers or sisters. I was scared to death to attend school most of the time. When Dad moved the family to Lancaster when I was eight years old, I changed schools, and once again I was terrified of all these strangers who always seemed to pick a fight with me. Later the principal, whose name was Elizabeth Martin, took a liking to me, and she appointed me captain of the school safety patrol, which is a fancy title for the school crossing guards. In essence I was a glorified patrol boy, but I was proud of the title and her trust in my ability. That was my first leadership position, giving orders and directing younger children across the street. This may seem insignificant to you, but it is indelibly imprinted in my mind after all these years."

I thought his response was incredibly interesting, but I wanted to delve into his letters to his platonic friend DeEtta, with whom he maintained an active correspondence for four years. There was one particular letter that I felt captured the essence of his leadership style, so I asked him about it. "I read your letters to your friend while you were in England. Do you recall the letter in which you couldn't understand why you were still a company executive officer after fifteen months and all your contemporaries at Toccoa had either been promoted or transferred to work on the staff of senior headquarters?"

"Give me a minute and I'll find it for you." After a short pause, he continued, "Here it is. Ah, yes. I was comparing my life as a commissioned officer with DeEtta, who had applied for a commission, but had been rejected. Trying to ease her disappointment, I said that she might envy the social life of an officer, but social status was not all that it was cracked up to be. I advised her that the social life of an officer was my only holdback to future advancement. While the other officers spent the majority of their off-duty time at the officers' club, I had no desire to do the same, and I refused to join the parties and social gatherings. 'Which leaves me,' I informed DeEtta, 'with the point to bring out that I am a half-breed, an officer, yes, but at heart an enlisted man. So I work and do my duty as I should, but when it comes to play, I am in a bad position and only in athletics with the men do I enjoy myself.'"

"What's that passage tell you about yourself, Dick?"

"What do you mean?"

"Don't you see? This is the key to your success as a troop commander. You never forgot the place you came from. A lot of senior officers in the army forget what it was like when they were lieutenants and captains. Your focus was never on personal aggrandizement or promotion. Your focus remained on the welfare of the soldiers in your command. It is as evident as the nose on your face."

Another one of Dick's letters validated my assessment. Six weeks before D-Day, Dick mentioned that he had not closed his eyes for more than forty-two hours since the company had been conducting maneuvers in the English countryside. Describing the scene to DeEtta, he wrote: "If you want to see a beautiful, pathetic, and touching picture, follow me. There you see a private, next to his machine gun along an English roadside on a cold morning. He's been on the march and fighting for just about twenty-four hours without stopping. He's tired, dead tired, so tired his mind is almost a blank. He's wet, hungry, and miserable. As his buddies sleep, he keeps watch, a hard job when you're so tired and know that when the sun comes up in another half hour, you'll be on the move. What does he do? Pulls out a picture of his girl, who's over 3,000 miles away and then studies the picture. In a state of tranquility, he dreams of days when he can enjoy the kind of life she stands for. Down the road comes an officer—It's me, nobody else would think of being up at a pre-dawn hour. 'How's it going, Shep? What are you doing?' Then together we study and discuss his girl's good features and virtues." A half-breed, yes, but Dick Winters remained an enlisted soldier at heart.

I next asked him about the importance of keeping a cool head in combat.

"That's what you are expected to do as an officer in combat," he responded. "To be good, you must first acquire a few brains and common sense. Next, learn to feel and think with the head and not the heart. Men are so many machines, capable of doing so much, in a certain amount of time. Try and save as many as you can. At times that is difficult when you figure percentage killed and wounded as to how successful the attack was."

Thinking back to our preliminary conversations about Easy Company and Captain Sobel, I asked Dick to elaborate about the importance of leadership by example. These conversations pre-dated the production of the miniseries, as well as his decision to publish his memoirs. So I asked him, "As an infantry officer myself and a professor at West Point, I know the importance of leadership from the front, but I was hoping you could amplify your feelings on the matter."

"The message I hoped that I instilled in the Corps of Cadets at the U.S. Military Academy is this: Lead from the front. Say, 'Follow me!' and then lead the way. As you know, 'Follow me!' is the motto of the Infantry School at Fort Benning. When Stephen Ambrose wrote *Band of Brothers*, he used my journals and reports as one of his primary sources. If you look at the chapter about Normandy, the title of the chapter is 'Follow Me!' Where did he get that title? I gave Steve my private memories of D-Day that I had recorded on June 22, 1944. I penned these memories after jotting down some key phrases while I recovered from my slight wound at Carentan on June 12." Handing me a copy of "Richard Winters' D-Day Memories," he said, "The underlined portions are notes that Steve incorporated into *Band of Brothers*. Take a look at page three and you will see that I recalled meeting a fellow paratrooper as soon as I landed on French soil. He was hesitant of taking the lead even with his tommy gun, so I said, 'Follow me.' Steve underlined the words 'Follow me' and made an editorial note that simply read 'Chapter Title.'"

"Who were the most effective leaders you met during the war?"

"Colonel Bob Sink certainly was one of the best. He set high standards and never compromised those standards. After the paratroopers of the 506th Parachute Infantry Regiment earned their jump wings, Sink granted a ten-day furlough, but cautioned the men to conduct themselves appropriately. Several paratroopers reported late for duty after their furloughs expired. Sink called another regimental formation and publicly humiliated one paratrooper from each of his nine companies. The adjutant called out the name of the last soldier to report to duty, and that paratrooper was marched in front of the formation, under escort. An officer stripped him of his unit patch, forced him to un-blouse his boots, and then escorted him from the field. What Sink was saying was paratroopers may be elite, but they had to follow the army's rules and regulations. I liked that. For some reason, Sink liked me, respected me. He was always the man instrumental in getting me my next job."

Dick then addressed the noncommissioned officers (NCOs). "We also had a solid group of NCOs in the company. Sergeants Carwood Lipton, Bill Guarnere, Bull Randleman, Joe Toye, and Johnny Martin were exceptional leaders who always led from the front. I always felt the best leaders were those who came up from the ranks. We had guys like Pat Christenson and Don Malarkey who were privates in Normandy, corporals in Holland, and later sergeants at Bastogne. Take Lipton for example. Carwood Lipton was a squad leader at Toccoa and later a platoon sergeant in Normandy. Prior to our jump into Holland, I promoted him to company first sergeant. Later, he received a battlefield commission to second lieutenant."

Dick smiled when he mentioned the next NCO. "And then there was Floyd Talbert. He had it all. We developed a personal friendship dating back to Toccoa. He was athletic and dedicated. You knew if your life were on the line, he would come through. At Toccoa, he was in 3rd Platoon, not mine. On the march to Atlanta, Talbert was slugging along with a machine gun. Behind him was Walter Gordon, who was supposed to carry the gun. I can still see the determination on Talbert's face. I promoted him to sergeant in Normandy. During the counterattack at Carentan, he held the right flank along the railroad. After Normandy, I promoted him to platoon sergeant when Carwood Lipton took over as company first sergeant. When Lipton received a battlefield commission later in the war, Talbert became first sergeant. He couldn't work with Captain Speirs—you will have to read his letter to see why he turned in his stripes. Talbert claimed that he was always comparing Speirs to me. We simply had different leadership styles, but I guess I should be flattered. I wrote to DeEtta about Talbert after the war. I told her that I was going deer hunting with an old sergeant of mine from Easy Company. That sergeant was Talbert. It wasn't the hunt as much as I just enjoyed being around this guy. We didn't have to talk to enjoy each other's company, nor did we have to talk in combat or during a battle. A word or two, or a wave of the hand, and we knew precisely what the other guy was thinking. That makes working just lovely. Of the enlisted soldiers in E Company, Talbert is the only one whom I would classify as a friend. These are the ones you always remember. The men who do their best, you never forget them."

Addressing the officers, Dick said, "You know how I feel about Harry Welsh and Lewis Nixon. Harry was a good officer, though he had a lot of faults in his makeup. He joined the regiment at Camp Mackall, North Carolina, in April 1943. Harry was my roommate at Aldbourne, England. He goofed a number of times later in the war, sometimes with dire consequences, but he was solid. Nixon was undoubtedly my best friend. At Toccoa, he commanded the first platoon and I led the second platoon. Our friendship evolved naturally. My first recollection of the impact I had on Nixon occurred on the troop carrier taking us back to England after Normandy. Nixon asked me to talk to the battalion officers on leadership. What could I say? That impressed me. Nixon was always there for me. He became a guy I could check with to receive counsel or a suggestion. Nixon kept me from second-guessing myself. As a combat leader, I also respected Ron Speirs, who commanded Easy Company longer than any previous commander. All were exceptional leaders."

"And what about the replacement officers?"

"There were many more non-leaders than leaders as the war progressed. By the time we entered Germany, I was so desperately in need of officers, I was satisfied to have warm bodies filling the leadership positions. Once we reached Germany, the replacements were ill-trained and not ready for combat. A good number were more interested in getting medals than they were in leading soldiers. At the same time, I was grateful that our days in actual contact with the enemy were scarce by the spring of 1945. The replacement officers never would have survived Normandy or Holland. They certainly would not have survived Bastogne. We had some good platoon leaders, but they were few and far between. Very few of them could cut it in combat, very few."

"Tell me about General Maxwell Taylor," I said.

"Ambrose thinks I am too hard on General Taylor, our commanding general in the 101st Airborne Division. I don't think so. He was more show than anything else. Once when my platoon was assigned security detail for Taylor's headquarters, I noticed that his orderlies had stacked six or eight pieces of firewood outside. The first thing that Taylor did when he emerged from his tent was to pick up an ax. He proceeded to put on a show by splitting firewood. What a phony. But that was the image he wanted to pass on to the men. I can't help but feel that this display was more for his ego than the benefit of the men to set an example of leadership. Later that morning, I was checking my outposts, making sure everyone was on the ball and that everything was exactly right. As Taylor got ready to leave the command post, one of my fellas sat up from sleeping and his helmet fell off his head. Taylor was driving by, and he stopped his jeep, took the soldier's name, and asked the identity of his platoon leader. Later, I received a notice to report to division headquarters. I was informed I was being fined fifty dollars because one of my men wasn't wearing his helmet. Fifty dollars at that time was a great deal of money, and it hurt. I felt that was so unjust, so unfair, and so unreasonable on Taylor's part. But I had other reasons why I didn't care for him."

"What other reasons?"

"At Bastogne, he left us. Ambrose says I am not being fair because Taylor had been ordered back to Washington before the Germans launched their attack, but I told him I didn't have to be fair. We were delighted that Taylor's division artillery commander Brigadier General Tony McAuliffe was in command at Bastogne. What we liked about McAuliffe was that he allowed us to do our jobs. You didn't have a lot of interference from McAuliffe. But with Taylor in command, he told you what you needed to do here—he had to run everything. You can't do a good job if you do not have a chance to use your imagination or your creativity. In my mind, Taylor was more interested in impressing his superiors than watching out for his men. Taylor was such a contrast with British General Montgomery."

"How so? I've never heard too many Americans sing Monty's praises."

"That's because the writers didn't know Monty or see him in action. Montgomery was the real deal. I saw him on a number of occasions, and he always impressed me as a commander who lived a lifestyle that was beyond reproach for his staff to follow. He set the example. He addressed every division that was scheduled to participate in the invasion. He called us together and had every soldier take off his helmet so he could see the troops better."

"Tell me about the importance of self-discipline."

Dick replied, "Self-discipline keeps you doing your job. Without it, you lose your pride and you forget the importance of self-respect in the eyes of your fellow men. Pride keeps you going on. This is what I feared I would lose—the loss of the will to measure up to my men."

Paul Fussell was one of the most prominent literary and cultural historians of the twentieth century. His *The Great War and Modern Memory*, coupled with *Wartime: Understanding and Behavior in the Second World War*, has been cited as "revolutionary" in its effect of understanding war. Knowing that Stephen Ambrose repeatedly quoted Fussell, I asked Dick, "Ambrose states that after so many days of continuous combat and the loss of so many leaders at Bastogne, Easy Company reached its breaking point. He quotes Fussell, who claims that every infantryman passes through three stages, depending on how long he remains in combat. The first phase is: 'This can't happen to me. I'm not going to get wounded. I'm too smart. I'm too good-looking. I'm too young.' The second stage is: 'Jesus, this could happen to me if I'm not more careful, so I've got to dig my foxhole a little deeper. I've got to sight this weapon in a little tighter.'"

"He's got it about right," Dick replied.

"Fussell continues with the third stage, which he states is the following: 'This is going to happen to me unless I get out of here.'"

"Right again," said Dick, and he added, "'I hope to hell when I am wounded, it won't be too severe.' After our first casualties in Normandy, we lost that youthful confidence in our own immortality."

I asked Dick to put aside his bravado and give a more honest answer to how close he came to breaking. "Did you come close to reaching your breaking point at Bastogne?"

It took Dick a minute to answer, "Most every man—myself included—had reached that third stage in Bastogne. Sooner or later, I believed that the odds were going to catch up to me, but there never was a fear that I was going to break. I just felt that I was going to be hit sooner or later. But as far as the breaking point, no. You don't see people getting hit around you every day, continuing on and on, and not think, 'How long is this war going to last? Is this going to go on forever? Am I ever going to see home again? I don't know. Not too damn sure I'm ever going to go home again.' Yeah, you just hope for the best. 'Sooner or later, I'll get it.'"

"Did this equate to a fear of death?"

"No, I just felt that I was no longer invincible. As I later reflected on the war, I had been lucky, mighty lucky, from the very first day. I saw so many get it and go out feet first. I just knew if I stuck around long enough, I'd have my turn sooner or later. I took way too many chances. I had to take them, with the position, prestige, and the job. Of course a fellow always hopes to live, and when he gets hit, please God, don't let it be too bad. I didn't want to be killed after all that I had gone through."

"Did any of the casualties affect you more than the others?"

"There was only one. He was a young kid, a private or private first class. I liked him as a friend. I can't even remember his name, but he had such a great personality. He was in the plane with Lieutenant Meehan when he was shot down over Ste. Mère-Eglise on D-Day. I don't know why, but he seemed 'special' to me. I felt worse about his death than I did Meehan's."

"Well, it must certainly have been lonely in command during Bastogne."

"Look, we had a job to perform," Dick responded. "Every commander is lonely. He is also isolated, because only he can make the decisions by which his men will live or die. Loneliness and isolation come with the territory. There is no need for dramat-

ics or the theatrical. The job of commanding is lonely by definition. A commander cannot show partiality or favoritism to any
soldier, officer or enlisted, in his command. There is simply no
time to develop personal relationships or worry if you are liked.
You do your best, and at the end of the day, you look in the mirror
and hope you were a good leader."

"Dick, you use the terms 'commander' and 'leader' almost in-
terchangeably. Is there a difference?"

"That's a great question. In my mind, a person can exercise
leadership by a position or title that he or she holds. A commander
is different. Yes, you may occupy a command position, but a good
commander must be willing to make the critical decisions where
an individual life is at stake. General Meade at Gettysburg is an
example. Meade arrives on the battlefield after the first day's
action has already been concluded. He meets his subordinate generals around midnight and has not had the opportunity to see
the battlefield in daylight. After receiving a briefing from one of
his corps commanders, Meade allegedly says, 'We may fight it out
here just as well as anywhere else.' General Teddy Roosevelt, Jr.,
said the same thing when he landed on Utah Beach on D-Day. His
4th Division landed on the wrong beach, but Roosevelt surveyed
the area and stated, 'We'll start the war right here.' These are
command decisions! Loneliness is the inescapable burden of a
commanding officer. On the commander's shoulders weighs the
fate of thousands and the nation that they serve. I hope that answers your question."

"And you were only twenty-six years old when you fought at
Bastogne."

"Twenty-six didn't seem so young at the time. Many of us
were twenty-six, and most were younger than that. The average

age of the paratroopers in Easy Company was approximately twenty-one years old. Things moved fast in those days."

I had read that Dick briefly considered making the army a career, and I was curious why he changed his mind. "Why did you leave the army when you obviously had such a bright future ahead of you?"

"You know I volunteered for the Pacific, but was rejected—we can explore that later. Guess the best way to explain things is to say the excitement was gone when the war ended. Most of my best soldiers had rotated back to the States or were discharged. A typical day in Austria where we were stationed wasn't too bad, but it wasn't fulfilling. Up about 0700 hours, breakfast, paperwork, inspect guards, quarters, kitchens the rest of the morning. After a little lunch, fool around for a while, and then take a sunbath for a few hours while I read or just lie and think. That's what I really enjoy, just drifting around thinking of nothing in particular. In the evening, we play a volleyball game, after which I take a run, some calisthenics, and we shoot the bull, maybe try and write a letter or read, but it's really just a lot of foolish talk. There is a limit to how much garrison life a fella can handle."

In two separate letters Dick went on to describe life in Kaprun, where he was responsible for overseeing the demobilization of twenty-five thousand German soldiers and displaced persons. "What a hell of a mess this whole place is," Dick wrote. "You have thousands and thousands of allied prisoners of war, millions of displaced persons, who are really slaves, brought here to work from other countries, and now thousands of German soldiers. They all want something. They need help, food, medical care, everything. Ye gods, I look at these people and think how they are lucky to be alive, really, for so many have died and others are crippled. Here they are, all wanting to go home, yet when they get there, millions won't have a home, food, or any families." Later he said, "It's so quiet here and despite the fact that I have 25,000 Krauts under my charge, there seems like nothing to do, no reason to work. With demobilization, everything that sustains morale in a military command—danger to the country, the potential for combat, and the fear of the unknown—virtually disappears overnight. Maintaining discipline and morale become a major leadership challenge."

"As a commander, what did you feel was the indispensable quality to ensure battlefield success?"

I think Dick was ready for the question because he answered almost before I had completed asking it. "I could talk a long time about this one, but I'll try to get directly to the point. I go back to your previous question. The big thing that I derived from combat was the necessity of maintaining discipline—discipline in our troops and getting the job done in combat. And, with that in mind, as we were coming home from France after D-Day, we were ordered to leave our weapons and anything that we had taken to France. We were supposed to leave it there. We would be given completely new weapons, ammunition, and equipment. However, for Company E, I brought back all the 30-caliber live ammunition I could find because I knew when we returned to England I would have to train the replacements. I wanted live ammunition for training purposes. I wanted to put those replacements under live ammunition in order for them to experience what it felt like conducting an attack. The only way to gain experience from overhead fire is by actually fighting through it. So we got back to England, and I conducted company field problems by using live ammunition for good purposes. It was dangerous. I was sticking my neck out.

If anybody would have been hurt or we had lost anybody, I would have been a dead duck. But I lucked out and it worked out okay. That training paid huge dividends when we jumped into Holland."

"As a leader, what aspect of your military service provided you the greatest satisfaction?"

"Knowing that I got the job done; knowing that I maintained the respect of my paratroopers. Soldiers looked at me in a different manner than they had before the battles on D-Day and on the Island. The greatest reward you have as a leader is the 'look of respect.' After the experience at Bastogne, the men knew me better than they had ever known me. If you are a leader, you lead the way, not just in the easy ones, but on the tough ones, too. The key to being a successful combat leader is to earn respect, not because of rank, but because you are a man."

There was only one question that Dick refused to answer. He cut me off immediately when I asked what made him so different from the other officers in Easy Company and in 2nd Battalion. "I'm going to skip that one, Cole. I don't want to share my ego."

As I reflected on Dick's answer, I returned to my initial question as to if leaders are born or if they are made. When he read Dick's thoughts on the subject, a fellow historian named Dennis Showalter helped me refine my personal thoughts and made an analogy with a bull's-eye target. Dick was too humble to assign any relevance to his innate leadership talents, and he attributed his success solely to hard work and dedication. "In essence, he denies the dichotomy between the born leader and the self-made commander," said Showalter. "He clearly demonstrates that the only way leaders can be produced in a republic is by cultivation. In other societies, birth and position within society may position a man or woman to leadership positions, but not in a democracy. In a democracy, leadership depends on self-awareness and self-referencing. The self is at the center. The next ring is spouse/partner. Then comes the ring of children, then family, then 'brethren,' then colleagues, and so on. When the order of the rings is disturbed, and even more when the bull's-eye fails to hold, the result is disintegration. Dick Winters knows himself; from that the rest develops. It is Dick's constant verifying his leadership attributes, not navel-gazing, certainly not strengths and shortcomings, but rather who and what he is, that defines his leadership."

CHAPTER V

Friendship

I came to love the way he lit up when I entered the room.
"Ah, it's my buddy" he would say.

—MITCH ALBOM, *TUESDAYS WITH MORRIE*

Several years ago, Dick and I reminisced about the relationships that we had formed during our lives. Dick took the opportunity to venture into an area in which I was particularly interested—friendship. By this time I had only known Dick about five years, but I struggled to recall him ever mentioning a single individual whom he considered a lifelong friend. He said that he had many acquaintances, but few close friends. That was the way he wanted it. "I like to count my close friends on one hand," he would say. I decided to pursue the matter and asked if we could talk about friendships and friends.

"I was very much a loner in elementary and high school. I spent the summer working for Edison Electric, where my father was one of three general foremen in the area surrounding Lancaster, Pennsylvania. Prior to enlisting in the U.S. Army in 1941, I had had only a handful of dates," he said. "In high school I was more interested in studying and athletics. That didn't change when I entered Franklin and Marshall College. As I put myself through college, I lived at home. As a result, I missed out, perhaps by choice, on the socialization that normally is associated with dormitory life and the college scene. My first date in college was compulsory by direction of my fraternity brothers. As it turned out, the date was a nightmare because of a combination of circumstances. The party was a dance and I couldn't dance. I didn't even know how to hold the girl. They told me to just go out there and walk to the music. So I did, but most of the time, I walked on the poor girl's feet. That was my first and last dance, for shortly afterward, I dropped out of the fraternity—too much money for a guy working his way through college."

"I'm chuckling, Dick, because I dated a lot in high school, but once I got to college, I was more focused on the Reserve Officer Training Corps (ROTC) and earning my commission in the U.S. Army. I just wasn't interested in the social aspect of college life," I said.

"Neither was I. Had a few dates my sophomore and junior years, but in my senior year, I didn't even take the time to look at a girl. Following graduation, I traveled to Vermont to work on a professor's farm in the mountains. After that, I went home to volunteer for the army instead of waiting for them to take me." He added, "Guess neither one of us set the world on fire in that department."

What intrigued me so much about Dick's attitude toward friendship was a letter that he had written to his pen pal DeEtta Almon just four days prior to D-Day. He began his treatise by remarking what a thrill it was to read in the *Stars and Stripes*, the soldier's overseas newspaper, that on D-Day all theaters, ball games, and nonessential business establishments planned to close, and people would be asked to go to church and pray. He went on to write, "The size and magnitude of a united feeling like that just sends the chills right up and down a fellow's spine. When we're at home, a fellow doesn't usually think beyond his local acquaintances. Go to another part of the country and it's your home state, and anybody from your hometown is a buddy. Go overseas and anybody from the United States is your buddy. So when you feel that way and think that all those people are sending their best wishes and prayers to you, a fellow can't help but feel good."

Friendships during the war were rare occurrences to Dick for no other reason than an officer must remain above the fray and not be encumbered by close attachment to any individual in his outfit. He chastised DeEtta when she wrote that some U.S. Navy officers with whom she worked had accompanied their enlisted sailors on picnics and how much DeEtta admired them for bridging the gap between officer and enlisted personnel. Her letter prompted Dick to write his analysis of why such relationships were self-defeating and detrimental to the efficiency of a military command. He wrote, "God almighty, I'd hate to be an officer in that outfit. Fraternization may work in the Navy, but I don't think it does, for I've noticed it throughout my career. You lack military discipline and respect for rank. I've been a buck private, and when I was an enlisted soldier, I didn't want to fool around with the officers. All I wanted from them was good leadership. Now I am a captain and I find that buddy stuff is out. I am all in favor of knowing each and every man, getting in bull sessions with them, etc., knowing their background, likes, dislikes, capabilities, and weak points. I want to be their friend and the guy they go to when they want a favor or they're in trouble. But I am not their buddy, I am their captain, when I say something, that's it—you jump. If you're going to have things like that then you can't go around on picnics with them and so forth. Of course, I know those officers are well liked who do things like that, but in the end, their ideas and principles break down. I've only been around three years in the army, but I can see that the old Army is the right Army, and the longer I am around, and the more I see of it, the more I am convinced. You can't make a decision as quickly and thoroughly if your buddies are concerned in a life and death situation."

Not surprisingly, Dick never allowed himself to get too close to anyone, including DeEtta. "As a matter of fact," he told her, "I wouldn't even kiss a girl's hand, for as a soldier, I don't want any more people than necessary to even know me. It's no good. If a soldier lives, O.K., get out of the army and forget it. If he doesn't, O.K., there are just that fewer people who feel the toll of the war." Of those who worked with him in the army, Dick said, "There are only a few of them who really know and understand how I feel and think about life in general. I guess there's really only one, Lieutenant Harry Welsh, who is as bull-headed as you'd expect an Irishman to be. At home there are my folks, and that's it. I don't think I have another soul who knows me."

I would add Lewis Nixon to that mix because I never heard Dick mention him in less than flattering terms. In the immediate aftermath of the war, Dick once classified Nixon as "absolutely the most unreliable man I've ever known in peacetime, but by far the best combat soldier in Easy Company." Dick paid Nixon the ultimate compliment by saying, "Nix's O.K. in the fight."

As I listened to Dick's comments about maintaining a degree of distance from his fellow officers and his men, I recalled my close friend Colonel Farrell, a fellow battalion commander who recently retired from the U.S. Army. "In Iraq," he said, "I generally kept my own counsel. I became very close with my command sergeant major. We functioned very well, and in the course of my command, we only had one disagreement. I do not remember the reason—I have blocked it out—but it lasted only a day or two. Other than that, we were very close and effective; however, as close as we were, I never shared the burden of command. He knew and accepted without reservation that that burden was mine. Similarly, with my two executive officers and operations officers, I became close, but only to a degree. I developed especially strong relationships with my company commanders, but again, I kept my distance to a large degree and I never shared my innermost thoughts." Though separated by sixty plus years, my friend's experiences were similar to those that Dick had expressed so eloquently to DeEtta.

At my request, Dick returned to the subject of friendship in one of his final interviews, conducted by magazine editor Christopher Anderson. Dick said, "I think about the people I worked with. They don't know me; nobody knows me. The neighbors, people whom I've lived with and worked for over the years, they have never known me. . . . I have always made an effort not to talk about myself. I talk about the war, but not about myself. I would like to keep it that way."

We next discussed Steve Ambrose's latest book, which Steve had written just prior to his death in 2002. Ambrose titled the book *Comrades: Brothers, Fathers, Heroes, Sons, Pals*. Although the book was not nearly as well received as Ambrose's standard biographies and histories, Dick was struck by the audio version, which he felt conveyed Steve's emotions about not only the men and women who had made an impression on his own life, but also friendships that illustrated a special bond on the subjects he had studied over five decades of research. Ambrose writes, "One of the joys of my adult life has been discovering male friendships. Friendship among men is difficult for Anglo-Saxon males of a middle-class background to define or practice. I was well into my fifties," says Ambrose, "before I discovered the pleasure of hugging a male friend. Now I do it habitually. . . . General Dwight Eisenhower wrote at the end of his life that he regretted his inability to give hugs to his fellows." Ambrose continues, "The four best words in the English language are love, wife, home and work. The fifth one is friend." I'm not sure I concur with Ambrose's order of merit, but the topic gets me thinking of Dick Winters's friends.

If I were asked to name Dick's closest friend, without hesitation I would say it was Bob Hoffman. Hoffman is a local architect from Lebanon, Pennsylvania. His association with Dick, which eventually blossomed into a loving friendship, dated to 1994 when Hoffman saw Dick's photo in the local paper on the recognition of the fiftieth anniversary of D-Day. Dick was pictured with another World War II veteran whom Hoffman knew well. Because Bob had an abiding interest in the 101st Airborne Division, he took his friend's suggestion and wrote a letter to Dick, requesting an opportunity to meet him. A month later, Hoffman received a call from Dick, who said he had received his letter, but he wanted to check out what kind of person Bob was. Because Bob was a chief executive officer of a hospital, Dick asked his physician to comment on Hoffman's character. Receiving a favorable report, Dick called.

In 2005, I asked Hoffman to share some of his memories of his initial meeting with Dick Winters. The rest of the story is told in Bob's own words: "Winters asked if I had read *Band of Brothers*, but I had not. He told me to read it and only then will we get together. I did and we did. It was one of those very rare times in life when we both had a feeling of comfort and sincerity. Our meetings became more frequent, and my understanding and admiration for Dick Winters increased geometrically. In the beginning we spoke a lot about the war, but long ago our relationship became more personal, revolving about the events in our daily lives. I truly think of him as a surrogate father. My family is gone. His personal support has been wonderful. He calls me 'Hoffman'; I call him 'Winters.' He remains in my thoughts every day."

Hoffman is being modest. What he gave Dick was something no one else could. In addition to arranging for Dick's medical care and facilitating the construction of a sunporch at Dick's home in Hershey, Bob significantly improved the quality of Dick's life. Hardly surprisingly, Dick enjoyed his company. Together they enjoyed countless meals, trips to the Emmys, the cinematic premiere of *Saving Private Ryan*, visits with President George W. Bush, and countless speaking engagements, ranging from the Federal Bureau of Investigation to local high schools. In short, when Dick was in Hoffman's company, he could simply be himself—and that was a rare gift. Later I discovered that Dick had inscribed a copy of his memoirs and presented it to Hoffman. His inscription read, "To Bob, this is copy #1. You're my man!" And that says it all.

My own friendship with Dick Winters and the veterans from World War II evolved over the years. While I was stationed at West Point, the common experience of military service established the foundation for the friendships that later emerged. My daughter thought it odd that here I was, an officer in my late forties, and my closest friends were in their mid-to-late eighties at best. "Dad, all your friends are in their nineties," she would say. "What are you going to do in five years?" "Maura," I responded, "I guess I'll be the man with no friends."

Her remarks got me thinking about friendship in general. Sometime the dearest friends one makes in life are those he or she makes late in life. There is a clear dichotomy between the friends you make in childhood and those whom you meet as an adult. When you are young, you encounter a limited number of acquaintances and you are forced to select your friends from that population. Those friendships are essentially defined by who you are—student athlete, member of the National Honor Society, if you are popular or not—and your persona is therefore essentially defined by a relatively small population. It is hardly surprising then that as life evolves and experiences multiply, many adults lose touch with their childhood friends. As you grow older, experience causes you to learn more about yourself, and if you are fortunate, you develop more confidence in the person you have become. As a result, you alone define who you are. You no longer need to be defined by your friends, so you can now select friends who buttress your self-confidence and share common interests. These friends exist to support you and to give you an opportunity to support them. Adult friends offer encouragement, support, and love.

Of all the veterans whom I befriended during my military career, Dick Winters was the most different from the others. Sixteen years after our initial meeting, I am at a loss to identify a single event that I would consider instrumental in the evolution of that friendship. But now in retrospect, as I reflect upon my relationship with Dick, I see a great friendship unfolding before my eyes—slowly at first, but gaining momentum with the passing years. I was not conscious of the evolution until long after Dick had passed, but the journey was quite pronounced. As I write this chapter, I recently noticed a journal entry on January 18, 2001, Dick's eighty-third birthday, which reads, "I spent several hours with Dick Winters today. He is the man with whom I most enjoy talking 'soldiering.' We addressed a myriad of topics, after which I asked Dick to come to West Point in mid-May and participate in my retirement ceremony. Hopefully he can do so. He seems willing to commit if the requirements surrounding the filming of 'Band of Brothers' do not interfere."

Two months later, Dick formally accepted my invitation when he called me late one evening. "Cole, Ethel and I will be only too happy to come to West Point on May 18 to officiate your retirement ceremony, but I want to make sure you really want us to be there. I'm going to ask you a direct question and I want an honest answer. Here is my question: 'Of the thousands of Army officers that you must know, are you sure that you want me to be a part of your retirement?'"

I responded, "Dick, I'm delighted that you will come. There is no one whom I can think of that I would rather retire me from the army. I assure you that the honor belongs to me and not to you. Thank you so very much."

As you might imagine the next two months sped by rapidly. When the word got out that Major Dick Winters of Easy Company, 506th Parachute Infantry Regiment, was presiding over my retirement, several agencies at the U.S. Military Academy asked me to solicit Dick to address their assemblies during his brief stay. Naturally, I took the liberty to inform them that my retirement was a personal matter and that Dick's schedule was full. On the day of my retirement, I dispatched an officer to Hershey to pick up Dick and bring him to West Point. I kept his presence a secret until the crowd of distinguished guests joined me in the John J. Pershing Room of West Point's Cullum Hall. At the designated hour, Dick appeared. In a retirement ceremony, the officer departing military service normally introduces his guests before the actual ceremony commences. What began as a low murmur grew into a thunderous ovation when I proudly announced that the man whom I had selected to officiate at my retirement was none other than Major Dick Winters of *Band of Brothers* fame. I saluted Dick as "my comrade-in-arms and brother." I could not have been more pleased when the assembly acknowledged his presence with extended applause. Nor could I have been prouder when Dick pinned the Legion of Merit on my uniform. In my valedictory remarks, I stated that I had not desired a formal ceremony, and that I preferred to leave without fanfare. I changed my mind because I had something important to say and I wanted my friends and colleagues to listen. While I have no intention to reiterate my farewell remarks, I did say that many had asked me how I felt about my "big day." I responded, "This is not a big day for me, it is an ordinary day. D-Day was a big day, and I assure you this hardly compares to D-Day." Later I paid tribute to the men and women of World War II, stating that in my career I had been privileged to know three great company commanders: Joe Dawson, whose company was first to penetrate the German defenses overlooking Omaha Beach; John Howard, who led the British glider company who captured Pegasus Bridge; and Dick Winters of the 101st Airborne Division. I concluded my remarks by stating, "I am honored to be associated with Dick Winters and the veterans of World War II. I feel privileged that they call me their friend, and I will always regard them as God's noblest creatures." At the conclusion of the ceremony, as the people flowed through the receiving line, I must confess that they seemed happier to shake Major Winters's hand than mine. Dick was the center of attention. And that's the way it should have been.

Later that evening, I hosted a small reception at the Hotel Thayer on the grounds of West Point. I asked Dick to sit next to me. My two children sat to my right, while Dick sat to my left. My daughter picks up the story from here. "As a thirteen-year-old girl straight from the eighth grade, I knew close to nothing of Easy Company, Brecourt, or Currahee. I did know, however, that whoever this guy was that my father had asked to retire him was probably a big deal. During our dinner, I, after bickering with my older brother because he wanted to sit with his girlfriend and not me, was lucky enough to find a seat next to the major. 'Sit next to me, Maura,' he said as I exchanged seats with my father. Conversation came easily. We laughed at jokes and talked about my father. At one point in the dinner, the major looked over to my brother, who was engaged in a private conversation with his date and paying little attention to the rest of the dinner party, and said, 'John, would you like to include the rest of us in your conversation?' Yes, poetic justice for our earlier argument! This was my first encounter with Major Winters. It was a short, delightful glimpse into a friendship that would develop over the years." As a sidebar, when we returned home that night, John looked at me and said, "Dad, that man is intimidating!" Intimidating or not, John grew to respect Dick as much as I did.

That evening I sent Dick a short note to convey my appreciation for his presiding over my retirement and how honored I was by the warm inscription that he wrote in *Band of Brothers*, which read, "Thanks for bringing us all together." I informed Dick that "in a lifetime of good friends and comrades-in-arms, I value your friendship above all others." And I meant every word that I had written.

In the autumn following my retirement, the HBO miniseries aired on national television. Dick was justifiably proud of the production, and he had every reason to be so. Much of the series was based on his private journal that had formed the basis of Stephen Ambrose's *Band of Brothers*. The achievements of Easy Company were now in the public domain, and the veterans were celebrities in their own right. I took the occasion to write an article for *Army* magazine that highlighted two extraordinary company commanders, one from World War II, the other from the Korean War. I selected Dick Winters for the former and Captain Lewis Millett for the latter. Both commanders had led their outfits with distinction and had led bayonet charges that defeated their enemies. I titled the article "Captains Courageous." It was published in the January 2002 issue of *Army*, and within one day, I received a call from Dick. My daughter actually answered the phone, and after a few minutes, she handed it to me and said, "Dad, Major Winters wants to talk to you."

"Good evening, Dick. What's up?"

He responded, "You know what's up. I'm reading this article in *Army* magazine and I'm absolutely speechless. I don't know what to say. I am just so overwhelmed."

Dick then requested additional copies so he could send them to his close friends, among whom were Tom Hanks and Steven Spielberg. A week later Dick called again and asked me to review the letter he was sending to Hanks. It was a wonderful letter that needed no editing from me. He again expressed his gratitude and informed me that "Captains Courageous" was one of the most wonderful gifts that he had ever received. Dick's comments were reminiscent of those of Captain Joe Dawson, who had read the article "Heroism under Fire," which featured him and two other Distinguished Service Cross recipients from World War II. As Joe said then, "Good buddy, you made this old veteran feel pretty special." I don't think I have ever received a nicer compliment.

Years later, my wife Mary and I visited Dick and Ethel, and no sooner had we walked into the house than Dick said, "Sit down, I have something for you." We sat on chairs on the sunporch as ordered, and he asked Ethel, "Please bring that print in here." Looking at us, Dick continued, "I've been thinking of something I can give you to express my appreciation, and I think I've found it. Here is the latest print in the 'Band of Brothers' series. It's called *Hang Tough, Bastogne 1944*. The artist is John Shaw, who painted one of the earlier prints in the series." Dick had signed the print "Hang Tough."

To say that I was flabbergasted would be an understatement. The print depicts an officer—Captain Winters—talking to three soldiers in the wintry Bois Jacques forest north of Bastogne. The narrative under the crest of the 101st Airborne Division describes the scene: "December 24, 1944, north of Bastogne, Belgium. Within the Bois Jacques forest, paratroopers of Easy Company, 506th PIR, 101st Airborne, filter back to their foxholes having repelled an attack earlier in the day. On this frigid Christmas Eve, Captain Dick Winters bolsters his men with his words 'Hang Tough.' Despite being surrounded and ill-equipped, the Band of Brothers would hold the line. Ultimately, the 101st Airborne would help turn the tide in the Battle of the Bulge."

"Dick, I'm speechless. This is the most beautiful print I've ever seen."

"This captures the essence of me as a leader. He's got me exactly how I want to be portrayed. Just as Easy Company was 'my' company, *Hang Tough, Bastogne 1944* is 'my' print since it encapsulates how I feel a company or battalion commander ought to lead from the front. Can you pick me out from the print?"

"This is you here," I said, pointing to the officer offering encouragement to the soldiers in the front line.

"Right, but what's your clue?"

"Well, it certainly looks like you, and this scene depicts an officer inspecting the forward line."

"That's true, but if you look closely, I am the only one who is cleanly shaven. That's your tip-off!"

Later, I watched a YouTube video of the presentation of the initial print to Dick. As the gentleman who delivered *Hang Tough, Bastogne 1944* explained to Dick, the artist examined a number of photographs recently taken in the Bois Jacques to capture the surrounding countryside in mid-December. While a team was actually photographing the forest, accompanied by some veterans from Easy Company, German veterans from the Wehrmacht were visiting the same area. When one of the Americans asked them why they did not attack in greater strength that Christmas Eve, the German veteran laughed and said, "You don't understand. You were the Eagle Heads," describing the 101st Airborne Division's patch depicting a screaming eagle. "My men did not want to come over here." No finer tribute can be paid to a combat soldier. Dick, particularly, seemed pleased to hear that remark.

Dick, himself, had expressed similar sentiments concerning the value of paratroopers in a letter that he had written two weeks before the European war ended. "The story of paratroopers can never be told as to the full significance of the role they played in this war," he said with obvious pride. "They have been proven beyond all doubt to be practicable, which was the only doubt I had in my mind a year ago. But even the ever-present threat of our employment is of no little importance in the general picture. And when we do drop, it's been proven that the [Germans] actually just take off, plain scared." Dick respected his adversaries as well as he remembered the fighting after D-Day. "Of course in Normandy that wasn't the case and as a result we had one hell of a good fight. Even when we bump into Waffen SS or panzer [tank] units on the line, they don't concern us as much as the knowledge that we've got paratroopers to shoot at. It's actually noticeable that the shooting and fierceness of the fight is much sharper against German paratroopers."

When it came time for Mary and me to leave, Ethel thanked me for coming and Dick made a special point of shaking my hand more vigorously than normal, saying, "Cole, I can never thank you for what you've done for me."

I often wonder how Steve Ambrose would have characterized my friendship with Dick Winters. He had written on brothers, peers, a lifetime of friends, his dearest friend, veterans, and combat friends. I suppose that Dick and I could have fallen into a number of these categories, but I like to believe Steve would have placed us in the chapter he titled "Faithful Friends," in which he described Meriwether Lewis and William Clark. Lewis and Clark became friends as adults, just as Dick and I did. Unlike us, their lives were entwined for three years as they led the thirty-man Corps of Discovery across North America. Lewis was the commander of the expedition by rank, but he made Clark an extraordinary offer and named his friend co-commander. Lewis then offered Clark a captain's commission, equal to his own, but the War Department did not have a vacancy for that grade. Although gravely disappointed, Lewis informed Clark that the War Department had refused his initial offer. Lewis then came to a resolution. Although Thomas Jefferson and the War Department referred to their trek across the continent as the Lewis Expedition, as far as the men could determine, they were members of the Lewis and Clark Expedition. Lewis referred to Clark as Captain Clark and Clark referred to Lewis as Captain Lewis. Together they led the Corps of Discovery to immortality.

That is how I like to think of my friendship with Dick. Unequal in military rank—in my mind Major Winters always outranked Colonel Kingseed—we formed a perfect friendship, a friendship based on trust and admiration, a friendship free of competition or seeking advantage. We gloried in each other's success and shared each other's bereavement when family members perished and old soldiers passed from the scene. I entered Dick's life very late in the game. Hoffman informs me that I was the last to enter Dick's inner circle. If I was, I'm proud of that because the last friendship a man makes is often the best one. Ambrose, with whom Dick and I shared a highly personal relationship, likened the last friendship to being a grandparent. "It is God's reward for having done your best." To this day, Dick Winters remains the best friend I ever had. I was privileged that he called me friend as well.

CHAPTER VI

Character

Humility must always be the portion of any man who receives acclaim earned in the blood of his followers and sacrifices of his friends.

—GENERAL DWIGHT D. EISENHOWER

The U.S. Military Academy's mission is to educate, train, and inspire the Corps of Cadets so that each graduate is a commissioned leader of character committed to the values of Duty, Honor, and Country and prepared for a career of professional excellence and service to the nation as an officer in the United States Army. The U.S. Naval Academy's mission is similar in that the Naval Academy strives to develop midshipmen morally, mentally, and physically and to imbue them with the highest ideals of Duty, Honor, and Loyalty, in order to graduate leaders who are dedicated to a career of naval service and have potential for future development in mind and character, to assume the highest responsibilities of command, citizenship, and government. Not surprisingly, all the service academies place high priority on character-based leaders.

How important is character to the U.S. Army and the other

branches of the service? To an officer in the army, character implies adherence to the seven army values of Loyalty, Duty, Respect, Selfless Service, Honor, Integrity, and Personal Courage. To an officer in the U.S. Marine Corps, the character of the Corps is reflected in its motto "*Semper Fidelis.*" Character is the foundation of leadership within all branches of the military service. Such traits remain as relevant to today's military leaders as they were in the military that fought and won World War II.

When Dick Winters selected the ten leadership principles with which he closed *Beyond Band of Brothers*, he listed "character" as the *sine qua non* of leadership. "Strive to be a leader of character, competence, and courage," he often said. For Dick, character had its roots in his upbringing in southern Pennsylvania. He cherished traditional family values, a Protestant work ethic, and a commitment of selfless service. He neither drank nor swore. Such behavior ran counter to his moral composition. He tolerated those who did, but never once did he cross that moral threshold himself. The Major Winters whom I knew viewed himself as a leader 100 percent of the time. To compromise his honor and his integrity would have proven anathema to Dick Winters.

I asked him one afternoon, "To what do you attribute your character?"

"Without hesitation," Dick replied, "I owe my character to my mother. A mother takes a child. She nurtures him, instills discipline, and teaches respect to others and how to live. She is first up in the morning and ensures the welfare of her family. She taught me to be respectful to women."

"I just watched *60 Minutes* last night and they interviewed Derek Jeter, the captain of the New York Yankees, and they asked him where he learned to be a leader. Do you want to know what he said?"

"What did he say?"

"Jeter attributed his leadership ability to his mother."

"I'm not a Yankee fan, but I'm glad to hear Jeter say that. He must be a pretty smart guy," Dick said with a smile on his face.

"Let me ask you another question. Why didn't you ever drink alcohol?"

Dick responded, "I don't like to talk about it much, but my grandfather was a confirmed alcoholic. I saw what it did to his family. So I never took a drink. It wasn't hard. I didn't want what happened to him to happen to me. It's as simple as that."

"Very interesting, Dick. I'm wondering how you define character."

"Character revolves around doing the right thing all the time. Character implies daily choices of right over wrong. I remember you once cited the Cadet Prayer at West Point, in which you said cadets strive to 'choose the harder right instead of the easier wrong and never to be content with a half truth when the whole can be won.' That gets to the heart of character. I would add that it is easier to do the right thing when everyone is looking. It is more difficult to do what you should do when you are alone. I like to think of character as every other virtue at the breaking point."

"Does war disrupt or reinforce character?"

"I can speak only from personal experience. War doesn't alter character. War merely brings out the best that an individual has to offer. Unfortunately, it also brings forth the worst in some men. If anything, war exposes the best and worst of those who are called to fight. I know of no man who lacked character in peace and then discovered his character in combat. But, back to your question, I believe that war reinforces character for better or worse."

To understand the importance of character in Dick's life, one only has to read a sampling of his wartime correspondence. Following the Battle of the Bulge, Dick responded to a letter in which DeEtta Almon asked if it was true that soldiers routinely "raise hell" when they are off duty. Dick replied, "It doesn't mean that everybody raises hell. Take it or leave it. I didn't, never have, never will, raise hell while I am in the U.S. Army. Why? First and most important, I've got my own conscience to answer to. Next, my parents, and then I am an officer in the U.S. Army. I am damn proud of it and with the rank and position I hold. I wouldn't think of doing anything to bring discredit to my outfit, my paratrooper boots, wings, the airborne patch, or the U.S. Army. Good morale within an outfit is usually reflected by good conduct away from it. That sounds like an idealistic high school kid, I know, but that's it. That's how I feel."

Dick's friend Bob Hoffman shares a memory of Winters and the importance of character. States Bob, "I can tell you that he was the same man when the journey of 'Band of Brothers' began as he was when his life's journey ended. When Dick initially viewed the transcript of the miniseries *Band of Brothers*, he was offended that Damian Lewis, who portrayed him on film, used excessive profanity throughout the series. Dick immediately wrote a letter to Tom Hanks, resigning from the project because 'I don't want these boys and girls thinking it is acceptable using profanity. You know that is not who I am.' Hanks issued a tepid apology, but he claimed it was too late in the production cycle to edit the offensive language. Dick held firm and steadfastly countered each of Hanks's points of rebuttal. Winters won again and you won't hear a single word of profanity from Lewis. So important was this indication of Dick's character that Hanks brought it up to me following the memorial service."

Sergeant Darrell "Shifty" Powers, one of the best soldiers in Easy Company, also objected to the profanity in the miniseries. As Powers told a close friend, "We would never have talked that way knowing that we might meet our Maker in the next moment." Then he qualified his remarks by stating, "At least us Southern boys. Those Yankees may have been different."

Doing the right thing was extremely important to Dick. Hoffman shares another vignette that further illustrates Dick's character. During the 2004 presidential campaign, Dick called Hoffman on a Sunday evening and said that the White House had called, asking him to introduce President George W. Bush at a Hershey Stadium rally. Dick declined, concerned that his Parkinson's disease had advanced to the stage that it would be hazardous to his own health to attend the rally. "Did I do the right thing?" he asked Bob. Hoffman said, "No! The old adage is that when the President of the United States asks you to do something, you do it." Dick then called the White House and said he had reconsidered and that he would be honored to introduce the president. An estimated thirty-three thousand people attended the rally. Following his introduction, Dick then saluted the commander in chief, the identical salute, sharp and crisp, that he had given when, on behalf of the paratroopers from Easy Company, he accepted the Emmy for the HBO miniseries *Band of Brothers*.

As I reviewed Dick's wartime journals, I was struck by how frequently he mentioned religious services. When I asked him about it, he replied, "Church was always important to my parents, and our family always attended services together. I never changed.

Religious services became the bedrock of my character. Easy Company arrived in England in September 1943. We were trucked to Aldbourne, a small village of several hundred people. The next morning, which was Sunday, I visited a local Norman church, and after services, I walked into the adjoining cemetery and sat on a bench. As I looked over the yard, I saw an elderly couple tending one of the graves. They then sat on an adjacent bench. The three of us talked, and they informed me that the grave belonged to their son who had been killed during the Battle of Britain. They invited me to join them for tea, and I graciously accepted their invitation. A day or two later, our unit requested billeting within the local community for the officers. The Barnes family volunteered to board two officers as long as I was one of the officers." Mr. Barnes was a lay preacher and his wife played the organ on Sunday. Dick continued, "Life with the Barnes family suited me perfectly. During the nine months prior to D-Day, I think I missed three Sunday services. Years later—I believe it must have been June 1991, a year before *Band of Brothers* appeared in print—I accompanied Ambrose on a *Band of Brothers* tour to the sites featured in the book. Aldbourne was not on our itinerary, but I insisted that we stop. When we arrived, our intrepid band viewed the stables where Easy Company had once billeted, and I returned to my old room above Mr. and Mrs. Barnes's store. The building now housed a general store and post office. I then excused myself for a few minutes to place flowers on the graves of Francis and 'Mother' Barnes. I next took a minute to reflect on this wonderful couple and sat on the same bench where they had first met me years ago."

"Did you see the Barnes family after the war?"

"Mr. Barnes passed away in October 1944, shortly before we

jumped into Holland. After V-E Day, I took a two-week furlough in England. I needed to relax. Physically I had always been in the hottest combat, but mentally, I was just like a fiddle. I knew something was wrong and I knew exactly what it was. Responsibility, work, the accumulation of past problems, concerns for the future had me in such a mental emotional state that I was becoming more like a military machine than an understanding officer and human being. With nowhere to go, I returned to Aldbourne and spent ten days with the Barnes family. Mother Barnes had kept my upstairs room just as I had left it. I spent the entire week just helping around the house, cutting the grass, and running the store. I regained a lot that I'd forgotten existed. When I returned to duty, I sent her a nice letter that I addressed to 'Dearest Mother.' Trying to find just the right words, I wrote, 'I was still walking around on that cloud that you had put me on during my recent visit. I really enjoyed those songs and hymns that were so dear to you, as well as those Bible readings and prayers. There were times when your influence on me permitted me to pass my thoughts and feelings along to other officers and men.' In August I saw her again when I received another week's leave. I couldn't think of a better place to spend my time than with her. Mrs. Barnes survived into the 1970s. I still keep the gifts that she and Francis gave me. She was truly a second mother to me and the one individual to whom I owe an incalculable debt."

Dick then added a second thought. "I'm not sure I've passed this on, but in the marshaling area before we loaded for D-Day, the paratroopers had the opportunity to attend religious services on a regular basis. What amazed me was the fact that with D-Day and a night jump into Nazi-occupied Europe staring us right in our faces, only a few extra men showed up for the services. I thought everyone would go, but only a few attended. That surprised me."

"To what extent were religious convictions expressed in your unit?"

Dick responded, "We had a good Catholic chaplain, Father Maloney. He took care of everybody who wanted to pray. He received the Distinguished Service Cross in Normandy. Religious services were an important factor in maintaining morale in a military outfit, but attendance was never strong. Each man made his personal peace within himself."

"Your religion was obviously important to you."

"Yes, but I never really considered myself a member of any specific religious affiliation. My mother grew up in a Mennonite community, but she never converted to the faith. What she did do was pass the message of self-discipline to me, as well as the values of honesty, hard work, and respect for others. I go to church, read the Bible, pray, and do what I think is right, but I've never had any assurance that I was going to heaven, and I'm not sure if I am saved. The way I feel about it, going to church is a privilege, an honor, and should be recognized as such. I didn't want to miss a chance to go. While in England, I attended a Methodist church, didn't miss but three Sundays in over eight months. The longest I was away from church was after jumping into Holland. I wrote DeEtta in mid-November that I attended services for the first time in two months. Of course, it wasn't exactly fancy, but it was a church. We held the services in a barn with some cows and horses crunching some hay and adding a delightful aroma to the setting. Later I attended a Roman Catholic wedding in a church in France. I enjoyed it."

"I feel the same way about attending Mass, Dick. By the way, I love your description of your 'personal cathedral' that you found amid the mountains of Austria after the war."

Looking at one of his letters, Dick read, "While in the mountains I found a church of my own. The aisle is two mountain ranges down which you can see for ten miles at least. At the end there's just a series of mountain peaks. A storm came up and the dark clouds covered everything but the far end, where the sun shone through on those magnificent peals. The color was all shades of rose, a light, soft rose, nothing hard or bright, but just rays of light coming through the clouds. There were the most beautiful stained glass windows I've ever seen, or hope to see. What a wonderful place to pray. What a magnificent church. I'll never forget it."

In another letter, written shortly after D-Day, Dick discussed the importance of prayer in his life. As he reviewed his experience since jumping into Normandy, Dick wrote, "I have found out just what is essential and what isn't in life. In my prayers before D-Day, I always thanked God for what He'd done for the world in general and asked that everyone be given a break in the future. For myself, I always thanked Him for a lot of things that I found out were insignificant. That I was still alive each night was the big thing, the only thing. And the only thing you ask for the future is that you'll be alive tomorrow morning and be able to live through the next day. That's all that matters, that's the only thing as far as wanting anything for yourself that's important. All other things are extra, nonessential, and you can't be bothered or burdened with nonessentials, not when battle is the payoff."

When he returned to England in mid-July 1944, Dick reminded me, that was the first time that he had heard church bells ringing since D-Day. "Those church bells that just tolled 2100 hours made me stop a moment for they brought back memories of the last time that I heard church bells ringing," he said. "That was in France, D-Day, H-Hour, and they weren't tolling a request for us to come to church, but an alarm to all the countryside that we'd arrived. What followed of course is history, but it sure gave me a funny feeling. Machine gun fire and rifle fire didn't scare me. But those bells, being all alone with only a knife, gave me the feeling of being hunted down by a pack of wolves." Even today, Dick stated that when he hears bells ringing at night, his thoughts return to that meadow outside Ste. Mère-Eglise where he landed shortly after midnight on June 6, 1944.

Before jumping into Holland, Dick reiterated the importance of church as he wrote DeEtta, "Well, tomorrow is Sunday and I am all set for church, buttons shined, boots polished, ribbons all over my tunic. Yes, I like to go to church. The way I feel about it, it is a very special privilege to be able to go at all and I don't want to miss a chance." Later he addressed reading the Bible. "I am no authority on the Book, never intend to be, so when I read it, it's not necessarily to improve my mind or to learn the proverbs so I can impress somebody by quoting them, but I read the Bible just for relaxation and atmosphere. I read wherever the Book happens to fall open, and sometimes it opens at just the right spot."

Since character was the topic of today's conversations, I reminded Dick of one of his first classes that he delivered at West Point in 1999. At West Point a cadet promises never to lie, cheat, steal, or tolerate those who do. That simple maxim constitutes the honor code that guides a cadet's conduct not just while at West

Point, but hopefully throughout his or her life. To quote General George Patton, "The honor code gives West Point its soul." So I asked Dick, "You have always considered yourself an honorable man. How do you reconcile your disobedience of a direct order at Haguenau when you falsified a report to Colonel Sink?"

"I was very surprised the cadets did not question me on that since I was fully cognizant of the importance of the honor code to the Corps of Cadets. Haguenau occurred during the fighting in Alsace-Lorraine in February 1945. Colonel Sink came to my head-quarters and directed that I dispatch a patrol to capture some prisoners. We had done so the preceding evening, and we had captured a few Germans for interrogation. On this particular day, Sink had a little too much to drink and his order didn't make any sense. We would have had to cross the Moder River again, and the freshly fallen snow had turned to ice. The enemy would have heard us a mile away. Well, what do you do? I replied, 'Yes, sir,' and then I promptly ignored the order. I did exactly the right thing and have never had any regrets. There was not time for preparation, the field to our front was wide open, and I would have lost too many men for no purpose whatsoever. I often wonder what I would have done had I been a career officer concerned about my own advancement. Would I have compromised my beliefs? That was an ethical dilemma of the first magnitude."

"To reiterate. You have no regrets?"

"Not at all. The war was nearly over. Everyone knew that the Germans were licked. Why lose a soldier when we had already accomplished the mission the night before?"

"I have to ask you another question concerning character," I said. "In many memoirs written by combat veterans, not just in

World War II, soldiers write something to the effect that once men begin killing, it is not easy to stop them. What's your take on that?"

"I never found men who enjoyed killing or that it seemed difficult to stop them from killing. I realize that war coarsens soldiers. They speak of killing in a more casual manner than they ever imagined before they experience combat. Killing is no longer abnormal or morally objectionable. It is accepted as a fact of life in a wartime environment. You talk tough and you act tough, probably to steel yourself if you don't make it through the next fight. But if a unit loses control, you have a leadership problem. I looked at the examples that we had in Easy Company, such as allegations that Joe Liebgott killed some prisoners. You and I have shared stories about Lieutenant Speirs doing the same thing in Normandy. I look at those examples, and I say that Speirs and Liebgott are doing this to establish a reputation as a real tough soldier. They are seeking the respect of everyone else in the company or within the battalion, whatever, and this is their way of doing it. Take Liebgott. I won't get into exactly what he did, but he prided himself with a collection of rings that he had accumulated. No excuse for that. He was simply showing off that he was a real tough guy. I didn't see the other men follow his example."

"Did you address officers differently?"

"I'll cite two examples to illustrate my point, Buck Compton and Ronald Speirs.

"When we were still in Aldbourne getting ready to go into combat, Compton—we called him 'Hollywood' because he had been a two-sport UCLA star who had played baseball with Jackie Robinson and football in the 1943 Rose Bowl—Compton would put a trench knife in his mouth and prance around the area saying that when he gets into combat that he's going to kill every German he comes across. It was nothing but an act. He wasn't that kind of a guy; he never did things like that in combat. It was an act, but it's the type of thing you remember all your life.

"Speirs was a different story. Ambrose describes Speirs as an officer with a reputation. Among the officers, his nickname was 'Sparky.' The enlisted men called him 'Bloody' Speirs because the stories surrounded him from Normandy. Allegedly, he killed a number of German prisoners and he also shot one of his own noncommissioned officers who refused one of his orders. Speirs earned respect from the men for what he did at Foy, but they never respected him as a man. First Sergeant Talbert turned in his stripes because he couldn't work for him."

"Were the stories about Speirs true?"

"I'm not going to comment, but there is one more thing I need to say about killing."

"What's that?"

"With respect to this matter of killing, there's a time when you are in combat and you have a German surrender to you. That's a touch-and-go moment. As he still has his weapons or is dropping his weapon, you are standing there and you have the drop on him. One false move on his part, in your mind, you can end up with somebody getting shot. It's a very delicate moment. It's not even a moment—it's a fraction of a moment—until he has dropped his weapon and you're in complete control. You're not sure if you should pull the trigger, that's a tough time. That's the time that character counts."

"Speaking of character, Dick, did you ever develop a hatred of the enemy?"

"No, I definitely did not. I hated what the Nazi regime represented, but because I was a soldier myself, I was able to differenti- ate between Hitler and the soldiers against whom I fought. Not hatred, but I wanted to eliminate them. They were still the enemy and they had to be controlled. There was nothing personal about it. As the war progressed, I developed a healthy respect for the bet- ter units that we faced. After the war was over, there was an op- portunity to meet the German soldiers and the German officers, at Kaprun, Austria. In working with these soldiers, I sensed that they were good soldiers and worthy of respect. I got to know Colonels Frederick von der Heydte and Hans von Luck and several other German officers years later through Steve Ambrose. They were first-class fellas—first-class all the way. Believe me, they don't come any better than Hans von Luck."

"You developed a strong relationship with von Luck, did you not?"

"I did indeed. He and Major John Howard, the opposing commanders at Pegasus Bridge in D-Day's very first engagement, attended several symposia organized by Ambrose at New Orleans. Howard and von Luck also conducted military staff rides to Normandy to discuss Pegasus Bridge. While visiting Ambrose at the University of New Orleans, they frequently lectured to his classes on World War II. One energetic student demanded to know how Colonel von Luck could have fought for Hitler. Hans von Luck protested the student's insinuations, but he willingly an- swered the question, telling the student that he had been a regular army officer since 1927 and had never been a Nazi or member of the Waffen SS. Howard leapt to von Luck's defense and so did I. The bond that links those who have served their country tran- scends generations and after a certain amount of time has ex- pired, it also transcends nationalities."

Character—character—the subject fascinated Dick. One day while we were talking about leadership and character, he received a package that he opened in front of me. The package contained an autographed copy of Senator John McCain's latest book, *Faith of My Fathers*. The family memoir was based on what McCain learned from his father and his grandfather, both four-star admirals in the U.S. Navy, and how their stellar example encouraged McCain to survive during his incarceration in the infamous Hanoi Hilton after the North Vietnamese had shot him down over North Vietnam. Senator McCain wrote a personal inscription inside the front cover that read "To Dick Winters—Thank you for your brave service to our Nation." Dick looked at me and said, "I have no idea who 'sparked' this very special gift, but I am honored. John McCain not only possesses solid character, but he is also a man of honor. Many leaders demonstrate character, but few are as honorable as John McCain. I suggest you read the book and you'll find you will understand, respect, and you will admire the man. He's honest."

"Yes, he is, Dick. Before we go on, I'd like to go back to your decision to apply for a transfer to the Pacific theater after Germany surrendered unconditionally on May 7, 1945. I'm more interested in the reasons you sought a transfer than I am in why your request was disapproved."

Dick responded immediately, "Within three weeks of V-E Day, I was bored and I'm thinking that I would like to transfer to the China-Burma-India theater of operations. I know this may come across as unduly harsh, but I found war invigorating. Had never seen that part of the world, so I requested an interview with the commanding general of the 13th Airborne Division that was scheduled for deployment to the Pacific. The commanding general was courteous, thanked me for my interest, but declined my request, stating that 'Major Winters, you've done enough.' He basically echoed the same thing that my mother had written, telling me, 'Do not go to the South Pacific. You've done your part. Be smart and come home.'" Turning to his pen pal, Dick informed DeEtta, "But mother doesn't understand. I am not going down there for the trip or any personal gain. I feel that God has been good enough to let me go through this war. As a result, I am combat-wise and in a position to do some good to help a lot of men. I know I can do the job better than, or as well as, any of the rest. How can I sit back and see others take men out and get them killed because they don't know; they don't have 'it.' Maybe I'll get hurt or killed for my trouble, but so what if I can make it possible for many others to go home. Their mothers want them, too, the same as mother wants me. So what else can I do and still hold my own self-respect as an officer and a man?"

I find it interesting that Dick couched his remarks not only from the perspective of a soldier, but also and more importantly from his perspective of a man with honor. I told him after this exchange that I always had tremendous respect for him as a soldier, but I attached greater significance to him exemplifying the highest qualities of an honorable man.

There was one postwar incident that in my opinion gave an indication of the true extent of Dick's character. Having witnessed such intense combat and having been away from home for three years, Dick made a point of fulfilling his obligations as a citizen as soon as he returned to Pennsylvania. "When I returned from the service," he said, "one of the first things I did was to go to the Internal Revenue office and insist that I pay my income tax on my income as an officer. The IRS man said, 'Son, you don't have to do this even though the regulations say you must. We will waive this return.' My answer was, 'Sir, I want to pay my part of the bill. I am proud to be an American!' He bowed his head and we figured out my bill, which I paid in full immediately."

There was one final component of character that I wanted to explore with Dick, even though I suspected that it might make him uncomfortable. That topic was love. I knew that Dick had grown up in a loving family, but his journal and his letters seemed to reflect an absence of love other than that directed toward Easy Company as an entity. I decided to tackle these issues one at a time.

"Dick I'm going to ask you a personal question. You don't have to answer it if you are not so inclined, but I'm incredibly interested in exploring a prevailing theme from your wartime correspondence with DeEtta, whom I know was your pen pal and confidante. DeEtta was obviously infatuated with you and wanted to explore a more permanent relationship, but you seemed impervious to her overtures. Frankly, I'm surprised that she continued to write as often as she did. As I reread your letters, particularly after V-E Day, I am reminded of the opening paragraph of Sir Arthur Conan Doyle's 'A Scandal in Bohemia,' in which Dr. Watson describes Sherlock Holmes's affinity for personal involvement with the antagonist Irene Adler. As the narrator of the story, Dr. Watson writes, 'It was not that he [Holmes] felt any emotion akin to love for Irene Adler. All emotions, and that one particularly, were abhorrent to his cold, precise but admirably balanced mind. He was, I take it, the most perfect reasoning and observing machine that the world has seen, but as a lover he would have placed himself in a false position. He never spoke of the softer passions, save with a gibe and a sneer.' That sounds to me a lot like Major Dick Winters in 1945."

Dick smiled and said, "That sounds a lot like me. Let me explain something about love in general and then we can discuss DeEtta later if you like. As a youth, I attended an old boys' school in Lancaster, Pennsylvania. From there I went directly to Franklin and Marshall College. F and M was not coed. Upon graduation, I entered the army, which was all male. At no time had I ever fallen in love. My mother had always impressed on me to respect women, but I did not know what love was at that point in my life. We'll get back to my pen pal momentarily, but in mid-July 1945, I addressed her questions concerning the composition of love. I remember writing DeEtta a number of letters on this subject. In one, I wrote, 'What is it anyhow, love? I am not being funny, I just don't know. Everybody talks about it, like you would a beautiful church, or a sunset, or a painting. It seems to be something holy. In fact, when someone asks me, "Haven't you ever been in love?" I say, "Well, I don't think so." Do you feel differently, act differently?' "

In the same letter, Dick digressed to what he had learned in ethics class while he attended Franklin & Marshall. In college, "They told us the Greeks were first to recognize three kinds of love: first, and evidently most important when you look at all the advertisements and newspapers, is physical. Second, mental and mutual understanding and fondness for man to man, man to woman, or any way you want. Everybody just likes the other guy for what he is. And third, just a little of both and when both parties are normal human beings, it's generally between a man and woman. Now, that's about the extent of my knowledge of love, for

I honestly don't know what it is, and what's more, I don't really give a damn until the war's over."

I found that last sentence incredibly revealing. As my friend Colonel Farrell noted when I asked what similarities he found between his own experience and that of Major Winters, "When I sent my family off three days prior to deploying my battalion to Iraq, when they departed remains one of the saddest days in my life because I thought it very well might be the last time I see my children and dear wife. I grieved in private, however, because I did not want anyone to see me that way. My wife was somewhat upset with me because to her, it seemed as if I pushed her and the children away, literally and figuratively. In fact she was right, because I needed to wall myself off, to steel myself against selfish emotions and concerns for my family and instead transition to focusing entirely on the unit and the mission. I knew the coming months would be physically and emotionally draining, which they were, because on the average week I was on duty 120 to 130 hours, and the battalion would require every ounce of energy I had."

Farrell's experiences are reminiscent of Dick's. Not until the war was concluded was Dick finally able to describe his inability to answer DeEtta's letters in the same tone as she had written them in. Two weeks before the war ended, he wrote, "I guess women are a bit different. Seems such a waste of time to me 'wasting tender thoughts' on a soldier. For tender thoughts are to me something I took off and left behind in the marshaling area prior to starting this war. There's no room for them. There's little thought about death, so how can one waste thoughts that are simply tender? Death? Yes, I think earnestly about the dead, but there is no time to mourn for them."

As soon as the war was over, Dick no longer worried about keeping his soldiers combat-ready and prepared to fight the enemy. So he took time to write and inform DeEtta, "You know, I am beginning to understand why I like to receive and read your letters so much and why I enjoy your friendship. During the past year, I didn't stop to dream about abstract and beautiful thoughts. So writing to you was just like writing to a sister, no more, no less. I didn't feel one way or the other. Now I realize a little why I've enjoyed your line. You're so damn understanding! When I went overseas you seemed to know and feel homesickness as I did. You felt the change in weather, customs of the English, the pinch of ice cream and candy. And then before D-Day, you felt the tightness of nerves that comes from waiting, which was something I didn't fully realize existed. I'll never forget your one letter saying, 'and when you're in a tight spot, remember you've got to come back.'" Not exactly the type of letter a woman wants to receive from someone with whom she wished to establish a more permanent relationship.

Dick's letter continued, "This isn't what you want to hear or have me write. Actually, I should write all about love, and how sweet you are, and all that stuff. I could if I wanted to. I know all those words from movies and magazines, but that wouldn't be right. I don't feel that way and I don't want you to think that way. What I want is for you to get married to some good guy who comes along. There are always a couple of good guys around. You need a husband and a family to be really happy. Those ideas about college and getting a degree after you're out of the navy, you're crazy, and you know it. You don't want that any more than you want to make the navy a life's work."

Dick and DeEtta maintained their correspondence until Dick returned home in November. The letters took on a different tone after the summer of 1945. Dick's attention shifted to returning to the States, and DeEtta, too, focused on life after the war. On December 15, 1945, Dick sent a Christmas card in which he stated, "Received your letter after 'farewell to arms,' and was glad to know my feelings were in tune with you. . . . Dad has this record of 'People Will Say We're in Love.' Reminds me of a couple I once knew, so there's that tricky smile on my lips and a wee bit of twinkle in my eye as I listen." They would meet once more after Christmas when Dick traveled to Washington, D.C., as DeEtta was discharged from the service. There was little chance to rekindle the feelings that they had once shared. By now Dick had withdrawn from even his closest friends as he attempted to readjust to civilian life. It was not an easy transition.

And there, things stood for half of a century.

Reflecting back on his friendship with DeEtta, Dick wrote two years after her death in 2001, "Her friendship meant so much to me. If I'd had a job and was making a living on my own, established, it could very well have been different. At night when I say my prayers, she's one of the people I remember."

"Any final thoughts on character from your war experience?"

Dick reflected for a minute and said, "Well, it probably sounds strange to you, but when I brought Easy Company to Utah Beach so we could board the LST [landing ship, tank] to return to England on July 11, 1944, I saw that beach for the first time with that vast armada of ships as far as the eye could see in every direction. Seeing the American flag fluttering over that beach, I felt weak in the knees and tears filled my eyes. Suddenly the flag meant something different than it ever had before. I have never looked at our flag since without that memory in my mind. Now I am an old man, but that feeling has never left me."

As I remember Dick Winters, it is his character that most stands out. Dick Winters was a man's man. His masculinity has nothing to do with macho posturing, but it has everything to do with character—and character, as Dick's story shows, is developed.

CHAPTER VII

Courage

The soldier is alone in his war with terror and we have to recognize the first signs of his defeat that we may come in time to his rescue.

—LORD MORAN

In the hundreds of hours that Major Winters and I discussed his experiences during the war, there was no topic that was off-limits. Leadership and character were his preferred subjects of discussion, but occasionally he opted to explore the darker aspects of his wartime experiences and the debilitating effects of war on his soldiers. I was not old enough to have fought in World War II. Yet I'm confident that I knew Dick Winters of Easy Company, because character and courage are not "sometimes things." The moral courage that any man displays is directly proportionate to his commitment and adherence to the values that govern his life. I once asked my cadets at the U.S. Military Academy, "Who were the leaders whom you most strive to emulate?" Some listed the great captains of history, but the majority identified small unit leaders like Colonel Joshua Lawrence Chamberlain, who commanded the 20th Maine Volunteer Regiment at Gettysburg; Lieutenant Colonel Hal Moore, who led the 1st Battalion, 7th Cavalry during the Battle of the Ia Drang Valley during the Vietnam War; and lastly, Captain Dick Winters of Easy Company. When asked why they selected these particular leaders, several cadets stated, "Because Chamberlain, Moore, and Winters were leaders of character first, competence second, and courage third."

With that as a backdrop, I decided to question Dick on his perception of how fear destroys the cohesion of a military command. He must have been thinking the same thing because on my next visit, he surprised me by initiating our conversation, saying, "We have spent a lot of time over the years discussing Easy Company, their wartime campaigns, and leadership under the strain of combat. As I rehash those conversations, I've noticed that you often question me about fear and moral courage. Why don't we talk about that today?"

"Sounds good to me, Dick. I've been interested in moral courage ever since I read British historian John Keegan, who examined the impact of war on the frontline soldier in his classic book *The Face of Battle*. General Patton once remarked that he found that moral courage was the most valuable and usually the most absent characteristic in men. I know we have discussed courage many times as you reminisced about Normandy and Bastogne, and some of these questions may sound redundant, but let's go into greater detail about what fear and courage consist of and how you as a commander overcame the fear that naturally accompanies soldiers in combat."

"First things first, moral courage is a far rarer commodity than physical courage. In that I agree with Patton. I have known many officers who were physically brave, but who did not have the intestinal fortitude to organize the chaos around them. Those officers who were most vocal about what they were going to do to the enemy often were the first to fall apart when the chips were down. Fear is not only debilitating, but its existence also destroys the cohesion of a command. It is the responsibility of a commander to identify the limits of courage, break the paralysis of fear, and motivate his soldiers to continue with the mission. Courage conquers fear."

"Did you personally experience fear? Did fear ever grip your outfit?"

"I suspect every soldier at one time or another experiences a degree of fear. Courage is not the absence of fear, but rather the willingness to rise above fear and do the things that you know need to be accomplished. All soldiers hope that they will measure up the first time that they get into a fight. I certainly was no exception, but I believe I had prepared myself very well that once I came under fire, I instinctively knew what needed to be done. I think I was more apprehensive, particularly before D-Day, than I was afraid. Maybe apprehension is the first stage of fear. I'm not really sure. You have to remember that Easy Company was an elite unit, as were all the paratroopers. We had trained for nearly two years before we jumped into Normandy. I think I saw far more excitement in the eyes of my men than I did fear. After Brecourt, we felt as if we were seasoned veterans even though we knew worse days were ahead."

"That leads me to my next question, Dick. In Easy Company, did you see much cowardice?"

"Absolutely not. As the war went on, the bonds among the men actually strengthened. No one wanted to let his buddy down. I think we discussed that some soldiers, like Joe Toye, went AWOL in order to return to Easy Company because if he had remained in a hospital, he would have been transferred from the paratroopers. Unit cohesion and the fear of abandoning your friend are powerful incentives. Even at Bastogne, Bill Guarnere risked his life to save Joe Toye. Cowardice in Easy Company? Never!"

"Does courage have limits?"

"I suppose so. Again, Steve Ambrose says that heavy artillery bombardment will make even the most seasoned veteran eventually break. I disagree. A leader has to overcome fear, convince himself that every enemy shell or bullet is not targeting him. The same is true in a company or a battalion. Leaders must ensure that strength in cohesion is a stronger force than fear. This is especially true in men who have been scarred by prolonged combat. Ambrose was correct when he titled the chapter in *Band of Brothers* 'Breaking Point' as he described the horrendous artillery barrage that inflicted so many casualties on Easy Company in the Bois Jacques. Company strength was below 50 percent, and many of the noncommissioned officers were killed or wounded. Without direct supervision by leaders, Easy Company, as well as the remainder of the battalion, could have easily been debilitated by an increased sense of mortality and fear. That is precisely why I made it a point to visit the front lines as often as possible. Soldiers need a sense that their commanders are in the game with them. Leadership by example is even more important in these situations."

"What signs appear when a soldier is reaching his limit?"

"I noticed that when men are at the edge of their physical endurance, they tend to develop that one-thousand-yard stare that you always read about. Tired soldiers will often take off their helmet and run their fingers through their hair. At times, they literally drop their helmets to the ground. This soldier is already losing his self-respect. The battle is half-lost. That's a sign for a commander to take immediate action. I didn't wait for the trooper to reach that stage. I proactively looked for these signs. Every soldier wants to do the right thing. You always know the proper thing to do, but doing it is sometimes more difficult. I never wanted a man to lose his self-respect."

"You once told me that married soldiers often hesitated before taking decisive action. Were married soldiers more prone to reach their breaking point?"

"I'm glad you asked that question because I was going to say that there is an additional point that I'd like to share that perhaps goes off on a tangent, but I think you'll realize that I have a point. When I observed Easy Company, I found that under fire in combat, whether it's rifle fire or artillery, the men who seemed to have their eyes glazed over quickest and put their heads down and kept their heads down, were those who were married. Either they were married or in love or had a fiancée back home. They were the first to show fear. Those who hadn't fallen in love or who weren't engaged seemed to be able to hold on longer. That's perfectly understandable in my opinion. My friend Nixon is a perfect example of what I'm trying to say."

"How so?"

"Not in the way you may think. Nixon and I were polar opposites, but I sensed that we shared mutual feelings and ways of looking at life. I could understand him and help him understand me and understand himself. Nixon had been married, but he had no love at home. I went to his house many times. He would invite, not just me, but he would invite a group of officers and company to his home on weekends. What I'm saying is—not from just what he told me, but from what I was able to observe of his married life—there was no love. Nixon did not have that burden of fear of not going back to his wife. As I think back and I put it together and compared our two lives, how different we were, yet how similar we were in many ways. Nixon didn't have this burden in combat, and I didn't either."

"In Lord Moran's *The Anatomy of Courage*, he addresses what he calls 'the care and management of fear.' He states that he developed the habit of watching for signs of wear and tear so that he might rest a soldier before he was broken. How did you break the cycle of fear, Dick?"

"Who is Lord Moran? I've never heard of him."

"Lord Moran was Winston Churchill's personal physician during World War II. As Captain Charles Wilson, Moran served as a doctor with the Royal Fusiliers throughout two and a half years of World War I. In later life Wilson, ennobled as Lord Moran, witnessed the pressures of high command as a member of Churchill's entourage. *The Anatomy of Courage* records Moran's experience and leads to his interpretation of courage in battle. According to Moran, fear is more common than courage."

"I'm intrigued. Tell me more."

"Moran states that there are four degrees of courage and four orders of men measured by that standard. Men who do not feel fear; men who feel fear but do not show it; men who feel fear and show it but do their job anyway; and men who feel fear, show it, and shirk. His experience during the Great War demonstrated that soldiers rarely fell into a single category and moved constantly up and down the ladder of fear. Moran goes on to say that 'modern war is concerned with the striving of men, eroded by fear, to maintain a precarious footing on the upper rungs of this ladder.'"

"Very interesting. Sorry to interrupt. Now, what's your question?"

"I asked how you broke the cycle of fear."

"That's right. As I said, when you notice a soldier literally falling apart before your eyes, you try to provide him some relief. I can think of two cases that illustrate what I'm saying. At Carentan one week after D-Day, I was standing in the aid station when I observed Private Albert Blithe leaning against the wall. I asked him what was wrong and he replied that he couldn't see. He was blinded by fear. I merely put my hand on his shoulder and told him everything would be okay. That's all it took. He looked at me and said, 'I can see. I'm okay now.' Sometimes all you need to hear is a calming voice to shake you from despair. The second case involves Joe Liebgott at Bastogne. I noticed that his nerves were frayed so I pulled him from the front line and assigned him duty as my battalion runner for a day or two. A day's rest from the front lines will literally accomplish wonders for a soldier's morale. A good soldier doesn't want to stay away from his buddies too long. He certainly prefers their company to yours. After two days, he will request to join his buddies at the front. As with Blithe and Liebgott, they were very anxious to return to the front."

Dick went on. "Sometimes you have to take more drastic action if a leader is involved. I already told you the circumstances surrounding Lieutenant Dike during the attack of Foy outside of Bastogne. What I had just witnessed was a classic case of combat fatigue at a very bad time. We had seen indications of this earlier, but Dike was sent to us as a favorite protégé of somebody from regimental headquarters and our hands were tied. Fortunately, Colonel Sink approved my action of replacing Dike with Captain Speirs."

Wishing to explore combat exhaustion, I redirected our conversation back to the Battle of the Bulge. "Speaking of Bastogne, I'm thinking about January 9, 1945, when many of your leaders succumbed to pressure as the battalion broke out from its encirclement. One of your lieutenants literally walked off the line, and then you relieved a company commander during the attack on Foy on January. The strain must have been enormous."

"Before you go on, I know you think I'm too hard on Lieutenant Compton for walking off the line at Bastogne. Let me explain myself. Buck was a great combat leader. He was a superb platoon leader in Normandy and Holland. In fact, I would say he was one of the best. At Bastogne, he broke after some of his friends were seriously wounded in the constant artillery barrages. There is a danger of getting too close to the men, and Buck crossed that line. When you see your friends getting maimed, it makes it more difficult to go on. That's why I always maintained a certain detachment from the paratroopers in Easy Company. Am I too harsh on Buck? Maybe, but a leader needs to rise above fear. The easiest thing to do is quit."

"Why didn't you crack?"

"I'm Pennsylvania Dutch. I don't quit. I made a commitment. Moral courage is based on physical fitness. Courage is a combination of willpower and determination."

"Surely there must be more than that. While others were breaking around you, how did Captain Winters maintain his sanity?"

"I was in excellent physical shape. I don't think there was a man in that outfit who was in better shape than I was, and it showed. I had trained hard. In England after we finished training,

I would run at night. Blackout conditions, but I would run. Then I'd come in and go to bed. I was in maximum shape. That was the physical side of things, but there is a mental aspect of stamina as well. I have always prided myself that I do my own thinking. I have my own philosophy. I have my own answers to the reasons things have turned out in my life. By taking full accountability for my life, I have been able to meet the standards that I set for myself. I don't know any other way of saying it."

"I view character and accountability as the twin components of leadership," I responded. "It's interesting that you cited accountability."

"Every commander must take full accountability for his actions. Stand up and be counted. As a commander, you are accountable for everything that your outfit does or fails to do. Don't worry about who receives credit when things go well. Don't play the blame game. In my case, the mantle of command provided me with the courage to succeed."

I next asked, "Did you see a lot of combat fatigue?"

"Not really in the beginning. In Normandy, I witnessed lots of stress, some in Holland, much more in Bastogne due to the intense cold, lack of sleep, and inadequate clothing. In Belgium, combat fatigue reached astronomical proportions. We had spent seventy days in the front lines in Holland and didn't have time to recover before we boarded the trucks to take us to Bastogne. On reflection, I realized what happened by the time the command arrived at Bastogne. The men had been on the front line since Normandy. Men were exhausted—no hot food, little sleep, no rest, constant tension, and intense pressure from combat. They were physically exhausted. Inclement weather and constant rain and snow made matters even worse. Physical exhaustion leads to mental exhaustion, which in turn causes men to lose discipline. The loss of self-discipline produces combat fatigue."

Because I knew that many combat historians attempt to set a limit on how long a soldier can stand on the front line, I asked Dick, "You once mentioned that Bastogne was so memorable because 2nd Battalion and Easy Company were under such intense artillery fire for a prolonged period of time. Will you say something about that?"

"That brings a smile to my face because I feel it is impossible to know unless you experience that type of combat. How can you possibly compare a man who has been under just one concentrated artillery bombardment for five minutes to a place like Bastogne, where he could be on the line for weeks and months. In one of Ambrose's books, he states that prolonged artillery bombardment will break any soldier. In civilian life, of course, we refer to combat fatigue as a mental breakdown. That is exactly the way it is in combat—it's a mental breakdown. The intensity—it becomes a problem for me to express my feelings here, but I'd like to share it with you. The intensity of a fire, or a heavy concentration, to be a leader, you have to be able to concentrate on that fire and move just as soon as it stops or the last round hits. Move. Get up. Start circulating among your men. Is everybody okay? Let's get up. Let's move. Keep your eye open for an attack. Get their attention. Move among your men as quickly as possible. And moving among them—the fact that they see you and they're talking to you—they know that you are there and you are talking to them, and it makes all the difference in the world to know that you are not in this thing by yourself. That's what officers must do—break the cycle of fear. If a soldier is concentrating on his own feelings and on his own fear, and he sees you moving around, he realizes that you're sharing the burden with him. That's why he can then move."

"Well, that's about the best exposition of a leader's role in combat, Dick, that I've ever heard."

Dick continued, "Courage will be spent if you relax your standards. An undisciplined soldier feels isolated and alone. Maintain the standards. Don't compromise your integrity. Never give up; don't ever give up. There is always one more thing that a leader can do to improve his situation and that of his command. I always felt that a leader's physical presence was indispensable to unit cohesion and morale. This is why Captain Sobel failed so miserably. Leadership by example always trumps leadership by fear."

I then asked Dick to reiterate what he had once told me about how he viewed casualties. "Tell me again how you coped as casualties mounted as the war progressed. Most commanders whom I have known experience a shame when their soldiers are killed and wounded and they are not."

"Well, it's hard to explain. When your men are dying and you do not, you feel ashamed. I don't know any other way of saying it. Soldiers in war, certainly in World War II and I suspect in every war, are generally young men in their prime. They meet death daily and in every form. They fully realize the hazards of their profession. They take chances because no young man expects to die before middle age. When the first soldier dies, that belief in immortality is shattered. As casualties mount and the core of the unit grows fewer, the remaining soldiers grow even stronger, often shutting off replacement soldiers. They don't want to know the replacements because they are often the first to die. If I recall when you asked a similar question during one of your earlier interviews, I responded that when I saw one of my men wounded, I was happy that he had a ticket home. A soldier killed in battle was at peace. He had lived his life among men whom he had loved. I took a degree of consolation in knowing that my men had lived rather than regretted that they had died. A soldier's real fear is not losing his life in combat, but placing his comrades in jeopardy. That's why ordinary men will perform in extraordinary ways, to ensure their buddies survive."

"That certainly answers my question, but that takes me back to one of my first questions concerning how a leader prevents or manages fear."

"I can only speak from experience, and I'm not sure if my observations apply to different outfits and commands. When I joined the paratroopers at Toccoa, the U.S. Army had already begun the weeding out process of eliminating those soldiers who lacked the physical and mental attributes of being a paratrooper. We did not have standardized tests that are now prevalent in the armed forces. If you made it through Toccoa and earned your wings after five jumps, you joined an outfit known for its *esprit de corps*. The same can be said about the American Rangers or the U.S. Marine Corps. Now back to your question. If you have selected the right personnel, then a leader must instill discipline. I don't mean the discipline that my pen pal wrote about when she described how her officers enjoyed fraternizing with the enlisted sailors, I mean perfect discipline. You often quote General Patton. As Patton once said, 'Discipline is the soul of the army.' George Washington said the same thing when he described the Continental Army in 1776. Discipline is manifested in how well a soldier keeps his uniform, how frequently he cleans his weapon, and the pride he has in his unit. I heard more times than I care to remember how a sailor would get into a fight as soon as another sailor would say something against his ship. I recall the story told of Private First Class Joe Hogan of Easy Company, while he was on furlough, that speaks for all of us on the subject of pride in Company E. During an argument with a soldier from another company about whose company was the better, Joe said, 'My Company E will lick your company in fifteen minutes, and if you wait until the guys who are AWOL come back, we'll do it in five minutes.' Unit pride leads to unit discipline."

"Dick, Eisenhower repeatedly said that morale is at one and the same time the strongest and the most delicate of growths. It withstands shocks, even disasters of the battlefield, but can be destroyed utterly by favoritism, neglect, or injustice. Do you agree?"

"Chalk another one up for the Supreme Commander. Leaders in war often view morale as one of their greatest problems, but as Ike also said, morale is one problem about which a leader can and must do something. I was fortunate in that I had the knack for maintaining morale within my command. Frankly, it wasn't difficult because I was consistent in the way I conducted myself and consistent in the manner in which I treated my soldiers. They always knew where I stood on any issue and what I would and wouldn't tolerate."

"How then do you explain why you didn't personally intervene while Easy Company was in England prior to the invasion, when the noncommissioned officers mutinied against Captain Sobel?"

"Well, I certainly heard the rumors about what the NCOs were planning, but they purposely kept me out of the loop. Whenever they met, one of the noncoms was charged with ensuring I was nowhere around. Should I have reported my suspicions to Colonel Strayer, my battalion commander? Probably, but following Sobel's attempt to court-martial me, I must confess I was not too inclined to give him the benefit of the doubt. In retrospect, what you tolerate, you condone. Perhaps I should have done something because deep down, I realized what they were doing was wrong. Luckily, Colonel Sink transferred Sobel from the regiment and the problem was solved."

"Anything else?"

"Just this. I know we have talked at length about leadership, but it is important to summarize a few things as they apply to morale. Leading in battle is the art of dealing with human nature and the human condition. I can't speak of higher command, but I know a few things about leadership at the small unit level. Leadership at all levels wins wars, but soldiers at the platoon, company, and battalion levels win battles. I think this is particularly true in a national army where soldiers need to understand the reasons behind an officer's orders. Would I have succeeded had I been promoted beyond battalion? I don't know. I do know that I felt comfortable at the small unit level. This is one reason why Easy Company holds such a tender place in my heart. I knew the strengths and weaknesses of every paratrooper. I could rapidly ascertain what I wanted to do, and I felt confident that I could convince the men to do it. After commanding Easy Company in Normandy and Holland, I know the men felt comfortable entrusting their lives to my care. I'm not bragging, because it is not my nature to do so. I'm stating fact. Knowing that I would never ask them to do anything that I wouldn't do myself led to Easy Company's confidence in me as a leader. They knew that I would never quit and that I would do everything within my power to bring them home after the war. I'm proud when I hear a paratrooper from Easy Company or 2nd Battalion remark about my courage under fire and my willingness to share their hardships. I told you once that wars do not make men great, but war sometimes brings out the greatness in good men. If I could choose my personal epitaph, that would be it."

CHAPTER VIII

Major Winters at Ease

The heart he kept . . . a secret to the end from all the pick-
locks of biographers.
—STEPHEN VINCENT BENÉT, *JOHN BROWN'S BODY*

As I reflect upon these vignettes, I am reminded that these are the stories that Dick enjoyed telling when he was most at ease. These are the tales that produced a twinkle in his eye and a smile across his face. These are the memories that he shared when he was in the company of his friends.

★ ★ ★

To truly understand Dick Winters, one merely needs to examine his personal letters from the time he entered the U.S. Army in the summer of 1941 until his return to the United States in November 1945. As with many soldiers, he began keeping a diary to record his military experience. At the same time, he developed a platonic relationship with DeEtta Almon of Asheville, North Carolina. Dick had met DeEtta in November 1941 when he accepted an invitation to join a Mr. Hazard, the director of the local YMCA, to attend religious services. After church, one of the good families demonstrated the truth and goodness of the fabled phrase "Southern hospitality." They invited the director and young Private Winters to their home for a Sunday dinner. The following week two Asheville girls approached Hazard for the names and addresses of some soldiers who might be appreciative of a package of brownies and fudge. According to Dick, "His friend Trent and I became the two lucky soldiers who received the benefit of the girls' goodwill toward the soldiers in the armed services."

Dick immediately sent a letter of thanks to the girls and mentioned that he would like to return to that lovely "city in the sky" and thank them personally. What evolved from that exchange was a wonderful friendship with DeEtta. In Dick's own words, "Between November 1941 and January 1946, when I was discharged from the army, she was my best friend and pen pal. She replied to every letter I wrote, and if I did not write, she continued to send letters. She kept me on the ball and helped me keep my head up." They would meet once after the war ended, to say good-bye. Both went their separate ways, their previous relationship a victim of a time and circumstances that had passed them by.

As Dick described it to me, there things lay until December 1995, fifty years after the war, when he received a telephone call one evening. The voice on the other end of the line was one of a young lady.

"Mr. Winters?"

"Yes."

"Band of Brothers?"

"Yes."

"Do you remember a girl by the name of DeEtta Almon from Asheville, North Carolina?"

"Oh, my goodness. Yes! I have many good memories of DeEtta!"

"I am her daughter Hazel."

That telephone call led Dick to reestablish contact with someone from his past whom he had held very dear. They exchanged several calls and letters, and in January 1996 DeEtta sent Dick two large scrapbooks that contained 117 letters that he, his father, and his sister Ann had written to DeEtta over the course of World War II. Dick and Ethel read each letter and later joined Hazel and DeEtta for a joyous reunion on May 14, 1996, DeEtta's birthday. "There was nothing improper in the letters. Our friendship was strictly platonic. I had nothing to hide from my wife," he told me. Dick and Ethel found the letters not only interesting, but also fascinating because the early correspondence revealed a period piece, a tableau of that innocent time before the war immeasurably altered Dick's life and that of the nation that he served. As Dick read the letters for the first time in fifty years, he remembered why the correspondence had been so important to him during the war. "For the biggest value a letter holds for me," he wrote DeEtta, "is that it takes my mind off my work and back to the land we dream of all the time. I like to hear how tough it is to get along back home. It makes me feel good to think of returning to that type of life someday."

DeEtta died in February 2001. Dick reminded me several times how much he regretted that she did not live to watch HBO's *Band of Brothers*.

When my own father passed on Memorial Day 2009, my mother asked me to clean out his desk in the back room of their home. I sorted through old papers and folders, most of which were yellowed by age. As I tossed one folder into the garbage, several sheets of carbon paper fell to the floor. Taking a closer look, I discovered the papers were actually copies of letters that Dad had sent to his mother during his first year in the navy. Most of us think of our fathers as we remember them in later life. Seldom does one have the opportunity to gain an insight into a father's past, when he was a young man with the entire world at his feet. As with Dad's thirty-four letters from 1938 through 1939, Dick's letters to DeEtta reveal a young man in his early twenties, coping with the realities of military service during the time of the greatest war of the twentieth century. As Dick informed me when he provided me a copy of "Letters to DeEtta," "These letters remind me of an innocent time when I was young and carefree, before the war changed me, and how I became the man I am today."

★ ★ ★

Shortly before my marriage in 2003, I brought a visitor to meet Dick Winters, my fiancée, Mary. By then, my routine of visiting Dick had fallen into a familiar pattern. I always arrived ten minutes early for my scheduled time at 4 P.M. Dick would say, "Military men are always early. I like that." Ethel would merely smile and then roll her eyes. We would then talk for an hour in Dick's upstairs office before departing to a local restaurant for dinner. Following our meal, we returned to the house for some lively after-dinner banter.

Since Mary was accompanying me on this occasion, I was anxious for her to meet Dick and Ethel. Dick had already arranged for a lovely dinner at the Canal House in Hershey, where the owner always reserved his private table in the alcove. Still, Mary was not sure what to expect and could not believe we were driving

LEFT: Private Dick Winters at Camp Croft, South Carolina, August 1941. "Just a rookie, and I sure look the part," wrote Winters.
DICK WINTERS'S PRIVATE COLLECTION

★

BELOW: Second Lieutenant Dick Winters upon graduation from Officer Candidate School, July 1942. Presented to the author by Mrs. Ethel Winters with the words "This has always been my favorite photograph of Dick while he was in the service."
COLE KINGSEED'S PRIVATE COLLECTION

Lieutenant Winters with his squad leaders at Camp Croft, South Carolina, August 1942.
DICK WINTERS'S PRIVATE COLLECTION

Lieutenant Winters instructing soldiers on the firing range while awaiting assignment to the paratroopers in August 1942. DICK WINTERS'S PRIVATE COLLECTION

First Lieutenant Dick Winters prior to deploying to England in September 1943. DICK WINTERS'S PRIVATE COLLECTION

First Lieutenant Winters returns home on leave following graduation from airborne school. "We all wanted those wings." DICK WINTERS'S PRIVATE COLLECTION

Brecourt Manor outside Ste. Marie-du-Mont where Winters saw his initial action on D-Day. Brecourt remained special to the major and he never spoke of it without a tear in his eye.   PHOTOGRAPH BY RICHARD E. THOMAS, COLE KINGSEED'S PRIVATE COLLECTION

Captain Dick Winters, Commanding Officer, Easy Company, 506th Parachute Infantry Regiment, 101st Airborne Division following his receipt of the Distinguished Service Cross for valor on D-Day.   ARMY SIGNAL CORPS PHOTOGRAPH

Captain Dick Winters, battalion executive officer, outside battalion headquarters at Schoonderlogt, Holland, October 1944.
ARMY SIGNAL CORPS PHOTOGRAPH BY AL KROACHKA

Same scene today at Schoonderlogt, Holland.
COLE KINGSEED'S PRIVATE COLLECTION

On the front porch of the Winters home in Hershey, Pennsylvania. Dick had invited me to his home "to answer any questions that I might have." It was the beginning of a wonderful relationship.
COLE KINGSEED'S PRIVATE COLLECTION

Major Winters discusses the Battle of Bastogne during one of his visits to West Point. "Strive to be leaders of character, competence, and courage," he emphasized. COLE KINGSEED'S PRIVATE COLLECTION

Dick and I at Hyde Park, New York, upon the presentation of the Franklin and Eleanor Roosevelt Institute's Four Freedoms/Freedom from Fear Award in May 2001. Major Winters represented the U.S. Army. COLE KINGSEED'S PRIVATE COLLECTION, PHOTO BY BG CHARLES F. BROWER, IV (U.S. ARMY, RETIRED)

Dick with NBC News Anchor Tom Brokaw
at Hyde Park.
DICK WINTERS'S PRIVATE COLLECTION

Major and Mrs. Dick Winters at
the awards banquet following the
presentation of the Roosevelt Institute's
Four Freedoms/Freedom from Fear Award
in May 2001.
PHOTO BY MATTHEW GILLIS,
COURTESY OF GILLIS PHOTOGRAPHY

Dick Winters presents the Legion of Merit to me on the occasion of my retirement from the U.S. Army
in May 2001.   OFFICIAL ARMY PHOTOGRAPH, COLE KINGSEED'S PRIVATE COLLECTION

Dick Winters and historian Stephen E. Ambrose. Dick always took great pride in the plaque above the door of his home that proudly proclaimed that "Steve Ambrose Slept Here." DICK WINTERS'S PRIVATE COLLECTION

LEFT: Dick Winters with actor Damian Lewis who played Winters in the miniseries *Band of Brothers*. Dick felt that Lewis did a marvelous job in the series, but following his initial meeting with Lewis, he pondered the studio's selection of a British actor for the role. "He's skinny and talks with an English accent. And they couldn't even find a guy with blond hair!" PHOTO BY BOB HOFFMAN, BOB HOFFMAN'S PRIVATE COLLECTION

★

BELOW: Dick and Ethel Winters, along with actor Tom Hanks and "Dr." Bob Hoffman at the Emmy Awards ceremony in 2002. "Am I the only one who thought Hoffman was a cardiologist?" asked Hanks. PHOTO BY MICHELLE KOPECKY, BOB HOFFMAN'S PRIVATE COLLECTION

In the refuge of his office, Dick Winters shares his stories and reflects upon his life.
PHOTOGRAPH COURTESY OF *INTELLIGENCER JOURNAL*, LANCASTER, PA

In one of his favorite pasttimes, Dick and Ethel Winters join Bob Hoffman; the author; and his wife, Mary at Dafnos's Restaurant in Hershey, Pennsylvania.   COLE KINGSEED'S PRIVATE COLLECTION

Dick Winters and Bob Hoffman share a laugh as Dick dons an M-1 helmet from World War II.
BOB HOFFMAN'S PRIVATE COLLECTION

Presenting Major Winters with the first copy of *Beyond Band of Brothers: The War Memoirs of Major Dick Winters* on his eighty-eighth birthday on January 21, 2006.
PHOTOGRAPH BY MARY KINGSEED, COLE KINGSEED'S PRIVATE COLLECTION

LEFT: The author with *Beyond Band of Brothers*. I wondered if I had measured up to the major's expectations. "For those who have served in combat, this is as close as it gets. For those who have not seen combat, they better listen," he said. "I'm so very proud of you." PHOTOGRAPH BY MARY KINGSEED, COLE KINGSEED'S PRIVATE COLLECTION

★

BELOW: Dick proudly displays the first copy of his memoirs to Bob Hoffman and the author. When asked by Hoffman if he had made the right choice in selecting me as his assistant, he smiled and replied, "I think so!" PHOTOGRAPH BY MARY KINGSEED, COLE KINGSEED'S PRIVATE C COLLECTION

The major with Mary Kingseed and the author. Mary joined me repeatedly on my visits to see Dick and Ethel. At one point, Dick turned to me and said, "Ethel must think Mary is very special because she never shares her photographs with anyone outside the family." PHOTOGRAPH BY ETHEL WINTERS, COLE KINGSEED'S PRIVATE COLLECTION

Dick Winters takes delight in displaying the Wheaties box that features "Major Richard D. Winters, Champion of the Band of Brothers."
PHOTOGRAPH BY BOB HOFFMAN,
BOB HOFFMAN'S PRIVATE COLLECTION

Dick was humbled when the Hershey-Derry Township Historical Society presented the Veterans Exhibit featuring "A Hero's Story: Featuring Major Dick Winters." Too ill to attend the opening ceremony, Major Winters was granted a private showing.
PHOTOGRAPH BY BOB HOFFMAN, BOB HOFFMAN'S PRIVATE COLLECTION

President George W. Bush greets Major Winters on a visit to Hershey in 2004. "When the commander-in-chief calls, you always answer the call," Dick said.
OFFICIAL WHITE HOUSE PHOTOGRAPH, DICK WINTERS'S PRIVATE COLLECTION

Major Winters enjoys a presidential embrace following President Bush's address to thousands of well-wishers on a visit to Hershey, Pennsylvania.
DICK WINTERS'S PRIVATE COLLECTION

In his last public appearance at the Starlight West Room of Hotel Hershey in February 2007, Mayor Alexander Sakkers of Eindhoven, Holland, presents Major Winters "The Medal of the City of Eindhoven" for his role in liberating Eindhoven in September 1944.
COLE KINGSEED'S PRIVATE COLLECTION

The author and Dick Winters confer during the presentation of "The Medal of the City of Eindhoven."
COLE KINGSEED'S PRIVATE COLLECTION

Major Winters was honored to sit next to Colonel Kevin Farrell during the ceremony where he became the first civilian who was honored by the citizens of Eindhoven, Holland. Farrell had recently returned from commanding a battalion task force in East Baghdad during the war in Iraq and was currently the chief of military history at West Point. PHOTOGRAPH BY PETER VAN DE WAL, KEVIN FARRELL'S PRIVATE COLLECTION

Mary Kingseed, Tom Hanks, and the author at the dinner following the memorial service celebrating the life of Dick Winters on March 18, 2011. I was honored to serve as the master of ceremonies for the memorial service. Hanks was the perfect gentleman, stating, "Colonel, I have done this type of program before. It's never easy. You did a great job!"
PHOTOGRAPH BY BOB HOFFMAN, COLE KINGSEED'S PRIVATE COLLECTION

Reflecting on his life at the end of a busy day, Major Winters takes a moment's rest. "Everyone wants a piece of me," he sometimes lamented, but he realized that this was the price of fame.
PHOTOGRAPH BY BOB HOFFMAN,
BOB HOFFMAN'S PRIVATE COLLECTION

This is how I remember Dick Winters. When he presented me the photograph, he regretted that he couldn't remember the photographer, but "I remember he took the photograph at my farm, where I finally found the peace and quiet that I promised myself if I survived the war." DICK WINTERS'S PRIVATE COLLECTION

The bucolic Bergstrasse Evangelical Lutheran Cemetery in Ephrata, Pennsylvania, where Major Winters is buried. His marker reads simply "Richard D. Winters, WW II 101st Airborne, 1918–2011." PHOTO BY THE AUTHOR, COLE KINGSEED'S PRIVATE COLLECTION

The author paying his respects to Major Winters by placing an American flag over his grave. "If I go first, I expect to see you over the next hill. If you precede me, I expect you to be waiting for me." PHOTOGRAPH BY MARY KINGSEED, COLE KINGSEED'S PRIVATE COLLECTION

A young girl is enthralled with the American flags that don the gravesite of Major Dick Winters. Knowing the major as well as I did, her presence would have brought a smile to his face and a twinkle to his eye.   PHOTOGRAPH BY CAROL WEBBER, CAROL WEBBER'S PRIVATE COLLECTION

The statue outside Brecourt Manor depicting the fighting spirit of the junior leaders of D-Day. The sculptor selected Dick Winters as representative of those leaders who spearheaded the invasion. Inscribed on the monument are the major's own tribute to those men who have paid the last full measure of their devotion: "Wars do not make men great, but sometimes wars bring out the greatness in good men."   PHOTOGRAPH BY RICHARD E. THOMAS, COLE KINGSEED'S PRIVATE COLLECTION

four hours to get together with someone whom she had never met and were going to dinner with a couple about whom she had only heard. Before departing New York, she asked, "Are you telling me that we need Dick Winters's permission to get married?"

"Wouldn't hurt, hon," I replied. Now familiar with my idiosyncrasies, Mary gave me an unadulterated smile.

On arriving in Hershey, I immediately pulled into the car wash four blocks from Elm Avenue and began washing the car. Mary, who had never seen me perform this task, seemed perplexed. Too polite to say anything, she was incredulous that after I finished washing the car, I pulled in to the station to vacuum the interior. After I cleaned the driver's side, I tossed the vacuum hose to Mary and asked her to do the passenger's side. That was the straw that broke the camel's back. Unable to control her laughter, she said, "You know, Cole, we are not picking up the king and queen of England!"

Remembering my first encounter five years earlier, when Ethel had remarked about my car's dirty windows, I replied, "Maybe not, Mary, but I will never pick up Ethel in a dirty car again."

Our visit and the dinner at the Canal House were fabulous, and Mary passed Dick's inspection, but not before she felt a moment of discomfort. After helping her to her seat, Dick looked her square in the eye and said, "Tell me about yourself!" Mary, used to standing before a high school class, could only stammer a response, which in turn produced nervous laughter. More questions followed and I received more than one kick under the table. To make a long story short, Dick granted his "approval" for us to marry. In the future, Mary and I made numerous visits to Hershey, but her initial visit was the one she considered the most memorable.

★ ★ ★

Damian Lewis, the British actor who played Dick in the HBO miniseries, tells a wonderful story about how he received the role of Major Winters. He likened the role to "a needle-in-the-haystack piece of casting. I had no real sense of who this guy was." Lewis was in his late twenties and had done nothing on this scale before. During the second audition, he began reading for the role of Winters. Following the final audition in London, he was invited to Los Angeles to meet Steven Spielberg and Tom Hanks. In L.A. he met Ron Livingston, who eventually played Lewis Nixon. Since they thought they had time on their hands, Lewis, Ron, and others went out on the town and partied until four in the morning. Three hours later, Lewis received a call from Spielberg's secretary notifying him that "Steve will see you at ten o'clock." In ninety minutes, Lewis claims, he consumed six cups of coffee and took three showers to get sober. When he arrived at Spielberg's office, several other actors were present, all of whom were vying for the coveted role. As Lewis recollected in a radio interview two months following Dick's passing, "I still don't know why I got the part. One of the actors looked exactly like Major Winters. It was uncanny how much he resembled the major, but fortunately, I got the part."

As the production of the HBO miniseries began in earnest, *People* magazine dispatched Lewis to Pennsylvania to meet the real thing. Dick, in turned, called Bob Hoffman and invited him to join Lewis and a reporter who was writing the feature article. It was a very upbeat day. Dick was extraordinarily pleased with the way that Lewis portrayed him in the series, but this was his initial meeting with the actor, and at first he was somewhat skeptical.

Dick and Hoffman invited Lewis and the reporter to his

favorite little restaurant, the Giddy-up Café in Hershey. At day's end, Dick and Hoffman stood on the curb in front of Dick's home on Elm Avenue and waved good-bye. Dick was all smiles as they departed, but he then turned to Hoffman and said, "Gee, he's skinny and talks with an English accent. And they couldn't even find a guy with blond hair!" Lewis, of course, is a redhead.

★ ★ ★

When *Band of Brothers* premiered in September 2001, the veterans of Easy Company became instant celebrities. Being invited to attend the Emmy Awards ceremony was a personal highlight for Dick. Steven Spielberg and Tom Hanks had personally invited Dick to participate in the onstage acceptance of the Emmy for Outstanding Miniseries, which they were confident was coming their way. Over dinner at a local restaurant, Dick shared the invitation with Ethel and Bob Hoffman, but he was unsure if he should attend. Ethel was reluctant to attend and was skeptical of the wisdom of her husband making a transcontinental trip to California. "No way you are going!" Ethel said, "It will be too much for you." The conversation became quite muted after that remark.

Returning to the house, Hoffman asked Dick point-blank if he wanted to go. When Dick responded in the affirmative, Bob proposed a scheme. Since he had arranged Dick's care with a local cardiologist, Bob suggested that if Dick's health improved, a nurse could accompany him and Ethel to California. That would assuage Ethel's fears of her husband traveling across the country. Everything progressed as planned until at the last minute, when the nurse cited complications that prevented her from going. The cardiologist then proposed that Dick take Hoffman along since

Bob knew better than anyone how to handle Dick's personal needs. Moreover, Dick had complete trust in him.

As they departed the airport in Philadelphia, Dick pulled Hoffman aside and said, "Hoffman, if anyone in California calls you 'Doctor,' just go along with it."

Bob looked at Dick and said, "Winters?"

"I haven't misled anyone, Hoffman, but if they are under that assumption, well, that's up to them," he quickly added.

From the moment the Winterses arrived in Los Angeles, the writers and producers of the series surrounded them, Steven Spielberg and Tom Hanks included. As Hoffman later recalled, the "closeness and dedication of the Easy Company veterans to their story and to each other was clearly visible. Skilled and famous artists in their own right, they spoke of a unifying spirit that brought all involved together with a single-minded purpose, a bonding which they all agreed was unusual to this industry and to this town." Hanks reinforced this feeling with remarks he shared with the Winterses following the awards ceremony. His thoughts were sincere, emotional, and private. As many times as dignitaries and famous men and women had courted Hanks, there was something in Dick's humility that struck a chord with him.

Upon arrival at their hotel in Hollywood, the manager escorted Dick and "Dr." Hoffman to adjoining rooms. By prior arrangement, and at Dick's insistence, they did not stay at the same hotel as the Easy Company families, who were staying at Los Angeles's St. Regis. Dick and Ethel's room contained a huge floral arrangement, engraved stationery, and name cards personalized for him. Hoffman's room had a smaller floral arrangement, engraved stationery, and name cards announcing to the world "Dr. Robert Hoffman in residence."

Dick and Hoffman next attended the HBO banquet for the thirty-seven Easy Company veterans and their extended families. Dick spoke only briefly, since he wanted the focus to be on the veterans and not on himself. "The company belonged to the men," Dick reiterated. "The officers were merely caretakers." Following dinner, Dick asked Hoffman to sit at his side to assist him in avoiding the "crush" of veterans and families seeking his autograph. All of the veterans referred to him as Major Winters. Not one addressed him as Dick—great respect and deference. Such admiration was typical of the members of Easy Company. Three years earlier, on the occasion of Dick's eightieth birthday, which was celebrated at the Veterans of Foreign Wars in Hershey, Pennsylvania, Forrest Guth rose to toast the honoree and felt compelled to seek Dick's approval. Forrest looked Dick in the eye and asked, "Major Winters, on this special occasion, may I have your permission to call you Dick?" The relationship between Winters and his men was that different.

By coincidence, the cast of the television situation comedy *Friends*, including David Schwimmer, who played the sadistic Captain Herbert Sobel in the miniseries, sat in the row immediately in front of Spielberg, Hanks, Dick and Ethel, and Hoffman. At one point, someone tapped Schwimmer on the shoulder and advised him, "The real Major Winters is sitting right behind you." Schwimmer turned to Dick and said, "Major Winters, I hope I wasn't too hard on you in the way I played Captain Sobel."

Without missing a beat, Dick looked him squarely in the eyes and said, "I assure you, he was much worse than you ever imagined."

Needless to say, the Emmy ceremony itself was an unqualified success. Accepting the award for Outstanding Miniseries was

Spielberg and Tom Hanks. Spielberg said, "Men of Easy Company won this in 1944." As the camera cut to the actual veterans, Spielberg continued, "These are the real men of Easy Company."

Dick, too, was energized and walked with a definite purpose as he went to the stage. The night before, he had asked Bob to write some thoughts on his speech. Hoffman did and suggested that he end with a salute. Following an introduction by Steven Spielberg at the awards ceremony, Dick addressed the audience: "Thank you, very much. This evening, I represent all the men of Easy Company who are present and accounted for and all who have passed on. Thank every one of you for your support. I salute you!" Short and sweet. Dick's speech was overwhelmingly well received and he was given a standing ovation.

Over dinner following the ceremony, Ethel thanked Tom Hanks for allowing Bob Hoffman to accompany them as it had made the difference in their coming. Hanks replied that there was nothing like traveling with your own cardiologist. Ethel, knowing nothing of the "medical masquerade" surrounding Hoffman, replied, "Cardiologist? Hoffman is an architect!" Hanks then spun around and addressed Hoffman, "And here I've been treating you with respect!"

The next morning at breakfast with the nine series writers, Erik Jendresen informed Hoffman that Hanks had tapped him on the shoulder at the bar after the Winters party had departed and said, "Did you know Hoffman is an architect, not a cardiologist?"

Jendresen replied, "Of course. I've known him since the beginning of the series' work!"

"Am I the only guy who thought Hoffman was a cardiologist?" laughed Hanks.

★ ★ ★

Two other events formed an indelible impression on Dick during his final years. In May 2001, the Franklin and Eleanor Roosevelt Institute conferred upon the veterans of World War II the Four Freedoms/Freedom from Fear Award. The Franklin D. Roosevelt Four Freedoms Medals are presented annually to men and women whose achievements have demonstrated a commitment to the four freedoms that President Roosevelt proclaimed on January 6, 1941: freedom of speech and expression, freedom of worship, freedom from want, and freedom from fear. Roosevelt considered the four freedoms essential to a flourishing democracy. Past recipients had included Presidents Harry Truman, John F. Kennedy, and Jimmy Carter; Coretta Scott King; Elie Wiesel; Katharine Graham; and Supreme Court justices William Brennan and Thurgood Marshall. In 2001, the institute selected five servicemen and -women to represent the United States armed forces of World War II. National Broadcasting Company anchor Tom Brokaw presented the actual awards to the five recipients who had served so gallantly during the war. Representing the U.S. Army was none other than Major Dick Winters. He stood in proud company, with navy corpsman Robert E. Bush; Navy Cross recipient William T. Ketcham, Jr., representing the U.S. Marine Corps; U.S. Air Force Colonel Lee A. Archer, Jr., the Tuskegee Airmen's only fighter ace; and Ellen Buckley, who served in the Army Nurse Corps.

I attended the ceremony at historic St. James' Church in Hyde Park, New York. Dick and Ethel were unaware that I would be there, but I wouldn't have missed it for the world. "What in heaven's name are you doing here," he asked. "You are supposed to be in the classroom."

"Dick, I'm here to thank you for what you and these men and women did for my generation and my children's generation. Thank you for your service to our great country."

The reception following the ceremony was spectacular. The crowd numbered in the hundreds, and the West Point Glee Club treated the attendees to a medley of patriotic songs from the World War II era. What was most gratifying was to see the young men and women from the Corps of Cadets of the U.S. Military Academy shake the hand of each recipient of the Freedom from Fear Award. Later, Dick called me aside and said, "I know you had something to do with us being here." I said that was not the case. "You're here for what you did over there. This is our way of saying thanks to your generation."

Three years later, Dick received an invitation to speak on leadership at the FBI headquarters in Washington, D.C. Several hundred senior agents were totally engrossed by Dick's presentation, which addressed a number of leadership challenges that he had encountered during the war. He urged the agents to maintain the highest standards of professional conduct and to always "Hang Tough!" When his presentation was over, Dick received his customary standing ovation. The applause became even more boisterous after FBI director Robert Mueller III presented an award to Dick. In his comments, he referred to a scene from the miniseries in which David Schwimmer portraying Captain Sobel refuses to salute Damian Lewis as Major Winters. Winters then instructs Sobel, "Captain Sobel, you salute the rank, not the man." Sobel reluctantly acquiesces and Winters smiles to Lewis Nixon. Director Mueller announced to the audience, "Major Winters, we thank you for joining us today. Unlike the scene in *Band of Brothers*, today we salute the man, not the rank." First-class.

* * *

Dick's last public appearance was at the Starlight West Room of the Hotel Hershey on February 28, 2007, when he received "the Medal of the City of Eindhoven" from Mayor Alexander Sakkers of Eindhoven, Holland. Dick was in ill health, and Ethel was probably correct in her assessment that the physical strain would be too much for him. Dick, however, wanted to attend the ceremony to express his personal gratitude to the Dutch nation that had endured four years of Nazi occupation. He recounted the reception on September 18, 1944, when members of the 506th Parachute Infantry Regiment, with Easy Company led by Captain Dick Winters in the van, entered and liberated the city of Eindhoven. "We had experienced a tough fight just to enter the city," recalled Dick. "The people were ecstatic to have their freedom returned. You could see it in their faces. They couldn't do enough. People would bring out chairs from their homes for the soldiers to sit down. They brought food and drinks. It was so different than anything we had experienced in Normandy. Of course, in France the people weren't sure we were going to stay, and that they were really liberated. But with Holland, they were sure we were going to stay. They had complete faith in us that we would stick with them—that they were free. If there is a lesson here, it is that freedom is so important that it should never be taken for granted."

Over a luncheon at the hotel, Mayor Sakkers addressed the assembly and stated that at last year's celebration in Eindhoven's city square, more than ten thousand residents gathered to hear Sakkers speak with Major Winters on the phone to announce the awarding of the honorary citizen medal. That conversation was broadcast on live television throughout the country. Sakkers then presented Dick with the medal and the citation conferring on him the status of an "Honorary Citizen of Eindhoven." He was the first non-Dutch recipient of the prestigious award. "Every citizen of Eindhoven is very proud that you are one of them," said Sakkers. "Thank you very much for all that you have done." The mayor continued, "The eighteenth of September will always be symbolic of gratefulness and of freedom that was earned in those days and is so important for everyone, every day."

True to form, Dick expressed his appreciation for such an honor, but that it was he who should be thanking the people of Holland for the role the Netherlands played in helping the United States establish itself after the American Revolution. Holland was the first European nation to recognize the fledgling United States after the fighting ceased in 1781. "Our actions in 1944 were a way of repaying our debt to you for coming to our rescue in 1782," Dick said. "Payback was needed and gladly given."

Dick's citation read: "The medal is granted for exceptional services rendered by Major R. D. Winters and all Allied Troops who risked their lives to bring about the liberation of Eindhoven and the surrounding region under life-threatening circumstances." In Dick's mind, the ceremony was a testament to yet another debt repaid. He was even more pleased when the Dutch edition of *Beyond Band of Brothers: The War Memoirs of Major Dick Winters* was released on the anniversary of Eindhoven's liberation.

PART THREE

★ ★ ★

Autumn

CHAPTER IX

Mrs. Winters

To Sherlock Holmes she is always *the* woman. I have seldom heard him mention her under any other name.
—ARTHUR CONAN DOYLE, "A SCANDAL IN BOHEMIA"

I suspect that Ethel Winters was the only woman whom Dick Winters actually loved. Ethel had met Dick in early 1948 when he was working as a personnel manager at the Nixon Nitration Works. Dick had seen Ethel, a recent graduate of Rutgers University, every morning when he stopped for breakfast at a local restaurant near the train station. It took time and more than a little bit of courage to ask her for a date. "I'll think about it," she said. And just as Dick routinely "checked people out the first time he met them," so did Ethel verify Dick's credentials. When she confirmed that he was who he said he was, she accepted his invitation. Several months later, Dick and Ethel were married, on May 16, 1948, in New Brunswick, New Jersey. Fifty years later, I sent them a congratulatory letter in honor of their golden anniversary.

Ethel became the unlikeliest of heroines, someone I grew to respect and admire almost as much as her husband. Early in my relationship with Dick, I determined that access to Dick Winters went through Ethel. She was undoubtedly "the keeper of the keys" of 117 Elm Avenue, Hershey, Pennsylvania. Just as Dick would "size you up" to determine if you possessed the qualities of a leader, a visitor had to run a similar gauntlet with Ethel. Until you convinced her that your intentions were sincere, that you had no intention of taking advantage of her husband, and that you were not seeking financial profit from your relationship with her family, your chance of crossing the portal of the Winters's home was virtually nonexistent. Not surprisingly, Ethel was not the easiest person to know, but once she accepted you, she became an ardent ally. There were many who felt that she was too controlling in limiting access to Dick, but to my mind, this was a private matter between husband and wife. I know for a fact that her actions were always guided by what she felt was in the best interest of her husband.

My first meeting with Ethel Winters occurred in late September 1999. It had been nearly eighteen months since I had met Dick when he had traveled to West Point. As fate would have it, Dick returned to the Military Academy in 1999 for a return engagement, to address the cadets attending a class on leadership sponsored by West Point's Department of Behavioral Sciences and Leadership. This time Ethel accompanied Dick, but she decided not to attend the classes, nor did she join Dick and me for dinner the evening preceding his lecture.

My own presence at dinner was not a sure thing. On the morning that Dick and Ethel arrived at West Point, I met his escort officer, who happened to be both a friend and colleague. The officer had been busy preparing his own classes and appeared a bit haggard.

"What's wrong? You seem out of sorts this morning."

"Well, sir, I need a lot of preparation for tomorrow's class, and now I find that I have to take Major Winters to dinner this evening."

Concealing my disbelief and sensing an opportunity, I replied, "Tell you what. I'm free this evening, so I'll take him off your hands."

"Thanks, sir, but you know I can't ask that of you since you are a senior officer."

"No problem. Just remember, you owe me one!"

Needless to say Dick and I enjoyed another fabulous dinner. Dick was anxious to outline his presentation and promised that he intended to present the cadets with an ethical dilemma of the highest magnitude. He refused to give me the specifics, but he wondered what their reaction would be the next morning.

On the day of the presentation, I finished teaching my own classes and encountered Dick's escort officer in the corridor. He seemed more flustered than before, so I asked, "Now what's wrong?"

His reply startled me. "Well, sir, I have just been tasked to drive Major and Mrs. Winters back to Hershey, Pennsylvania. It's a four-hour drive, and then I have to return tonight to West Point for tomorrow's classes."

Frankly, I could not believe my good fortune. "Well, I'm not teaching tomorrow, so I'll drive them home." The opportunity to talk "soldiering" with Dick Winters over an extended period was just the sort of opportunity that I did not intend to miss.

He protested in vain, but I insisted, telling him, "But remember, this time you really owe me!"

Dick's presentation to the cadets was masterful. He outlined his actions at Brecourt Manor on D-Day. At one point, he asked pointedly, "How many of you think of yourselves as killers?" Every hand shot up. "You are missing the point," he told the cadets. "West Point must produce leaders, not killers. As future officers, you must direct the action. As a leader, your responsibility is to ensure your soldiers function as a team and not as independent fighting men. The team is more important than the individual."

Afterward, I questioned Dick about this, and he responded, "Talk is cheap. They thought they needed to be killers. I wanted them to think things through and to remember their responsibilities as officers."

Two hours later, I met Ethel over lunch at the West Point Officers' Club. As soon as we had finished our meal, I pulled up the car and we began our journey to Hershey. Dick sat next to me and Ethel seemed comfortable in the backseat. She appeared content just to be knitting as we left the Military Academy. The distance from West Point to Hershey is approximately two hundred miles, and you would think that there would be ample time for conversation. I took the opportunity to provide Dick a little more of my own background, growing up on a farm in western Ohio. We shared a number of laughs, but I did not hear a word from Ethel. Had I said something wrong? Had I inadvertently offended her? One hundred thirty miles into our journey, I finally gained a reprieve when Dick suggested that we pull off Interstate 81 for a comfort stop. I waited patiently in the car until I saw them exit the restroom.

No sooner had they returned to the car than Dick asked, "How would you like to see my farm?"

"Dick, I would love to see the farm!"

"Just continue driving and I'll tell you when to pull off."

Back in the car, Ethel had still not uttered a single word. We reached the farm outside Fredericksburg, Pennsylvania, two hours later. It was approximately mid-afternoon. As we arrived, Ethel thanked me and went straight into the house. I accompanied Dick for a tour of the premises, too scared to inquire why Ethel seemed so reticent while we were driving. I could not believe that my driving had been so torturous that I had driven her into absolute silence.

For his part Dick was in his element as soon as we arrived. This farm was exactly what he had prayed for if he survived the war, "a quiet piece of land somewhere in the Pennsylvania countryside" where he could live out his life in peace. It was evident that he treasured the land every bit as much as my own father, who constantly reminded me that the good Lord will never make additional land, so you have to treasure what He has made. We walked to the small pond where Dick took some feed from his pocket and scattered it to the koi. As he was feeding the fish, I couldn't help but think: Here is one of the fiercest warriors from World War II, a company commander who conducted two combat jumps into enemy territory, and he is feeding fish without a care in the world. Looking at a nearby fence post, I noticed three turtle shells nailed to it. Somewhat fascinated, I asked, "What are those?"

"Oh, a couple years ago some snapping turtles decided that they would feast on my fish, so I had to shoot them," he replied.

"Are you still a good shot?"

He winked and said, "I'm pretty good! Why don't you spend some time with Ethel, and I'll be up in a minute."

Now that we were out of the car and in the house, Ethel was chatty. I told her how much I appreciated, and how honored I was, at being invited to see the farm. She replied, "You ought to feel honored. No one, no one, sees this farm. This is our private retreat. Dick has invited Stephen Ambrose and Tom Hanks, but he doesn't usually allow anyone else to visit." She then added, "You mentioned the story told by Ambrose in *Band of Brothers* about Dick walking down to the pond and a flock of thirty Canadian geese took off. One goose stayed behind because it had a broken wing. Steve suggested that Dick shoot the goose and freeze it to serve it at our next Thanksgiving dinner. As Ambrose tells the story, Dick replied, 'I couldn't do that!' Steve said Dick was incapable of violent action, but what he did not know was that Dick went to the pond every day to feed the goose since it could not fly. That's the reason he couldn't shoot it. He had been nursing it back to health." That vignette told me more about Dick Winters than I could have imagined.

Back in the car, I drove Dick and Ethel to Hershey, a short distance away. Once again, Ethel grew silent. Now I pride myself on being a decent driver, but something was wrong. As we arrived at that small white house on Elm Avenue, I finally had my answer. Chuckling, Ethel turned to me and said, "How do you see out these darn windows? They are so dirty!"

At the U.S. Military Academy at West Point, new cadets are informed they have three acceptable responses: "No, sir/ma'am!" "Yes, sir/ma'am!" and "No excuse, sir/ma'am!" Chastised, I simply responded, "Ethel, I have no excuse." Dick and Ethel could hardly contain their amusement as we went into the house.

Since I had the return drive to make, I stayed but an hour. Dick showed me his upstairs office, a private room where I was destined to spend innumerable hours over the next ten years. Ethel and I shared some light moments before I announced that it was time to depart. I turned to thank Dick, but he had quietly disappeared. "Ethel, where is Dick? I want to thank him for his hospitality."

"Never mind him. I think he is outside."

As she opened the door to escort me to the car, I looked at the street, and there was Major Dick Winters, with Windex in one hand and a rag in the other, cleaning the front windshield of my Camry. Ethel had set me up, keeping me occupied while Dick snuck out the back. Completely mortified, I ran to the car. Dick smiled and said, "Get in. You do the inside." It was not a request, it was an order, and I complied. Of course it is more difficult to clean the inside windshield since it is virtually impossible to get your hand to the area just above the dash. Poking his head in the side window and with a grin on his face, Dick asked, "Are you doing a good job?"

"I'm trying, Major Winters," I said. "I'm trying!"

Even I was laughing by this time. As I pulled away, I looked back, and there were Dick and Ethel waving from the front step. Two honks on the horn and I was gone.

Two weeks later, I paid my respects on the Winterses when I stopped briefly en route to a lecture I planned to deliver the following evening at the U.S. Army War College in Carlisle Barracks, Pennsylvania. Dick and Ethel joined me for dinner at Friendly's Restaurant near the Hershey Park. When it was time to depart, I asked Dick to show me where Brecourt Manor was located on my map of Normandy. We talked briefly and then it was time to push on to Carlisle. As Dick wrote later, "As you turned left on Route 39 from Hershey, Ethel remarked, 'He's okay.'" Coming from Ethel, this was the ultimate compliment.

As a footnote, four years after the "dirty car" incident, I had just returned from the Gettysburg battlefield, and I noticed my car was not as clean as I would have liked. Instead of pulling up in my usual spot in front of the Winters house, I purposely parked up the street at a distance, where Ethel could not observe the car from her office window. As fate would have it, when I departed, she said she wanted to discuss something with me and accompanied me outside. As she finished, she gazed at the street and asked, "Where is your car?" I sheepishly pointed it out several houses down Elm Avenue. Her response was predictable. "Cole, your car looks pretty dirty from here." I couldn't believe it. I responded, "Ethel, you have to be kidding. I purposely parked it there so you wouldn't see it. You never walk me outside. Guilty again!"

Years later, my wife Mary and I paid a scheduled visit to the Winters home on the occasion of my sixtieth birthday. Since we had some additional time on our hands, Mary decided to shop at the Hershey outlets. As we were preparing to depart, the car battery died. Fortunately, I had my jumper cables present, so after a friendly resident assisted us, I drove the car to a repair shop two blocks from the Days Inn on Chocolate Avenue, where we usually stayed while visiting the Winterses. The mechanic informed us that he needed to keep the car overnight, but he could provide a ride for us if necessary. It was only ten minutes before Dick and Ethel were expecting us, so I took him up on his offer. Ethel was anticipating our arrival and laughed when ten minutes later Mary and I pulled up in front of the house in a wrecker. As I knocked on the door, she opened it and smiled. "Not your usual means of transportation, Cole," she said. I chuckled and then responded, "Wild horses couldn't keep us away."

As was her custom, Ethel accompanied us into the living room, where Dick was awaiting our arrival. No sooner had we sat down than Ethel reappeared with a glass of iced tea for me and a bottle of ginger ale for Mary. "I like to keep your favorite beverages on hand in the event that you stop by," she said. As Dick discussed the progress of sales of his memoirs, Ethel then asked Mary to accompany her to the office where she handled the volumes of correspondence written by Dick's admirers. "I have something to show you, Mary," she said and then opened a box of family photographs taken over the last four decades. Dick smiled and said to me, "Ethel never shows those pictures to anyone. She must really like Mary. Those photos are very personal to her. Tell Mary, 'Welcome to the club.'"

My children enjoyed knowing Ethel as much as they did her husband. My daughter Maura fondly remembers her meeting with Ethel that took place when we visited once between Veterans Day and Christmas. Christmastime in Hershey, Pennsylvania, is a memorable event. The town that Milton Hershey built is arrayed in holiday trimmings and bright lights. On this occasion, Dick and Ethel asked us to join them for a Christmas concert at the Hershey School. In addition to holiday carols, the band played nostalgic songs from the 1940s and a series of patriotic anthems. Halfway through the show, one of the band members requested that all veterans rise. As Maura recalls, "The major proudly stood up and looked over at my father, still sitting. He ordered my father to stand up! Of course, my father is undeniably proud to be a veteran, but in the presence of the major, it was hard for him to stand and be considered an equal. Well, the major would have none of that. It was then that I realized that the friendship between my father and the major went beyond two guys who both happened to be in the army at some point in their lives. They respected each other and respected each other's sacrifices, no matter how large or small those sacrifices were."

Something funny occurred during that same visit. After the concert, we were pretty exhausted, but Ethel invited us to the house to relax. As Dick and Maura sat in Dick's upstairs office to talk about Normandy, Ethel entered the room and made a reference to Sergeant Bill Guarnere shooting horses outside Brecourt Manor. A somber expression passed over Dick's face, and he said solemnly, "You weren't supposed to say that. That's a military secret." Ethel rolled her eyes and smiled at Maura. When Maura and I returned to the hotel later that evening, she said, "That's when I realized that Mrs. Winters wasn't only the major's wife, she was also his friend (and our friend, too)."

Over the next few years, our relationship grew stronger. I'm not sure why, but it took a long time to gain entry into Ethel's inner circle. Perhaps she needed a confidant as well, and maybe, just maybe, I served that role. She had been skeptical at first. A mutual friend later informed me that Dick had recounted a conversation with his wife following our first dinner out. "I think he wants something," she cautioned Dick. However, she overcame her skepticism, and when she had concluded that I was not interested in profiting from her husband, Ethel relaxed her guard. She told me one day why I had received "most favored nation" status. "Cole, a lot of Dick's friends are probably envious that you have so much access to Dick. I don't care what they think. You are the only person I trust. I am so sick of everyone trying to become famous and make a fortune on Dick. It feels sometimes like the vultures are gathering, and when you have someone so vulnerable, it is so stressful. There are so many requests for autographs, memorabilia, and books. You have never asked for anything. I want you to remember one thing: We picked you, you did not ask. Thank you for that."

I advised Ethel to keep up her guard and to inform those who desired to see Dick that he was just not able to receive visitors. Still the requests never ceased. The Winterses were forced to change their phone number in an effort to keep messages to a minimum. Finally, the clamor for more of Dick's time became too invasive, so in early 2007, Ethel passed me a note in which she stated that she was invoking new rules for future visits—no books for signatures, only afternoon visits, and brevity when visitors arrived. "These guidelines don't apply to you, Cole," she added, "because you and Mary already abide by these rules."

For the last six years of Dick's life, Ethel remained his constant companion and principal provider. When Dick required greater attention, she quit her volunteer work at the Hershey Public Library to be at his side. She handled all Dick's personal correspondence and managed his visitors. She copied Dick's files and photographs, as well as typed his wartime letters. When the correspondence became too burdensome, she passed off what she considered the most important to me to respond to. Ethel also managed the family's legal and financial matters and coordinated the memorial service. At times, I attempted to get her to relax and to forget the problems associated with full-time care. Knowing how much she used to enjoyed reading, I suggested some books that I believed might offer a degree of comfort, such as Mitch Albom's *Tuesdays with Morrie: An Old Man, a Young Man, and Life's Greatest Lesson* and *The Five People You Meet in Heaven*.

Always grateful for a suggestion, she politely refused. "I can't deal with death any more." This was the tender side of Ethel Winters that the public never saw and that I witnessed firsthand.

She was extraordinary in every respect, but she cherished her privacy. In a sense she wore the hero's mantle uncomfortably, but her selfless devotion to her husband and to her community serve as quiet inspiration that heroes can be found far from the battlefield.

One final note concerning Ethel Winters. As Dick and I prepared the final draft of *Beyond Band of Brothers*, I proposed a dedication to the soldiers of Easy Company. He looked at it and grimaced. "Let me think about it," he said. "I'm a bit uncomfortable with that. Give me another alternative."

Taking a pen, I scrawled something on the page and handed it back. The note read simply, "To Ethel."

"Now you have it!"

★ ★ ★

Ethel Estoppey Winters followed Dick in death fifteen months after her husband's passing. I had promised her after Dick's memorial service that she hadn't seen the last of me. I paid my respects every quarter over the course of the following year. Our conversations often dealt with minor tasks that she requested I handle on her behalf. On one occasion, she asked me to take a photograph of one of her previous homes in New Oxford, Pennsylvania. When I presented it to her, she mounted it in a double frame along with a photograph of their home on Elm Avenue. "I can't go back to Elm Avenue," she said. "The house holds too many memories." As I looked at her expression, I could see she was reflecting on her sixty-two years of marriage and the family that she had raised. She seemed perfectly content.

As Dick had, Ethel finally found the inner peace that had always been slightly out of reach. When she passed away on April 11, 2012, I was conducting a leadership seminar in Normandy. I felt bad that I could not attend her memorial service, but I was there in spirit. To this day, my enduring image of Ethel will always be of her greeting the men and women entering the Hershey Theatre to pay homage to her late husband. Were I to describe her in a single word that day, it would be "elegant." I never saw her look as beautiful as she was that afternoon. Immaculately attired in a yellow pantsuit, she was beaming as she shook as many hands as possible. Small wonder why she seemed so happy—her life's work was done.

CHAPTER X

Seeking Solace

Submission in war does not necessarily qualify a man to be
the master of the peace.

— WAR CORRESPONDENT ERNIE PYLE

If there was one guiding principle that provided direction to Major Winters's life in the years I knew him, it was his eternal quest for quiet and peace. This quest certainly preceded our relationship. If you watch the HBO miniseries *Band of Brothers*, you might think that the search began on D-Day, June 6, 1944, when Lieutenant Winters touched down outside Ste. Mère-Eglise. The quest actually began months earlier, while Dick was still in England. Not yet in combat, he found his thoughts turning to home and a life following the war. "My plans," he wrote, "are different. Now I think I'll do as Dad suggests—keep some ready cash on hand to rest and play until I'm ready to work—for two or three weeks and then take off, get a job on a tramp steamer as a deckhand or on a liner in some capacity and just sail around until I've seen the world, or until I am tired of traveling. Then I'll start looking for a way to earn a living. It's not practical, fantastic and all that, but, brother, I know this idea of thinking you can go home and adjust yourself to that old type of life by just changing uniforms is wrong. And I don't want to be around home while I am adjusting myself."

"Quiet is easy to achieve," Dick repeatedly said, "but true peace must come from within." That was where the farm came in, a quiet piece of Pennsylvania where he could forget about the war. Without that refuge, Dick's thoughts always returned to the war, those horrendous battles, those fallen comrades, those lucky ones who suffered the million-dollar wound and returned to the States while the survivors went on.

He approached the subject of what he referred to as "flashes from the past" only after we had known each other for five years. He turned to me once, changing the subject that we had been discussing, and said, "Don't you think it's strange that fifty-eight years after the war, I can't get these images out of my mind?"

"Not at all, Dick. Every soldier bears the emotional scars of combat long after war ends. War is only attractive to those who know nothing about it. I remember how one of the war's correspondents, I think it was Ernie Pyle, but I'm not sure, said at war's end, 'All we can do is fumble and try once more—try out of the memory of our anguish—and be as tolerant with each other as we can.'"

Dick nodded and said, "I promised myself that if I survived the war, I would find a piece of land somewhere and spend the remainder of my life in peace and quiet. I bought that farm in 1951 just outside of Fredericksburg, Pennsylvania. My farm provided me the quiet, but not the peace. The farm still allows me the quiet contemplation that I need." He continued, "I once asked my daughter Jill to record some of her memories of the men whom she had met over the years. When she finished, she added a few thoughts about the farm. She said that we were not cash rich, and there was so much manual labor. The 'Farm,' I remember she capitalized it, was the defining fact of her life. That's exactly how I feel. After the war, I needed tranquility in my life. You've been to the farmhouse several times. I built my quiet and what I hoped was my inner peace, one brick at a time. You grew up on a farm. I suspect you appreciate how one feels about owning land.

"My dad felt the same way. When I was a boy, oil speculators were purchasing as much land in western Ohio as possible in the hopes of striking it rich. One company offered Dad hundreds of thousands of dollars to drill on the farm. Dad turned them down, saying that they could offer him a million dollars and he would never sell a single acre. Years later, when Dad could no longer work the fields, we children proposed that Mom and Dad consider moving to the neighboring town, where medical care was more accessible. Dad wouldn't hear of it. 'The only way you're getting me off this farm is by dragging me by my boots.' The land was that important to him."

Dick then told a story about a woman from New Zealand who sent a photograph of herself and asked him how it is possible to find peace. He responded, "I see there is a bench in your photograph, so I guess you found a quiet moment to relax and contemplate your life. As far as finding peace, you must find that in your inner soul. Contentment and satisfaction in your life are the result of knowing that you have been honest, done your best, and treated those who are a part of your life with kindness."

I was anxious for Dick to elaborate on his personal quest for peace during the war, so I asked if his men suffered any false illusions as to what combat would be like and how he personally dealt with the loss of the soldiers who had trained together since Easy Company was assembled in 1942.

"I don't believe that as paratroopers, we faced the shock of our first fatality to the degree that most outfits do in combat. Every paratrooper encounters the possibility of serious injury or death on every jump. In training we had gone through this many times. Each man must make up his own mind how he would handle such a situation. Each man must conquer fear himself. I had a way of looking at fatalities and serious injury that I've stuck with over the years. I certainly used it in combat. In one of our previous conversations I mentioned that I looked at those soldiers who had been wounded in action as lucky. Sometimes they earned a ticket home. The war was over for them. The rest of us had to keep on fighting, day in and day out. And if you had a man who was killed in action, you looked at him and hoped that he had found peace in death. I feel like that is what we are all looking for in life. Call it an escape mechanism if you like, but this is how I handled things personally."

Listening to Dick describe his "escape mechanism" reminded me of my colleague's description of his experience during the Iraq War when he said, "To prepare myself for deploying my battalion to Iraq for a year or more and in anticipation of combat, experiencing loss/casualties, and engaging the enemy, I literally walled myself off from friends and family outside the battalion. I sent my wife and children home three days prior to my scheduled deployment because I wanted to go through the pain of saying goodbye and the separation prior to my actual deployment. I realized that my duty and my obligation to my battalion took precedence over my duties as a father, husband, and son. My parents and my family understood that I would not return home to the United States for any reason, to include death or illness of a family member. My mission and my soldiers demanded and would receive my complete dedication. I did not want to be distracted by thoughts of home or missing my children."

Now in deep reflection, Dick continued, "The war changed me. I returned to the States bitter, a different man than the young man who had enlisted in the army in 1941. I was hardened when I returned. First impressions were more important than they had previously been. I looked at things differently. When you return from a wartime environment, you have to adjust to society, the life that you are going to be sharing with others just to make a living. Though I was comfortable in a combat environment, I wondered if I would feel at home among civilized people who wouldn't be able to understand how a soldier thinks and feels. I came to understand that I would have to make changes to be accepted into life at home. This takes time and it's never easy. While on the front lines in prolonged combat, I often wondered about my friends back in the States, old friends I had grown up with, some of whom had avoided coming over either by becoming conscientious objectors or working in war-related factories that the federal government had declared essential. I understand everyone doesn't have to share my belief that military service is the only form of service in wartime, but I took immense pride in my contribution to the war effort. We who fought the war were part of something noble. Military service is an honor, a privilege. Funny thing is that when I finally returned home, I had no desire to pick up with those friends who managed to skip the whole thing. I completely shut them out. I wouldn't come downstairs when they knocked on the door. Even today, when I look at a man or a woman, I can't help but judge them. Does he have leadership capabilities? Would she be good in combat? Does he or she have what it takes?"

Reflecting on what Dick was telling me, I recounted something that fellow World War II veterans had once said about Dick Winters. Leonard "Bud" Lomell was the American Ranger who personally destroyed the guns at Pointe du Hoc on D-Day. As with Winters and several other veterans of D-Day, Lomell became a personal favorite of historian Steve Ambrose. On the occasion of one of my visits to Lomell's home in Toms River, New Jersey, Bud talked at length about Dick Winters and recollected a conversation he'd had with Dick years earlier. Asking Dick to reconcile his current pastoral lifestyle with the man who had killed so many of the enemy, Bud said Dick responded, "I did what I had to do." Another veteran, Captain Joe Dawson, a commander in the 1st Infantry Division, whom Ambrose claims was the first company commander to penetrate the German defenses on the bluff overlooking Omaha Beach, expressed a similar sentiment in response to the same question. Dawson was describing himself, but he could have just as easily been describing Dick Winters when he said, "There is a distinct difference between Joe Dawson the warrior and Joe Dawson the man. They were two entirely different people. One could never have survived the other's world." Perhaps that explains the difficulty Dick encountered when he returned home in November 1945.

"Well, Dick," I replied, "you have done pretty well. You have a beautiful family and you are an inspiration to thousands of men and women. Count yourself lucky, my friend."

"I know, but I'm still missing something."

That "something" was the writing of his memoirs, the ultimate closure of his wartime experience. Here is how it came about. Home Box Office had premiered the miniseries *Band of Brothers* in September 2001. By now Major Dick Winters was a household name. Nearing eighty-four years old when the series appeared on national television, he was still able to travel locally for speaking engagements and to make public appearances, albeit on a limited basis. Several authors had already contacted him for permission to write his story, and area politicians and news commentators were constantly bombarding him with requests for interviews. Dick greatly admired historian Steve Ambrose and was eternally grateful to Ambrose for telling the story of Easy Company. A plaque above his door proudly boasted that "Stephen Ambrose Slept Here." But Ambrose had told the story of Easy Company, and Dick wanted to tell his own story. Was the war seen through the eyes of the commander worth sharing? Had he measured up in his own eyes and those of his soldiers? Was there still a story to be told? In Dick's mind, the answer to all these questions was a resounding "Yes." I later discovered that he had discussed his decision to publish his memoirs with Bob Hoffman, who recommended that I assist. "He's exactly who I was thinking about," responded Dick.

Coincidentally, it was shortly before Thanksgiving 2003, and my daughter Maura and I were already planning to visit Hershey on our annual trip to see my parents on the farm in Ohio. Arriving in Hershey, we joined Dick and Ethel for what had become our annual Thanksgiving Saturday dinner. At their home, Dick excused himself and went upstairs. Ethel waited a few minutes and then escorted us to his office. In Dick's den were retired U.S. Air Force Sergeant Major Herm Clemens, Easy Company historian Jake Powers, and the ever-present Hoffman sitting in a circle. Dick welcomed us and directed us to our respective seats. Needless to say, all of this had been carefully choreographed. "Maura, you sit next to me," he said. "Cole, you sit over there." As Maura sat, Dick passed her a page facedown, from a yellow tablet. As she turned it over to examine it, Dick put his finger to his lips and shook his head back and forth, implying not to say a word. He then turned to me.

"I've been thinking about something for a long time now, and I have talked it over with these guys. If you are willing, I would like you to help me write my memoirs. I have copies of all my correspondence to the men of Easy Company over the years, all the operational reports from battalion, and a copy of my personal journal for you. We will split the royalties fifty-fifty." Turning over the paper that he had previously given Maura, he handed it to me. The page read "Untold Stories of Band of Brothers by Major Dick Winters and Colonel Cole C. Kingseed." "What do you say?"

"Well, Dick, I would be happy to help you. It would be my great honor to help tell your story. I'm not interested in the money. A fifty-fifty split seems inherently unfair. I'm thinking more like a 95 to 5 percent split, and I'm not talking about me receiving 95 percent."

"Well, we'll talk about that later." Extending his arm, he shook hands with me, and that was that—no formal contract, just a handshake. I felt like I was walking on air. Later that evening, Maura brought me back to reality. "You know, Dad, Major Winters told me before he told you that he wanted you to write his memoirs. He likes me better than he likes you."

After we packed the six plastic boxes into the car, I drove home in silence. I couldn't help but contemplate the enormous trust that Dick had placed in me. It took me more than a week just to read the files, and as I did, I gained a clearer mental image of Dick Winters the soldier than I had had before.

One week later, the phone rang, and when I answered it, I heard a familiar voice. "Cole, this is Ethel. Dick is concerned about the financial arrangements and wants you to come down at your earliest convenience."

"Of course, I'll be there on Saturday."

The week went fast and by mid-Saturday afternoon, I was again sitting in Dick's office. After exchanging formalities, he turned to me and said, "I've been thinking about the royalties and what you said last week. I don't ever want money to come between us, Cole. Rather than dividing the royalties fifty-fifty, I want you to take all the royalties. I don't need them at my age and I have already provided for my family. I prefer you take the royalties and put Maura through school and use them for anything else you need."

"That's very generous, Dick, but I don't want the royalties either. I wouldn't feel right about accepting money and making a profit from my friendship with you. How about this? I will keep enough to pay taxes, and we can give all the rest to charity. Every time we receive a royalty check, I will provide you with a detailed account as to which charities the funds will be directed. How does that sound?"

"I like that."

Another handshake and the deal was complete. In the ensuing years, every dime, every nickel was diverted to church organizations, women's groups such as the National Breast Cancer Foundation, Ronald McDonald House, and servicemen's and -women's organizations to assist America's wounded warriors. I cannot tell you how often Dick would say, "Isn't it wonderful to give the money away?"

It took me the better part of a year to prepare the book proposal for what eventually became *Beyond Band of Brothers: The War Memoirs of Major Dick Winters*. Although I had published several books in the past, I hoped to reach a national audience with Dick's memoirs. By late 2004, I was writing feverishly and Dick was checking the drafts in earnest. Dick made three decisions early in the process that proved extraordinarily critical in his desire to reach a broader audience. He would tell his story in the first person, he would capture the popularity of the miniseries by including *Band of Brothers* in the title, and we would tap into the Internet to publicize the book. A good publisher would assist in the latter. My role was merely to serve as the pen in Dick's hand. He had already completed the research and provided me with all the necessary materials. My job was relatively easy since Dick had already written the book in his mind.

As I look back on the six months of actual writing, fact-checking, and rewriting, a couple vignettes seem worthy of note. In the beginning, Dick kept his own counsel as he proofread the initial drafts of the various chapters. That didn't last too long. Ethel was as familiar as he with many of the stories since she had transcribed the majority of his journals from the war. Her assistance proved invaluable in preparing a coherent account of the memoirs. She kept us both on our toes. "What about this?" "Is this what you are really trying to say?" "I don't think this is as clear as it should be."

I was most concerned with what Dick would say when he read the chapters outlining his experience as commander of Easy Company from D-Day through Operation Market Garden in Holland

in September/October 1944. Could I capture the mental tough-
ness that was required during Dick's actual experience in combat?
My answer arrived late one evening when Dick called. "Cole, I
don't cry very often, but I read each chapter and I cried after every
one. You really touched me. You got it right!" How was that for
an endorsement?

By 2005, as we moved to complete the manuscript, I could
sense my friend was failing, and I conducted my final interview.
The session lasted five hours and the strain was beginning to show.
"Cole, I'm finding it more difficult to concentrate at times. I need
you to tell me exactly what you require from me. I'm not sure I
will see the project to its end."

"Not to worry, Dick. We have enough material. I will prepare
a final list of thirty or so questions and you can record your answers at your leisure on tape. I'll take care of everything else."

It took a week to develop the questions for Dick since I knew
it was the final opportunity to capture his innermost thoughts. It
took him another two weeks to respond, I suspect for the same
reason that I had taken time to prepare the questionnaire. The
next two months passed rapidly. In mid-February, Dick called
around ten in the evening, rather late for a man in his late eighties.
"Dick, what are you doing up at this hour?"

"For those who have served in combat, this is as close as it
gets. For those who have not seen combat, they better listen. Cole,
I'm so damn proud of you."

On March 16, 2005, Dick and I completed a draft of *Beyond
Band of Brothers*.

Two notes from the Elm Avenue residence arrived at my home
in New York and allayed my fears that I had not measured up to
Dick's expectations. Dick wrote, "I finished reading this in late

afternoon, before dinner. You had said you found Maura with tears after she finished reading your last chapter. I found myself not only in tears, but also in an emotional state where I found it impossible to think about eating. I am physically and mentally exhausted! I ended up with a bowl of soup an hour later and that was dinner. . . . Ethel and I feel while we have great respect for Ambrose as an author, we feel that you and your approach to tell our story in the first person are far superior to the job that Steve Ambrose did. I have never seen or felt the story covered more thoroughly, as honestly, and with a positive word for each man. I am speechless in knowing how to thank you and congratulate you!"

Ethel added, "Cole, this book is beautifully written. I admire your mastery of the English language. I just wanted to say that after reading so many accounts of the battles of Easy Company, I think your clarity and careful progression of events finally made me able to follow them and picture them. Other accounts got so muddled that I finally gave up and just read the stories. I congratulate you on covering such difficult engagements. I, too, felt emotionally drained after reading about the deaths of so many of the men. They were not just names to me, but I had known them. In my mind, I can still hear their voices when the phone rings. 'Hello, Ethel, this is Carwood.' Or 'Hello, Ethel, this is Steve.' Ambrose's voice is just as clear today as it was years ago and I miss them all."

Two weeks later I forwarded the completed manuscript to our publisher in New York. I called to relay the news, and there was a pregnant pause on the end of the line.

"Cole," Ethel said, "Dick would like you to stop by the next time you are in town."

"I'll be there tomorrow, Ethel."

"You don't have to make a special trip, just give us a call when you are in the area."

"Ethel, if Dick wants me, I'll be there tomorrow. See you at four o'clock."

Twenty-four hours later, Ethel ushered me into their home. I had arrived ten minutes early. "Why am I not surprised that you are early?" she said. "Dick is in the next room."

Sitting in his chair in the living room, Dick smiled as I entered. "Good to see you, Cole. What news do you have for me today?"

"Dick, I mailed the manuscript to Berkley Caliber yesterday morning. Your memoirs should be in print ten months from today, sometime next February."

"You don't need anything else from me?"

"Not a thing, Dick. We made our deadline and everything is in their hands."

As if a tremendous burden had been lifted from his shoulders, Dick closed his eyes, sat back in his chair, and sighed, "It's finished!"

And that was the last time that Dick Winters and I ever discussed World War II.

As we closed the book on Dick's wartime experiences, I reflected a lot on what Dick had achieved. Since the days of ancient Greece, it has been a premise of Western culture that an ordinary man can go to war and then return to the ways of peace. Perhaps Ernie Pyle was correct when he wrote, "When it's over, all of us together will have to learn how to reassemble our broken world into a pattern so firm and so fair that another great war cannot soon be possible." Dick's experience shows it's not that easy—but it can be done, in contrast to current tendencies to insist that the trauma of combat changes one utterly and permanently.

On reflection, I think that's why Dick insisted that we conclude the memoirs with a final thought. "War brings out the worst and the best in people. Wars do not make men great, but they do bring out the greatness in good men. For those of us who served in Easy Company and for those who served in other theaters, we came back as better men and women as a result of being in combat. But each of us hoped that if we had learned anything from the experience, it is that war is unreal and we earnestly hoped that it would never happen again."

* * *

In the months that followed, Dick waited anxiously to hear the latest news on the publication process. Even though he knew the memoirs would not be released until early February 2006, his chief concern was whether or not he would live to see the actual book in print. In early autumn, the publisher announced that the memoirs would be available for preorder on the Internet. More importantly, they determined a precise date for the release of *Beyond Band of Brothers*. The date was February 6, 2006. When I announced the date to Dick and Ethel, a quizzical expression formed on Ethel's face and she excused herself and left the room. Five minutes later she returned and said to Dick, "February 6 is the eve of when both of our mothers passed away in 1970. I can't help but think that this is a sign. Your book will be a great success." And so it would be.

* * *

January 20, 2006, was one of those great days, on par with my retirement from the army in May 2001. Dick had just celebrated his eighty-eighth birthday and he eagerly awaited the publication of his memoirs. My wife Mary and I had scheduled a visit to see the Winterses and to dine with Bob Hoffman that evening. In my possession were the first two copies of *Beyond Band of Brothers*, which I intended to present to Dick as a birthday gift. In mid-afternoon, I purchased a half-dozen roses for Ethel before we arrived at the house. When we arrived, Dick, Ethel, Mary, and I sat in the living room, and I immediately updated Dick on the release date for his memoirs. Then I asked Mary to give me the Brooks Brothers box that we had previously gift-wrapped to appear to be a shirt and tie. "Happy Birthday, Dick. I hope you have enjoyed your birthday." He opened the box, and words cannot capture the look of satisfaction and contentment on his face when he grasped the books in his hands. Tears welled up in his eyes when he read my inscription, "To Dick Winters, who crossed my path ten years ago and changed my life forever." His first words were, "Wonderful! What else can I say?" I could sense the pride and accomplishment that he felt seeing the book project to its conclusion.

At this stage of Dick's life I usually limited my visits to around a half hour, but Dick and Mary were enjoying such a wonderful conversation that we lost track of time. While Mary and Dick were talking, I met Ethel in the kitchen and hugged her and thanked her for all the support. I also presented her with a copy of the book since she had played such an instrumental role in its writing and in its publication. To Ethel, I wrote, "To Ethel, without whose support this book would never have been written." I was pleased when she showed the inscription to Dick.

Dick then inquired when I intended to see his friend Bob Hoffman. When I informed him that we were meeting for dinner that evening, he asked if he might join us. Naturally, I responded in the affirmative if he was up for it. He looked at me and responded, "That's just it. I would love to join you. I need room to breathe. I must get out of this house."

Dinner of course was fabulous. Mary and I picked up Dick and Ethel and drove them to the restaurant. As we approached it, I looked at Dick and said, "We did it. Mission accomplished!" He replied, "You hit it right on the head." We spent the next hour talking and laughing. To my surprise Ethel invited us back to the house for dessert. While we were sitting in the living room, Dick smiled and said: "Now I can hear all of you. This is what I like, sitting here surrounded by my friends."

I was reminded of what Dick had repeatedly said in his memoirs about how one would know if a man had succeeded. You will see it in his eyes. Witnessing Dick Winters in that environment, at that precise moment, confirmed his message. He just seemed so pleased. Later Ethel pulled me aside and whispered, "Thank God he lived to see this day."

As we left for a drive to the hotel, Bob turned to Dick and said, "Do you think you made the right choice in having this guy write your memoirs?"

"I think so! Cole, thank you."

It was nearly nine thirty when Mary and I finally reached the hotel, content that we had made a great man happy.

Within a month, *Beyond Band of Brothers* topped out as number ten on the *New York Times* best-seller list for nonfiction. By mid-April, Dick's memoirs were already in their seventh printing. Sales remained brisk through Memorial Day, when the book returned to number ten on the best-seller list. Before tapering off,

Beyond Band of Brothers occupied the best-seller list for six weeks, and the extended best-seller list for thirteen additional weeks. Two years later, the paper edition was released, and it was widely successful as well. To date, the cloth version of *Beyond Band of Brothers* is in its thirteenth printing, and the paperback edition is in its fifth printing. The book has also been released in the People's Republic of China, Thailand, the United Kingdom, the Netherlands, Canada, and the Czech Republic. Ever humbled by the reception of his memoirs, Dick's only comment remained a single word: "Wow!"

Ethel, too, was pleased that Dick's memoirs met such a receptive audience. In the family Christmas card for 2006, she wrote, "One of the year's surprises was the success of our book *Beyond Band of Brothers*. That it made the *New York Times* best-seller list was something we had never expected. The best story of the year was a phone call from a doctor friend who reported that as he was going through customs in Brussels, the Belgian customs official noticed that the doctor was from Pennsylvania and asked if he knew how he could get in touch with Dick Winters!"

Of greater interest to Dick was the disbursement of the royalties. True to my word, every six months after publication, I presented Dick and Ethel with a list of the charities to which I had written checks. They seemed pleased to see that the vast majority of the royalties found their way to servicemen's and -women's organizations, church groups, health-related organizations dedicated to finding cures for breast cancer and other diseases, support of local museums, and the Ronald McDonald House in Hershey, Pennsylvania. In appreciation for building the Utah Beach Museum in Normandy and for keeping the memory of Easy

Company alive in France, Dick was insistent that I provide a degree of financial support to Charles de Vallavieille at Brecourt Manor. After our semiannual report, Dick would turn to me and repeat, "Isn't it wonderful to give this money to those who need it more than we?"

And wonderful it has been.

CHAPTER XI

Growing Old

That world which I knew in its blossoming youth is old and bowed and melancholy now; its soft cheeks are leathery and wrinkled, the fire is gone out in its eyes, and the spring from its step.

—MARK TWAIN

I first met Dick Winters when he had just celebrated his eightieth birthday. And every birthday thereafter, I sent a card conveying my best wishes on his having reached another milestone. To the best of my knowledge, aging didn't bother him. I suspect that in his mind he had already lived a number of lives, and one more didn't seem to faze him. In one of our earlier conversations about his life's journey, I broached the subject of how the war changed him as a man. He replied in what I thought was a rather strange way, dividing his eighty plus years into unequal segments.

"I spent the first twenty years of my life growing up in a close-knit community in what I can only describe as small town America. Everyone knew everyone else's business. The people I remember were middle class and shared similar values. After graduating from Franklin and Marshall College in June 1941, I could start life in the real world in one of two ways. I could either find a job now that the Great Depression was showing signs of recovery or I could volunteer for military service. Under the Selective Service Act, each male was eligible for one year of service. I decided to volunteer for the U.S. Army and not wait until my draft number was called. That way, I could fulfill my obligation and then be free of my military commitment."

"Interesting that you should say that, Dick, because most of the veterans I know who enlisted before the end of 1941 never intended to spend more than a year in service and then return to civilian life. Pearl Harbor changed all that."

"It sure did. I was on a short furlough in North Carolina when I received word of the Japanese attack. Instead of returning to Pennsylvania the next summer, I realized I was now in for the duration of the war. And that began the second phase of my life. It only lasted four years, but I crammed a lifetime of memories, some good, others bad, into those four years. Although only twenty-eight years old when I was discharged from the U.S. Army in January 1946, I felt that I had aged twenty years during the war."

"Tell me about that transition."

"When I joined the U.S. Army, I was young and carefree. The entire world lay at my feet. Life was simple then. Army life certainly wasn't challenging. Most of the soldiers at Camp Croft, South Carolina, were from east of the Mississippi River and shared similar backgrounds and outlooks on life. Since I planned to leave the army after a year, I wasn't too caught up with the daily grind. Until news of Pearl Harbor reached us, I had hardly displayed any ambition. As I reflect upon that period in my life, I realize how protected my life had been before the war began. I had come from a loving family, but my world was so narrow in scope. My intellectual horizons needed expanding."

"How did Pearl Harbor change you as a person?"

"Now that the United States was at war, I decided to dedicate myself to self-improvement and demonstrate my leadership potential. My commanding officer recommended me for Officer Candidate School, and I graduated in July 1942. I was now a commissioned officer, and I applied for airborne duty. In August I was assigned to the 506th Parachute Infantry Regiment at Camp Toombs in northeast Georgia to begin my airborne training. With the paratroopers, I was thrown into an outfit that was truly representative of the country as a whole. It was my first real time away from home, and I didn't really know what to expect. Unlike my first year in the army, men arrived at Toccoa from every region of the country. Most were strapping young men with fire in their eyes and a can-do attitude with which I could easily identify. The vast majority of the men were physically fit. Those who were not fit were mustered out and returned to their former outfits. Every activity had a serious ring to it because we knew that sooner or later we would be in combat. We trained hard for a year and then deployed to England in September 1943. The next nine months proved incredibly strenuous."

"How so?"

"Now that we were in England, we were a step closer to the war. As paratroopers, our mission would be to land behind enemy lines and fight outnumbered until we could be reinforced. Fortunately before we jumped into France on D-Day, we were mentally and physically tough, and we had complete confidence in our ability to do the job. I significantly changed during those nine months prior to D-Day."

"Tell me about that change, Dick," I said.

"You recall my letters to DeEtta Almon? You do. Well, I wrote a letter one month before D-Day in response to a letter she had written in which she noticed a change in me." Taking a copy of the letter from his folder, he continued. "Now, I want you to listen to what I'm saying because it is important. When you are an officer, you are responsible for the lives of the soldiers in your command. You think about kids like this one paratrooper I knew well and you soon become old beyond your years. In the three years since I had entered the army, I had aged a great deal."

Discovering the appropriate passage he wanted to highlight, Dick read verbatim. "'It seems as if college days and days of civilian life when I did as I pleased, are long past. It must have been a dream, a small and short, but beautiful part of my life. Now all I do is work. Work to improve myself as an officer, work to improve them as fighters, as men. Make them work to improve themselves. Result—I am old before my time, not old physically, but hardened to the point where I can make the rest of them look like undeveloped high school boys—old to the extent where I can keep going after my men fall over and sleep from exhaustion. I can keep going as a mother who works after her sick and exhausted child has fallen asleep, old to the extent where if it's a decision or advice needed, my decisions are taken as if the wisdom behind them was infallible. Yes, I feel old and tired from training these men to the point where they are efficient fighters. I hope it means that some will return to those girls back home.'"

I interjected, "And this was all before D-Day?"

Three months later, Dick returned to the subject of aging in another letter. "'Well, yesterday, I celebrated my third anniversary in the army. As I look back, it seems like a lifetime in some respects and as if I've aged three times three. Then again, it isn't so long and I've been pretty lucky right along. There are not many in this outfit that have done as much in the same period of time. In fact, I know of none. Then, too, if I stick in this parachute outfit for two or three more years, salt my money away at about the same rate that I have been, I'll have a pretty darn good foothold on this financial situation.'

"By war's end," Dick continued, "DeEtta would not have recognized me. She wrote and expressed feelings of love and hope for a rapid reunion, but I was so focused on the job at hand. I had people asking me questions about weapons, targets, harassing fire, grazing fire, chow, transportation, and a base of fire. I didn't know that 'love' existed. I told DeEtta that my job as battalion commander necessitated that my thoughts and feelings be hard, cold, impersonal, and effective. Told her we would tackle questions about love, devotion, and all that stuff after the war so I could use my head and not my heart. On rereading her correspondence, I note that I often referred to her as 'Hey, Squirt' or 'My Wave,' all somewhat humorous, but rather impersonal to say the least. As I said, after four years at war, I had aged a lifetime."

"Understandably so. Tell me about life's next phase."

"Phase three of my life began when I met Ethel and we started to raise a family. I worked hard, maybe too hard, because I was not at home as much as I would have liked when the children were young. Yet a man does his best to provide a decent life for his family. I did my best and hope that it was good enough. I don't want to talk about it anymore."

"Okay, let's move on. You told me that Stephen Ambrose changed your life in the fall of 1988. What happened?"

"He did indeed. And you are now an integral part of this stage of my life. Easy Company held a reunion in New Orleans in May of that year. Ambrose, who had published a two-volume biography of General Eisenhower, discovered the veterans were in town. Ambrose and his assistant Ron Drez introduced themselves, and Ambrose decided to write a story about Easy Company. Ambrose announced that he was gathering interviews for his next book on D-Day. I decided not to join the meeting, but to let the men speak out. All the veterans wanted to tell their stories, their memories. I mailed my written account to Ambrose later."

Dick went on. "After a few months, Ambrose contacted me and I agreed to assemble a number of Easy Company's veterans. We met first at Ambrose's home in Bay St. Louis, Mississippi, and six months later I hosted Ambrose, Harry Welsh, Joe Toye, Forrest Guth, and Rod Strohl at my farm outside Fredericksburg. Our discussions covered a range of topics. From these discussions emerged Ambrose's book *Band of Brothers: E Company, 506th Regiment, 101st Airborne from Normandy to Hitler's Eagle's Nest* that he published in 1992, the fiftieth anniversary of the formation of Easy Company at Camp Toombs. You know the rest of the story. In preparing the manuscript, Steve hosted a number of us on a return to the battlefields. It was most memorable. When we returned to the States, I wrote Steve a warm personal letter in which I said, 'That sure was some trip! I figured this would be the big trip of my life, and I can truthfully say I was not disappointed. This whole tour was very emotional for me—from Aldbourne, every step of the way, every single day, right through to Salzburg and then our special visit with von der Heydte. You made it all possible, you made it a reality, and you've given me memories I'll never forget.'"

"And how did the miniseries come about?"

Dick smiled and said, "It was shortly before Christmas that he called and left a message on the answering machine. It said, 'Dick, this is Steve Ambrose. I have a letter from Tom Hanks, and he wants to buy the rights to *Band of Brothers*. I presume he wants to play Dick Winters, but I told him that Herbert Sobel is closer to the mark. Anyway, I just wanted to share the good news with you.' So Ambrose sold *Band of Brothers* to Steven Spielberg and Tom Hanks. Since that time, my time and Ethel's have revolved around keeping E Company's story in the news. It has been an amazing journey. And here I am now, nearly ninety years old, sitting in my front room with you."

"Dick, you don't sound like a ninety-year-old man to me," I said.

"Well, I am, and I intend to stay around a little longer."

"You aren't afraid of getting old?"

"I'm not," he replied. "Why should I be? I've led a good life. Listen, most men my age sit at home, never leave the house, and regret how their lives turned out the way they did. I've made a few mistakes in life, but I have no regrets."

"Were you pleased with the miniseries?"

"For the most part. I was surprised that Spielberg and Hanks selected so many British actors to portray Easy Company's soldiers. Guess they felt no American actor could do the job properly. I told Captain Dale Dye, who played Colonel Sink, that I thought my old regimental commander would have been highly pleased by Dye's portrayal. Captain Dye seemed to like that. I objected to the amount of profanity in the series and the one gratuitous sex scene when Easy Company arrived in Germany, but overall I was very pleased with the finished product. I was particularly pleased that so many men finally received recognition for what they accomplished during the war."

Over the next few years, I witnessed Dick pass through several stages of infirmity. My father had gone through a similar process, so I had experienced how difficult it now was for him to accomplish rather simple tasks. Gone were the days when Dick could take the step in front of his house or climb the stairs to his upstairs office. I recall how surprised I was the first time that I saw him use a cane. Ethel confirmed that he needed the cane for support anytime that he left the house. She also informed me that Dick was in the early stage of Parkinson's disease. This troubled me deeply, and when I departed Hershey, I shook his hand and informed him that he was my dearest friend. He responded how honored he was and that he intended to do his best to live up to my expectations. As I left the house and walked to the car, I turned around and there was Dick at the front door with a final salute and a wave.

The cane was soon followed by a walker, and two years later by a wheelchair. Through it all, Dick's spirits never dampened. Later, Ethel installed an electronic chair to convey Dick from the main floor to the second level of their home, where his bedroom and office were located. Now my monthly visits took place in the first floor living room rather than his upstairs office. I genuinely missed our conversations in his office because he often closed the door so we could talk in private without interruptions. Dick always seemed more relaxed when his military memorabilia and those things that he treasured most surrounded him.

Aging is tough. In one of the family Christmas cards, Ethel wrote, "Getting older is a nuisance as we find we have had to cut down even further on the activities we enjoy, but we are still able to recall all the good times and trips of the past. Especially treasured are memories of experiences we shared with family, friends, and the men of Company E. None will ever be forgotten."

Dick's health significantly deteriorated beginning in 2005. We were anxiously awaiting publication of his wartime memoirs, but now that the manuscript had already been submitted to the publisher, he seemed far weaker than he had been earlier in the year. I visited Dick on May 18, 2005, four years to the day since he presided over my retirement ceremony. I noted in my journal that night that Dick seemed more tired than usual and he had not been eating well. Since he now required daily care, Ethel had relinquished her volunteer work at the library to stay at Dick's side. My thoughts that evening were simply that his body was giving out. Two weeks later, Ethel called and invited me to pay my respects on June 6. She informed me that future visits were in jeopardy until Dick's health made a significant improvement. I wondered if this would be Dick's final commemoration of D-Day. I said a prayer that the old warrior would recover and live long enough to see his memoirs in print. The Almighty answered my prayers, and Dick was soon on the path to recovery.

My visits now centered on dinners restricted to Hershey, an activity that always improved his morale and lifted his spirits. Then came the inevitable day when Ethel informed me, "You need to park in back, Cole. Dick can no longer use the front step. Bob Hoffman has installed a ramp outside the sunporch and this makes it easier to get to the car." And by July 2007, the dinners ceased. I remember how strange it sounded when Dick asked me where I intended to eat in Hershey now that he wasn't able to depart the house. I could tell how much he detested being confined there. Yet, on this particular visit, although he seemed slower in speech, he possessed much more color.

Looking for any technique to bring Dick comfort and to add to his enjoyment, I devised a new scheme of bringing a small gift whenever I stopped by the house. Two of the most noteworthy gifts were bags of M&M candies with the words "Hang Tough" on each piece of candy and a box of cereal that brought him immense satisfaction. I had recently conducted a leadership seminar for General Mills and had remarked to one of the corporate leaders present that I recalled an advertising gimmick in which customers could pay a small fee and have their image on a box of Wheaties. Since he was in charge of General Mills' Food Division, he asked, "Do you want your picture on a cereal box, Cole?" "Not for me," I replied, "but I do have someone in mind." Two months later, I brought my special surprise to Dick and Ethel. All I had told them was that I was bringing something that was very practical. When Mary and I arrived, we sat in the living room and I carefully removed the cereal box from my bag, making sure that when I handed it to Dick, I presented the box with the back facing him. "Well, Cole, this is very nice. I've always liked Wheaties."

"For Pete's sake, why don't you turn the box around?" I said.

Rather than turning it completely around, Dick turned it to its side and began looking at the ingredients listed on the side of the box. Too polite to ask for an explanation, Dick said, "I'm not sure I know what I'm supposed to say, other than thank you very much."

"Dick, you're killing me. Look at the front of the box!"

Now, as he turned the box toward its front, his eyes lit up when he saw his face on the cereal box, under which were the words "Major Richard D. Winters, Champion for the Band of Brothers." All he could say was "Wow!" Ethel later inquired if it were possible to obtain additional boxes, but I reluctantly informed her that only two such boxes were in existence. For the next two years that box of Wheaties occupied a prominent place on their mantel. Today, the Wheaties box sits in a special exhibit commemorating Dick's military service at the Hershey Derry Township Historical Society building in Hershey, Pennsylvania.

Other gifts followed, including a book commissioned by the Army Historical Society that featured a chapter I had written entitled "Infantry Heroes and Legends." Mary and I presented Dick with this book on his ninetieth birthday. Dick received a full-page portrait in *U.S. Army Infantry* as well as a summary of his World War II experience. He seemed particularly delighted that I had selected him as one of the three infantrymen who best personified the infantry motto of "Follow me!" Following small talk, Dick suggested that we adjourn to the kitchen in order that we could examine the book and share some special memories. Once there, Ethel and Dick showed us the very edelweiss that Dick had sent his mother in the summer of 1945. Mary then asked how many Christmas cards that they had received this year, and Dick proudly proclaimed, "About two hundred, and I read every one of them." Later I accompanied Dick back to his chair in the family room, where he apologized for not being able to take us to dinner. He informed us that he seldom departed the house anymore, and as a result, he no longer had much contact with the outside community. As a result, his mind was no longer challenged as much as it used to be. To compensate, Dick said he had become a voracious reader. Still he regretted not leaving the house, but "I need to spare myself the embarrassment because I can no longer think fast enough." Before departing, I asked if there was anything I could do for him, and he replied instantly, "You're doing it by coming to see me."

By Christmas 2007, Ethel had imposed a closed-door policy on visitations for good reason. As she wrote in their Christmas message, "We have found that when the hearing is so undependable that phone voices are hard to hear, when the eyes become so weak that reading is a chore, and the pen in hand has a mind of its own, the best thing to do is hunker down and pull up the drawbridge. So many times we don't return phone calls, never read mail from strangers, don't sign anything, and have put a 'Do Not Disturb' sign on the door. It simplifies life tremendously." She went on, "We apologize for neglecting our friends and the closed door policy. Do you think it means old age has arrived? Anyway, we are hanging very, very tough. You do the same."

During his declining years, Dick relived many of the battles that he had fought a lifetime ago. Such a phenomenon is common among combat veterans. As a young sailor, my father served aboard a destroyer in Pearl Harbor on December 7, 1941. The USS *Macdonough* earned thirteen battle stars during the Pacific war, and Dad saw more than his share of action. Yet, in his declining years, his dreams focused on the night his ship was rammed by another American ship in the dense fog of the Aleutian Islands. Had the destroyer been struck a yard fore or aft to where the collision occurred, the *Macdonough* would have sunk with all hands. As Dad told me, "You could literally walk off the deck into the ocean." The *Macdonough* didn't sink, and it was towed back for repair, but I was always struck that it was the memory of this collision, rather than the many battles in which he fought, that still seared Dad's memory. And then on the last day of my father's life, Dad, who was a ship's cook during World War II, asked my mother why his nurse hadn't returned from the galley with his breakfast. In the afternoon, Dad inquired why his shipmates had not come to see him. At the time, Dad was one of only two surviving members of the original crew from the USS *Macdonough* that had witnessed the "day of infamy."

As with my father, recurring nightmares from the war tormented Dick. Ethel once said, "Dick fights the Battle of the Bulge virtually every night." The anniversary of D-Day also caused troublesome flashbacks. Dick informed me once, "I know I did everything within my power to ensure as many soldiers made it home from the war as possible, but when you survive, and your soldiers don't, you feel guilty. It haunts me today that I lived and so many of my paratroopers died. As the veterans of Easy Company pass on, I am reminded of those who never returned from the war. I see their faces. I can almost hear them calling me." As Dick shared these dreams, I realized that he, too, had become one of war's casualties, a moral casualty, but a casualty nevertheless.

Yet when I spoke to Dick in late 2008, he appeared in the best spirits that I had seen him in in two years. He was jovial, articulate, and still awestruck at the success of his memoirs. Always a fighter, Dick continued to surprise his doctors with his recuperative abilities. For the next two years, our conversation turned to far more pleasant things, always away from the war and those issues that might excite or agitate him. Visiting him during his final years was wonderful and exhilarating for both of us. In spite of his deteriorating health, Dick radiated joy and warmth, maintaining that twinkle in his eye and clasping my extended hand with both of his hands when it was time for me to depart. He always thanked me for taking time to see him, perhaps not appreciating that these visits benefitted me more than him. On one of my final visits, I asked Dick what he considered beautiful in life now that he had surpassed the ripe age of ninety.

"I sit here in this house and I gaze out the window. I see the flowers and the birds. I behold the wonder of nature. Everything seems so beautiful."

CHAPTER XII

Legacy

If we would create something, we must be something.
—VINCE LOMBARDI

As I reflect on my association with Dick Winters, I am always struck that he remained very conscious of his image as a leader. That image had nothing to do with power or authority conveyed by title or position during the war when he led Easy Company into battle. Rather the image had everything to do with obligation and responsibility: obligation to the organization, its values, and its goals; and responsibility to the soldiers entrusted to his care, his family, and the young men and women whom he hoped to influence. A leader's legacy is reflected in the following questions: What am I about? What do I stand for? How do I want to be remembered? From that perspective, Dick Winters bequeathed an incredible legacy to mankind.

I once asked him, "In your opinion, is leadership a responsibility or a burden?"

"It's definitely a responsibility, although once or twice in my life, when I was run down and disillusioned, I must confess that I yearned for the days when I was a young private at Camp Croft. The happiest days of my army career were there, making twenty-one dollars a month, yet always having a little money at the end of the month. I traveled more, did more, and had more fun than at any time since. During the war I now had real responsibility. In addition to being responsible for my company and battalion, I was accountable for my men. I wore the bars. I no longer had time for fun."

In a separate letter to DeEtta after the fighting in Normandy ended, Dick remarked on a public relations photograph in which he was directed to look stern and not to smile. He then discussed the pressure of command. He wrote, "I don't feel quite so hard inside as I did in Normandy, but I guess I still look the part. As for a twinkle in my eye, sometimes I think it must have been frozen to death. There may be a day when it will warm up, but never as long as there's a war on. I've got to push the company. What a job, being papa to a hundred sixty odd men and seven so-called officers. And, what a headache it is at times. Ever since the second week of the invasion, casualties have been my greatest concern. Victory is ours, but the casualties that must be paid is the price that hurts."

As Dick struggled to define his personal legacy, he began enumerating his ten principles of success. First and foremost was the development of leaders of character, competence, and courage. He then listed leadership by example, followed by physical fitness. Unlike many leaders who emphasize succession planning, Dick chose to concentrate on succession readiness. Said he, "Delegate responsibility to your subordinates and let them do their jobs." He was thinking of General Taylor and his tendency to micromanage things. Such practices tend to curtail initiative and creativity.

Humility and self-reflection followed, as did the ability to make calm, rational decisions under pressure. Anticipate problems before they occur. And of course he repeatedly reiterated the satisfaction that comes from doing the best that one could do. I suggested that we use "Hang Tough!" as his capstone principle, but he said that wasn't enough. "These principles are my leadership legacy, so let's add 'Never, ever, give up' to Hang Tough! If you do that, then we'll have it right."

Despite his physical deterioration, Dick maintained a vigorous schedule of speaking engagements, mostly at local schools and service-related organizations. At times the public adulation touched a nerve. Dick called me one afternoon and lamented, "Everyone wants a piece of me. All I want is peace. Why won't they leave me alone?"

"Dick, that's the price of fame," I responded. "You need to take all of this as a huge compliment. The days when you can sit comfortably inside 117 Elm Avenue are gone forever. The great American public wants to see you, touch you, and write you in the hope that by their being in your presence, your leadership and more importantly your character will somehow rub off on them. That was the basis for my question about leadership being a burden or a responsibility. I hate to tell you this, but it's going to get worse long before it's going to get better, my friend."

"I know, but I could use a little break," he replied.

After an hour, I added, "Dick, you once said that you can assess your value as a leader by looking into the eyes of your men. I think you can get a pretty good idea of your effectiveness by the letters you have received from the members of Easy Company. I'm thinking of the letter that Talbert sent you shortly before he died. He said, 'Dick, you are loved and will never be forgotten by any soldier who ever served under you. You are the best friend I ever had. . . . You were my ideal, and motor in combat. . . . You are to me the greatest soldier I could ever hope to meet.'"

"The feeling was certainly mutual. Floyd Talbert will always be special to me. I have said this more than once. If I had to pick out just *one* man to be with me on a mission in combat, it would be Talbert."

"Tell me about the letter that 'Burr' Smith wrote you."

Dick took Smith's letter from his folder and read, "'You were blessed (some would say rewarded) with the utter respect and admiration of 120 soldiers, essentially civilians in uniform, who would have followed you to certain death. I've been a soldier most of my adult life. In that time, I've met only a handful of great soldiers, and of that handful, only half or less come from my WWII experience, and two of them came from ol' Easy—you and Bill Guarnere. The rest of us were O.K.—Good soldiers by-and-large, and a few were better than average, but I know as much about 'Grace Under Pressure' as most men, and a lot more about it than some. You had it!'"

"I believe that Shifty Powers's daughter also wrote you, did she not?"

"Yes, she sent me the nicest letter after reading Larry Alexander's fine book *Biggest Brother*. There is a section in the book that says that Lieutenant Colonel Robert Cole, the Medal of Honor recipient from Normandy, thought himself invincible. When Shifty read that passage, he said, 'I saw Major Winters on top of a dike in Holland, in a totally exposed position, waving and yelling commands and directions to his men while Germans were doing everything they could do to shoot him. Major Winters always put himself at risk where his men were concerned. Because of Major

Winters's leadership, many men came home who might not have had he not been in command. Many of the veterans you led have stated that "I don't know how Major Winters survived the war because of the risks he took to lead us." ' When you hear something like this from one of your men, it makes you feel both humble and proud. Shifty was a great soldier. I don't think the miniseries did him justice. I was fortunate to have him in Easy Company."

"Receiving approval and earning respect from your men ought to make any leader proud," I said. "Tom Brokaw calls the generation that survived the Great Depression and fought and won World War II 'the greatest generation.' Do you agree?"

"We veterans appreciate what Brokaw did to increase the awareness of what our comrades accomplished during the war, but I never felt that this country owed our generation anything. For me, it was an honor to serve my nation. We were at war. The fate of democracy was at stake. I could not have lived with myself had I avoided military service. The current generation owes me nothing. I served out of patriotism, not because someday I hoped to receive admiration and respect from an adoring nation. I don't expect special treatment from anyone. 'Selflessness' as opposed to 'selfishness' is what I preach."

"I suspect that you have attended a good number of funerals of your paratroopers over the course of the last several years. Their ranks grow thinner every day, it seems."

Dick sighed and said, "I delivered the eulogies at Nixon's and Harry Welsh's funerals. How could I not? Joe Toye's family also asked me to deliver the eulogy and to serve as a pallbearer. I was honored to do so. Next to Talbert, I felt Joe Toye was the finest soldier in the company. When a soldier's family asks you to participate in their loved one's funeral, you have to think that you must have done something right as a leader."

In addition to his contemporaries with whom he served during the war, Dick's reach found popular appeal among America's corporate leaders as well. Years ago, I watched Rand Harbert, a senior vice president in one of the nation's largest insurance companies, walk across the pasture field where Dick destroyed the enemy guns outside Brecourt Manor on D-Day. As he visualized the battle, Rand stooped to his knee and placed a handful of dirt in a plastic bag as a keepsake of his pilgrimage to Normandy. Later he read *Beyond Band of Brothers* and became caught up in the raw emotion of what Dick achieved during the war. Bastogne particularly resonated with Harbert. As he later stated, "I often think about Dick's leadership during the Battle of the Bulge. Worst winter of the twentieth century and arguably the toughest battle conditions in the history of modern warfare and Dick's team performs exactly like they always did—flawlessly. To me, that Christmas in the Ardennes and what they accomplished define leadership. The impossible made possible due to the belief Easy Company had in one man. When I am having a 'tough' day, I find myself thinking about Dick and what he faced in Belgium. I quickly realize that I have never faced an obstacle that compares to his task in the winter of 1944."

Doug Lovejoy, one of this country's leading insurance salesmen, notes, "I've often wondered if Dick Winters considered the residual influence of his leadership. In the context of personal reflection, did he ever ask himself, 'Will the record reflect that my men and I measured up in the chaos and brutality of war? In our attempt to lead by example, will those who come behind us find some true north to help guide their journey?' His leadership legacy influences me today. His leadership mantra 'Hang Tough' echoes in my mind; his example is helping guide my journey."

Lovejoy's reference to "true north" reminded me of the closing of one of Dick's letters on the eve of D-Day, when he wrote, "The old north star is a soldier's guiding light when he's lost, alone, and feeling mighty funny in the pit of the stomach. That's when he feels good, when he can look up and know that there's somebody else looking up there also."

Damian Lewis—Lewis has always been quick to point out that he merely represented Major Winters in the miniseries, he did not portray him—claims that Dick formed the backbone of the series in that he was the spine that ran throughout all ten episodes. Lewis recalls that when the actors attended the cast boot camp run by Captain Dale Dye, he and the others were pushed to the limits of physical exhaustion. "We were in character for ten days," Lewis remembers. "It was an extraordinary bonding, but boot camp was where I separated from the rest of the actors." Lewis couldn't come out of character because "I knew that Major Winters had separated from his men since he needed to make impartial decisions that might mean life or death to the members of E Company." In a radio interview following Dick's death, Lewis added, "Major Winters had a Henry the Fifth attitude. England's King Henry the Fifth delivered the original Band of Brothers speech on the eve of the Battle of Agincourt in 1415. As Rudyard Kipling once said, he walked with kings, but he maintained the common touch." That is a perfect description of the character that manifested itself in Dick's persona.

Political figures as well fell under Dick's shadow. Former Pennsylvania governor and future secretary of Homeland Security Tom Ridge met Dick in 2001 when he attended the Pennsylvania premiere of *Band of Brothers*. When the miniseries began, the studio decided that regional premieres were the most efficient manner to bring *Band of Brothers* to the widest possible audience. Consequently, Governor Ridge and other local politicians traveled to Irvine Auditorium of the University of Pennsylvania, where Ridge had been designated to serve as master of ceremonies for the event. Easy Company veterans, including Dick Winters, sat along the aisle to watch the initial two episodes of the miniseries. Following the ceremony, Dick and Ethel moved to the lobby, where they waited for Bob Hoffman to join them for the return trip to Hershey. While the Winterses waited, Hoffman engaged the governor in a casual conversation that focused on Easy Company. Ridge listened to Hoffman and said he wanted to meet Dick Winters. As Hoffman tells the story, he approached Dick and advised him that the governor wanted to meet him. "No, I don't want to do that," Dick responded.

The governor's security team came forward and said, "Major Winters, Governor Ridge wants to meet you." They then escorted Dick to a room where a small podium stood. Dick, who was not pleased with the delay and had no interest in meeting Governor Ridge, stood stoically behind the podium and began to pout, placing his chin in his hands. Three to four minutes later, in walked Ridge. Seeing Dick in that pose, Ridge stood opposite him and mirrored Dick's pose, placing his chin in his hands. The sight must have appeared comical—two grown men, standing across from each other, with their chins in their hands, staring each other down. Eventually, the two finally broke the ice, and fifteen minutes later, Ridge and Winters were swapping stories. From this inauspicious beginning grew a wonderful friendship. Years later, the duo served as co–grand marshals of a Veterans Day parade, and they maintained a healthy correspondence until Dick became too enfeebled to write. Both also stood on the platform when President George W. Bush visited Hershey during the 2004 presidential campaign. Since he had been "present at the creation" of this budding friendship, Hoffman was always sure to remind his friend, "Winters, you owe me big-time!"

There is another humorous incident related to President Bush and Major Winters. During a subsequent presidential visit, Dick and Hoffman were waiting in an isolated room for Air Force One to deliver the president. While the minutes ticked by, Dick turned to Hoffman and said, "Hold it a minute! Do you think this old man can touch the floor with the palms of his hands?"

"Winters," said Hoffman, "I think this old man can do anything he sets his mind to do."

Taking his cue from Hoffman, Dick stood up from his wheelchair, balanced himself, and began a rocking motion front and back until he actually touched the floor with his palms. Knowing that discretion is the better part of valor, Dick then turned to Bob and said, "Whatever you do, don't you ever tell Ethel!"

Another Pennsylvania politician, Dauphin County State Representative John D. Payne (R-106th Legislative District), spearheaded a campaign to award Dick Winters the Medal of Honor for his heroic deeds on D-Day. U.S. Senator Rick Santorum (R-Pennsylvania) echoed Payne's remarks. During the war, General Eisenhower delegated nominations for awarding the Medal of Honor, our nation's highest award for heroism under fire, to division commanders. The 101st Airborne Division commanding general, General Maxwell Taylor, placed an artificial constraint of one awardee from his division for actions in the Normandy campaign. Taylor selected Lieutenant Colonel Robert Cole for leading

a bayonet charge near Carentan as the nominee from the Screaming Eagles. Cole received the medal shortly thereafter, but he was
later killed in Holland. Winters received the Distinguished Service
Cross despite the fact that Colonel Sink had nominated him for
the Medal of Honor. Sixty years later, Payne's effort to repair this
injustice garnered widespread support throughout Pennsylvania.
The Pennsylvania House of Representatives approved a resolution
sponsored by Payne that urged Congress to award the medal to
Winters. Said Payne, "We think Dick is deserving of this honor,
and it needs to be reviewed again. I don't think he received a fair
review." As is customary, the secretary of the army had to approve
the nomination before it was sent to the White House for approval. Dick's nomination reached acting secretary of the Army
Les Brownlee before it was passed to a U.S. Army colonel to research Payne's request. For whatever reason, the officer rejected
the nomination, and Brownlee quietly approved the colonel's recommendation. If I sound upset with the outcome by the secretary
of the army, it is partly because I wrote the citation for Dick's
award, but more importantly, I feel Dick's action at Brecourt
Manor met the criteria for awarding the Medal of Honor.

Dick, of course, refused to endorse the efforts of his friends
and associates to award him the Medal of Honor, even on a personal basis. He never looked for personal recognition and refused
to attach his name to any such effort on his behalf. Even during
the war, he shunned the public recognition that accompanied pro-
motions. Following his promotion to major and assignment to
battalion command, he wrote, "It sure was an honor to get the
battalion for it means I've come straight up from junior second
lieutenant to commanding officer in the same battalion in a period of two and a half years. As far as the promotion in rank goes,

I don't give a damn, but I do like the job and the responsibility that goes with it." When Sergeant Major Herm Clemens asked Dick if he could initiate the recommendation to upgrade his Distinguished Service Cross to the Medal of Honor, without hesitation, Dick shook his head, and said, "No." "I left too many men in Europe, they are the real heroes" was his reply. Clemens was persistent and tried again to persuade Dick. "Do what you want to do, but I won't be part of it," Dick replied.

Personal recognition was simply alien to Dick's nature. In a letter to an admirer who wrote in 2005 that he had personally lobbied the White House to upgrade Dick's Distinguished Service Cross, Dick merely expressed his gratitude for the many people who were seeking the medal on his behalf, but other than that, "I have no comment."

In the years that I had known him, Dick's only mention of the Medal of Honor was contained in one of his letters to DeEtta written after V-E Day. Writing to his friend, who had recently attended a White House reception during which President Harry S. Truman bestowed the Medal of Honor on several recipients, Dick wrote, "But don't think you'll ever have to be looking for a place to stand when I get decorated by the president. For yours truly that will never happen, I hope. Twice I came very close to achieving that honor. In Normandy I was as hot as a baked potato. It scares me when I think back on what I did. That was the time they recommended me for the Congressional Medal of Honor. But at that time, they thought you had to kill an army and we had no setup for writing decorations. So I wear the Distinguished Service Cross. In Holland when I made that bayonet charge, remember, if I'd have had a machine gun instead of my M1, I'd have had the better part of 250 Krauts, I feel sure. . . . All came out O.K. for I had my small group and machine guns coming up and we cleaned them up, and that's the object anyhow. Anyway, I don't think I want the Congressional Medal of Honor. For a paratrooper it costs you about two of those nine lives we're supposed to have. I feel like I've used all nine already and it's only due to an administrative error that I am still here."

Representative Payne was also instrumental in having a bridge that crosses the Swatara Creek between Swatara Township and Derry Township on State Route 322 dedicated as the Major Richard D. Winters Bridge. At the unveiling ceremony, Representative Payne said, "The 106th Legislative District can be proud to have a true American hero living in our midst, and naming a local bridge in his honor is a fitting tribute to his valor. We pause to remember how Major Winters distinguished himself during a war in which the fate of the free world hung in the balance." Dick, of course, was unable to attend the dedication ceremony on October 4, 2005, but Payne delivered a copy of the sign to him, to hang in his Hershey home.

As I reflect upon the legacy of Dick Winters, I envision the literally thousands of lives that he touched in his lifetime, both in war and peace. Many use their fame for selfish purposes, but not the quiet man who resided on a farm outside Fredericksburg, Pennsylvania, and who spent his last years in neighboring Hershey. His generous gift of the royalties from *Beyond Band of Brothers: The War Memoirs of Major Dick Winters* alone could have made him a rich man, but he refused to profit from the sacrifices of his men. Nor did he charge for his autograph that after the release of the miniseries would have generated hundreds of thousands of dollars had he been so inclined. When friend Bob Hoffman served as chairman of the Lebanon County United Way fund-raising drive, Dick made an exception to his rule and signed a thousand prints of military artist James Dietz's painting *Silencing the Guns*, which depicted the action at Brecourt Manor on D-Day. Dick's signature generated $50,000 worth of donations, every penny of which found its way to the United Way. Hoffman was simply overwhelmed, but not surprised, when he accepted a check for the entire amount and deposited it to the United Way's account. "It's absolutely spectacular. It's wonderful. I don't know how to say it any other way," Hoffman said. Though Dick could not attend the ceremony in which the donation was recognized, a local newspaper account recorded Hoffman's remarks as "Major Winters is with us in spirit, although he is not here in body. He's one of the most humble persons I've ever had the honor of knowing." To the best of Hoffman's knowledge, Dick's gift of $50,000 was the largest gift by a private citizen during the fund-raising campaign.

When Dick spoke at school auditoriums, the auditoriums were standing room only. His story resonated with thousands of young men and women. Even before the miniseries premiered, Dick wrote to advise me, "As you know, HBO promised, during a visit to Hershey in November 2000, that an educational program for young school children would be part of the overall program. It is a wonderful feeling to see them keep that promise."

I had the occasion to speak about Major Dick Winters at the U.S. Army War College in Carlisle, Pennsylvania, on a cold wintry night in early February 2008. Nearly two hundred people braved the elements to hear his story. At the Hershey Public Library, hundreds more attended an event to hear my recollections of the friendship that created an inseparable bond between us. When the Hershey Derry Township Historical Society opened a veterans exhibit that it named "A Hero's Story: Featuring Major Dick Winters," the building was filled to capacity. For Dick, the recognition was never personal and the fame simply served as a "direct reflection of the sacrifices of the men of Easy Company, men who were so brave that I still search my soul to find the proper words to describe their heroism and their willingness to sacrifice everything for each other."

Not to be outdone, Berkley Caliber, the publisher of *Beyond Band of Brothers: The War Memoirs of Major Dick Winters*, distributed 2,506 copies of Dick's memoirs to the fighting men and women of our armed forces on duty in Afghanistan. The number of copies represented the number of Easy Company's battalion affiliation (2) and the number of the parachute infantry regiment (506) to which they were attached. By last count, Dick's memoirs were in their thirteenth printing, a testament to the man and his legacy.

From the personal perspective, I summarized Dick's impact on me and my children's lives in a letter that I wrote on Dick's eighty-seventh birthday, in 2005. I wrote:

For as much writing as I do, this letter is very difficult to write. I think I do a far better job writing history than I do expressing my true feelings. First things first: Mary, John, and Maura join me in wishing you the happiest of birthdays. Reaching the exalted age of eighty-seven is an achievement in itself—must be the result of hard work and good living.

I looked for the perfect card, but was unable to find one that reflected my deep admiration and sincere respect for a man, who next to my own father is the finest man whom I have ever known. Your willingness to share the last decade with me has enriched my life more than I can say. On reflection of the past several years, I recall a sermon I heard as an undergraduate in 1970, in which our dormitory priest said, "You can never touch others without being touched yourself." Dick, in a lifetime of heroic achievement, you have touched literally thousands of lives, a good many in war, far greater numbers in peace. I should consider myself fortunate if I could imagine that I would ever become such a positive influence on mankind.

Thank you especially for the many kindnesses that you have bestowed on my family. To John and Maura, you are the most inspirational man they know. To Mary, you are a wonderful friend. To me, you are not only my friend, but you are my dearest friend.

★ ★ ★

So where does this leave us in our attempt to define Dick Winters's legacy? When in doubt, go to the source, and so I did. "Dick, you have led a wonderful life and you have given so much to the young people of this country. What is Dick Winters's legacy to future generations?"

"That is easy and I'm going to answer it this way. It is the same that I have been saying for many years: 'Hang Tough!' By that, I mean simply 'Do your best every day, whether at school, at your job, or anywhere else. You don't have to have all the answers. There's no way you should expect that from yourself. Just satisfy yourself so at the end of the day, you can look at yourself in the mirror and say, "Today, I did my best." If you do that, you are being honest and everything will be okay.' Does that answer your question?"

"Yes, it does."

"Okay, then, but let me reduce this to a two-step process," he added. "Number one: Be honest. Every man or woman can define honesty and integrity differently. Just look at yourself and talk to yourself. Make it clear to one and all. Number two: Be humble. Never let power or authority go to your head. I have always made an effort not to talk about myself. I talk about the war, but not about myself. I would like to keep it that way."

Dick continued, "The last thought I want to share with you is this, and I hope that it doesn't sound out of place. As I look back on the war, I think that war brings out the worst and the best in people. My soldiers and I came back as better men as a result of being in combat, and most would do it again if necessary. But all hoped that we had learned from experience that war is unreal and we sincerely hope that we never have to do it again. We must find a better way to resolve our differences. And now that we are ending this tape, I think we have completed this job."

PART FOUR

★ ★ ★

Winter

CHAPTER XIII

Saying Good-bye

There is nothing more I should do now and therefore I am not likely to be more ready to go than at this moment.

—ULYSSES S. GRANT

I actually said good-bye to Dick Winters on multiple occasions. The first parting took place on June 6, 2005, when my son John joined me for a leadership program that I was conducting at Gettysburg. Knowing that John had just graduated from the University of Notre Dame, Dick invited us to swing by the house en route to the battlefield. It had been four years since John met Dick on the occasion of my retirement from the U.S. Army. As always, Ethel met us at the door and escorted us to the living room, where Dick was resting in his favorite easy chair. A year earlier we would have left the house to eat at a local restaurant, but those trips were mostly a thing of the past now. On this visit, Ethel had ordered sandwiches and she had also cooked a large bowl of soup. John and I only stayed for ninety minutes, as Dick was not himself that day. Still, I was honored that he wanted to share D-Day with me. This was a day that Dick usually preferred to spend in quiet reflection. As we drove to Gettysburg, I must have been saying a silent prayer, because John asked what was wrong. "John, you were looking at a dying man. Better say a prayer for Dick because I'm not sure he will see another D-Day."

A number of subsequent emails from Ethel seemed to confirm my worst fears of Dick's declining health, but the old warrior recovered. I remain convinced that the publication of his memoirs a year later gave Dick renewed desire to live. My fear had been that once the memoirs were released, Dick would lose that will. That, fortunately, was not the case. On the contrary, the serenity he enjoyed had the opposite effect. Then there were the repeated visits with my daughter Maura and my wife Mary that he always enjoyed. One visit still sticks in my mind. After Dick presented Mary and me the beautiful print entitled *Hang Tough, Bastogne 1944*, Maura lamented that Dick now liked me more than her. I mentioned Maura's concern to Ethel, who wrote back, "I assure you that Dick prefers the company of women to men, particularly young pretty ones." Now fortified by Ethel's missive, Maura was quick to inform me, "Dad, I've stolen Major Winters from you once again!" And so she had.

When Maura prepared to leave for college in Ohio, we planned another visit to allow her to say good-bye. Dick had called while we were at lunch and had left a message. "Cole, this is Dick Winters. I'm looking at the calendar here and I see you and Maura are scheduled for a trip here on September 4, [2005] and I see that you are planning to return the same day. That's quite a day." He then added, "In visiting with Maura, I have many, many good memories and I agree with you that she is quite a wonderful girl. I'd like to keep the memories alive for the future, such as the time she was with us the day we sat down and decided to write the memoirs."

The answering machine cut off Dick's message in mid-sentence, but his breathing sounded so labored that I deemed it prudent to email Ethel to ensure everything was all right before we departed home the following morning.

Ethel responded that same evening and said that Dick wasn't feeling up for a visit at this time. Perhaps Maura might want to write Dick a note telling him how much he meant to her. The letter would be in lieu of a visit. Ethel later informed me of the real purpose of her message urging Maura to write. She wrote, "These days Dick is mostly silent even with his own family. After sixty years of marriage, we know each other's thoughts. A simple nod of the head or a hand gesture are often sufficient. I think the biggest reason that he prefers to cancel your visit is that he knows he has trouble speaking and he is afraid of disappointing Maura. He is not the man she once knew and he is afraid of that. He may think it is better if she remembers him as he was." Needless to say, we respected Ethel's wishes. The fact that Dick had called indicated that he was genuinely concerned and that was sufficient for Maura and me to postpone her visit.

So as not to make Dick feel badly that he had requested a postponement, I took it upon myself to send him a brief message that read: "I hate to ask you this, Dick, but I was wondering if you would not be too upset if we postpone our visit until the semester break over the Christmas holidays. Maura doesn't really do very well saying good-bye to good friends. The past week has been very difficult for her and she is afraid she will cry if she has to say good-bye to you. 'I don't want Major Winters to see me this way,' she told me. What she prefers to do if you have no objection is to drop you a letter before she heads west. She promises to visit when she comes home after her first semester. 'Tell Major Winters

I want to see those boots again. I also want to know how he likes his memoirs. Remember Dad, he told me about his memoirs before he asked you to help him write it. And Mrs. Winters and I were the first to read the entire book before it went to the publisher.' She still thinks she 'stole' you from me. Just the other night, Maura reminded me that during my retirement dinner, you sat next to her. That meant a lot to her, Dick."

That evening Maura penned her "Tribute to a Friendship." She wrote: "When I sat down to write this, I surprisingly found a great deal of difficulty deciding where to begin, what to say, even what to think. Should I record things in chronological order or should I let my mind, as well as my writing, wander from memory to memory as they emerge in my thoughts? Should this be a formal piece or should I portray conversations, looks, and emotions in a way I would describe them to a friend on the couch? None of the answers I decided upon seemed to answer my questions. If anything, this is an honest and telling account of my friendship with a soldier seventy-one years my senior."

Maura then went on to describe her first meeting with Dick and a number of special memories before she captured the essence of her friendship:

Over the next two years, my father and I took repeated trips to Hershey. I looked forward to them in the same way I looked forward to visiting my grandparents' farm. In many ways, the Major and Mrs. Winters became like another set of grandparents. Our conversations were casual, yet they never lost the air of respect held by both parties. That was the thing about the Major. For some reason, unbeknownst to me, I think he respected me as much as I respected him. This idea was so alien to me. Winning some race in track was just about the most important thing that I had ever done in my entire life. The fact that the Major treated me like an adult made me actually feel like I was on the same playing field as all the real adults in the room. This made my trips to Hershey that much more of an honor.

She continued,

Well, five years have come and gone and we've all aged a little. I start college in about two weeks and I fear that the visits to the Major whom I still love and cherish, will be harder and harder to arrange. The conversations I once had with the Major in his office I can still find in "We Stand Alone Together," the last disc from the miniseries. More importantly, I find our conversations in the dark corners of my mind. These conversations have never and will never be forgotten. On occasion, I find my mind wandering to the first time I was in the Major's office and he showed me his jump boots. These memories keep our friendship alive and thriving. When I first met the Major, he was the famous Major Dick Winters. Well, yes, he is still famous, that's just not how I see him anymore. He is my friend, my family. I love the Major and Mrs. Winters in the same way I love my Grandpa and Grandma. I have learned more about people, life, leadership, and myself in those short visits than I ever could have imagined. In light of this, I thank Dick for a lifetime of knowledge and happiness. I feel so very blessed to have spent even a moment's time in his presence and will never forget the memories I have of one of my best friends. Farewell.

I would have liked to have seen Dick's expression when he read Maura's letter.

Ethel responded a week later to wish my daughter a happy birthday and good luck in college. Then she said, "I wanted to say that Dick and I both thank Maura for her beautiful letter. Dick carried it around for several days before he was emotionally ready to open it. I'm sure it is something he will treasure forever."

Two months later, I received a call on behalf of the band director at West Point. "Would it be possible for Major Winters to write an inspirational message to the new cadets who will form the West Point Class of 2009?" was his request. I jotted down a few words based on Dick's leadership principles and forwarded them to Sergeant First Class (SFC) Douglas Richard, who had made the initial call. Richard then penned a musical score to Dick's message. When I next visited Dick, I presented him the text and a compact disc of "Hang Tough," his message to the U.S. Corps of Cadets. He was overjoyed, especially when SFC Richard stated that "Hang Tough" was the highlight of the performance and that the new cadet class had stood up and cheered. While the band performed the score under the direction of Major Timothy Holtan, Sergeant Major Rick Gerard read Dick's letter to the incoming cadet class. When he announced Dick's name, three thousand heads turned to see if Dick was standing on the hill overlooking the amphitheater at Trophy Point. As I mentioned to Dick, "Still in shock from their first five days at West Point, your message on leadership reminded them why they had come to the U.S. Military Academy in the first place."

Three weeks later, Dick received a letter from a high school hockey coach who related a story about one of his team captains who was an exceptional hockey player and was offered an appointment to West Point. "After a few months of consternation," the coach wrote, "the opportunity to challenge himself at West Point, where he could hone his leadership skills, won out over his desire to pursue college hockey down a different path. He left Minnesota a few weeks ago to attend the initiation 'boot camp' and I received a letter from him today. He is now called Cadet Matt Hickey. In that letter, he excitedly told me about a letter that was written by you entitled 'Hang Tough' to his Class of '09 and read at their 4th of July induction ceremony. Out of the many things you covered, it was your ending that he found most profound. You told them that to be a leader, you must do two things: first, say 'Follow me' and second, simply 'Show the way.' Simple, direct, respectful—the Dick Winters approach. Matt found it quite inspirational. I just sent him a letter marveling at how you continue to serve your country—yet another lesson for us." In closing, the coach informed Dick that he was thinking of using "Show the way" as his team's motto for the upcoming year.

When Ethel left the room after I presented Dick with the disc, I leaned over to him and said, "Don't you quit on me! We are going to see this through to the end. The finish line is in sight." He merely smiled as I informed him that my greatest fear in assisting with the memoirs was that I would let him down.

Dick looked at me and responded, "I can tell by the look in your eyes that you didn't."

After I had departed, Ethel wrote me and thanked me for the compact disc, stating, "Every time he listens to it, he cries." I was sure glad that I brought a degree of happiness to Dick in his final years.

Over the course of the next several months, I continued to bring small surprises to cheer up my dear friend whenever I visited. In October he was quite pleased to see the dust jacket for his memoirs, now scheduled for publication the following February. On the cover was the official U.S. Army Signal Corps photograph of Dick in England following the Normandy campaign, when he was photographed for receiving the Distinguished Service Cross. The editor had also raised the print of the book's title and Dick's name. On the reverse cover was a paratrooper descending in full harness. When Dick saw the cover, his reaction was summarized by one word: "Wow!" He seemed so pleased with the progress of the publication process. I hoped that seeing the dust jacket would rejuvenate him and motivate him to hang on to see the finished product. I thought he looked better physically than I had seen him in several months, but I was only at the house for fifteen minutes.

On my next visit, I presented Dick with an aerial photograph of Brecourt Manor and the adjacent fields. The photographer was a Canadian admirer who'd spent $2,000 of his own money to hire a helicopter pilot to overfly the de Vallavieille farm. Dick was so pleased that he informed Ethel he intended to frame the photograph and hang it in his office. I also let Dick know that we were now within one hundred days of the release of *Beyond Band of Brothers*. Moreover, the book was now available for preorder on Amazon, and it had climbed to the three- to four-thousand-level of sales on Amazon's listing. I was delighted to tell him that the publisher had made a decision to print forty-five thousand additional copies for the initial printing.

I had hoped to see Dick on the anniversary of D-Day in 2006—it was a special time for us—but he was too ill for a visit. I delayed my visit to the following week. My concern following the visit was evident in my journal, in which I recorded: "Saw Dick Winters yesterday. He doesn't look well. I fear my old friend is entering the final stage of his life. I am so proud that in his declining years, I have been able to add a touch of happiness. He is so pleased with the progress of his memoirs that are now in their eleventh printing. Ethel informed me that the last few days have been particularly difficult for Dick. I pray that the good Lord will protect him and not let him suffer when it is his time to join his comrades from Easy Company."

Under the loving care of Ethel, Dick once again miraculously recovered, but the days when we would dine outside the house were long since over. The monthly visits continued, but I confined myself to a single hour since Dick's stamina was not what it used to be. In July 2008, I visited Dick at Ethel's invitation. "We'll be eating lunch," Ethel said, "but stop by to say hello." Unlike previous visits, the door was locked, and I thought that Ethel had forgotten that she had extended an invitation. I knocked on the door twice before she opened the door and invited me inside the house. I asked her how Dick was, and she merely moved her hand up and down, signifying little improvement.

Dick was sitting at the table in the kitchen, his once-proud head resting softly on his chest as if he lacked the strength to sit upright. Dressed only in an undershirt and shorts, he seemed a shadow of the man I once knew. A towel lay across his legs. As always, he perked up when he recognized me. His handshake was weaker than I had ever remembered. After we exchanged pleasantries, I presented Dick with the large print edition of the paperback copy of his memoirs, as well as a photograph of the new Easy Company monument near Brecourt Manor in Normandy. He said it was a beautiful monument and then inquired who had paid for it. I didn't know.

Ethel then rose and said she had something to show me. Not

finding it at her desk, she excused herself and asked that I remain with Dick while she went upstairs. No sooner had she departed than Dick turned to me. Raising his hand in a familiar gesture, he whispered, "Cole, thanks for everything."

"No, Dick. I thank you."

I was taken aback as I perceived he was bidding his final farewell. I think old warriors have a strong instinct regarding their own mortality. I thanked him for allowing me to be part of his life and I reminded him how much I treasured his friendship. Before Ethel returned with some correspondence she wanted me to answer, I reiterated that I was only a phone call away and I would take care of anything that needed to be done. "You can count on me, Dick."

He merely acknowledged my response with a smile—a soldier's bond.

I couldn't help but think this was our final meeting, but as Dick repeatedly reminded me, "No words are necessary; you can see the respect in the eyes of the men." I like to think our last glimpse into each other's eyes was testament of our enduring friendship.

Later that evening, I wrote my children and related the details of my visit. Maura wrote back, "In my mind he will always be two characters: the young, intelligent commander and the older, funny officer at your retirement. It seems like only yesterday we were going down to Hershey for Veteran's Day and Easter. Remember when we went to the Hershey's Chocolate World and we rode that ride? I think I was a freshman in high school. Wow! That was about six and a half years ago. I guess that's a lot when you are as old as Major Winters. You are very lucky you have the kind of relationship that you have had with him. He is the epitome of 'hanging tough.'"

The following day Ethel informed me that Dick's condition had deteriorated. She outlined the funeral arrangements that she had discussed with him. When the time arrived, she said, the funeral would be a family affair. A public memorial service would be held later. "Cole, I've talked to Dick, and we would like you to be the master of ceremonies of the memorial service," she added. "Any of Dick's friends who want to speak at the memorial service are free to do so. Newspapers will not be given the obituary to print until the private service is completed. It is not pleasant to think about, but it will save a lot of confusion and anguish at the time. There is no immediate danger, but be on call if I need you."

I had the distinct feeling we were talking about days, possibly weeks, not months.

To this day, I am bewildered that Dick recovered as well as he did. Without Ethel, he would not have survived very long. I thought of my own father, who passed through the same stages of infirmity in his final years. Ethel, like my mom, kept a vigilant watch over her husband. For my part, I struggled with coming up with new ideas to keep his mind alert and to keep Dick entertained. By the end of 2008, he seemed in the finest health that I had observed in four years. Things were certainly looking up.

To celebrate his recovery, I collected my most intimate memories of the times we had shared since our initial meeting a decade ago. Having put the memories into a folder, I delivered my reminiscences to Dick and Ethel in early January, for Dick's ninety-first birthday. Dick had often prefaced his remarks with the phrase "I'm thinking of the time when . . ." As we examined the folder, he smiled when he read how pleased I was when he accepted my request to preside over my retirement from the U.S. Army. "The past two days have been wonderful," he had written shortly afterward. "Thanks for bringing us all together. Always remember to Hang Tough!" And when I informed him that as Maura and I watched the HBO miniseries in the fall of 2001, she reminded me that actor Damian Lewis had done a great job, but the "real guy" was better. I concluded with my favorite memory. "Dick, I'll always cherish our many luncheons and dinners at Dafnos, Bob Evans, the Canal House, Hershey Hotel, Houlihan's, and Friendly's, to name but a few places where we laughed and solved the world's problems."

I last visited Dick Winters on October 30, 2010. Three weeks earlier, I had grasped his hand and told him how much he meant to me and that he was my dearest friend. He looked at me and directed me to "hang in there." Now, at the end of October, Dick was definitely approaching his final days. He did not look very well, and I suspected he did not have much time remaining. Ethel, too, tired easily, but her spirits were high. When Mary and I entered the house, I wondered if it would be our final visit. Dick laughed when we reminisced about the first time he had met Mary and demanded "Tell me about yourself!" I reminded Dick that to Mary's eternal consternation, he would always remain my best friend and Mary merely my best female friend. He just smiled with that familiar twinkle in his eye.

While Mary and Ethel conversed, I took the opportunity to speak to Dick in muffled tones. I think we both realized that the end was approaching, but he refused to concede defeat. "I'm comfortable where I am now. I realize my time is short, but I am at peace," Dick said. I couldn't help but think that his mind was already over that next hill, where his wartime comrades were standing at attention, awaiting their commander's arrival.

We mostly spoke about the beauty of the autumn leaves, the birds, and the flowers outside his window. As I rose to leave, I leaned over and whispered, "Dick, the country was blessed to have had you in its hour of need. I will always cherish our time together. I love you as my brother." These were my final words to Major Dick Winters.

"Don't ever change that," he responded with a tear in his eye.

CHAPTER XIV

Fallen Eagle

You will take with you the satisfaction that proceeds from the consciousness of duty faithfully performed; and I earnestly pray that a Merciful God will extend to you His blessing and protection.

—ROBERT E. LEE IN HIS FAREWELL ADDRESS
TO THE ARMY OF NORTHERN VIRGINIA

When I departed Hershey on October 30, 2010, I realized the chance of seeing Dick again was limited. How a person faces death is a true testament to his or her character. Dick Winters was no exception. Despite the warm reception that Mary and I had received, he was definitely on a downward spiral. We had planned to make our annual pilgrimage to Hershey over the Thanksgiving holiday, but Ethel wrote two days before to inform me that she and Dick were moving from their house on Elm Avenue to an assisted living facility ten minutes away in neighboring Campbelltown, just east of Hershey. There were a number of legitimate reasons for the move: her own deteriorating health, Dick now requiring more professional help, and the financial burden for in-home nursing, which had become excessive.

Still, the news came as a shock. I called and shared it with Bob Hoffman. He, too, felt that Dick was nearing journey's end. All this was reminiscent of my own father's passing. I prayed that when Dick's time came, the Almighty would take him quietly in his sleep.

Five days before Christmas, Ethel wrote a short note extending to my family her warmest wishes for a merry Christmas. She then added, "We are having tough times here. He is very weak and is in bed a great deal of the time. No visitors but family at this time. We take it day by day and he is in God's hands now." The end was obviously near. She graciously granted me plans for a short visit after Christmas, but on New Year's Day, she apologized and said the visit, albeit short, was now out of the question.

"Please cancel any thoughts of a visit next week. Dick would not want you to see him fighting his last fight," Ethel wrote. I understood her situation and hoped against hope that she would relent and allow me five minutes to bid Dick a proper farewell. She didn't and she was right. Dick and Ethel had obviously talked the matter over. Neither wanted Dick's closest friends' final memories to be of a frail, disoriented man on death's portal. Far better to remember the Dick Winters who had officiated over my retirement ceremony and to whom I had given the first two copies of his wartime memoirs. Those memories seemed so much more real now. There was so much more I wish I had asked him when I had had the opportunity. If only we could have shared one more hour or, even better, one more meal. If only I could have told him once more how much I loved him and how much I treasured his friendship. How much I now yearned to have him grasp my right hand in his and hear him say "Hang Tough!" one last time.

I responded, "I'm very sorry, Ethel. Of course, I will comply with your wishes. Know that you and Dick, as well as the children, are in my prayers during this difficult time. I love Dick as my brother. I am available for anything you need."

The following morning, I awoke to a beautiful wintry morning along the Hudson River Valley. A carpet of freshly fallen snow covered the Hudson Highlands in a scene reminiscent of a Currier and Ives landscape. My thoughts, however, turned to my friend, and I prayed that he would reach his ninety-third birthday in a few weeks. Walking to my office, I turned on the computer, as was my habit every morning, to check emails and conduct routine business.

Awaiting me was a note from Ethel.

Dear Cole.

Tell no one, but Dick passed away at 1:25 this morning. I am really happy for him since he has been suffering so. I know he is at peace with all his men. The funeral is not yet scheduled, but will be family only. A memorial service will be at the Hershey Theatre at a later time.

Love,
Ethel

I immediately expressed my deepest sympathy, writing:

Dear Ethel,

I am very sorry that Dick has left this world, but I am happy that he is now at peace and has joined his comrades. I remember my Dad kept asking Mom on his last day, 'Why haven't my shipmates come to visit me?' His last conscious thoughts were of his men. He has now joined them in eternal peace.

You and the family have my deepest sympathy. When the time comes, let me know what I can do.

I then collected my thoughts and notified my daughter and son that Major Winters had died. They knew by the tone of my voice what had occurred. "It's Major Winters, isn't it, Dad?" my daughter said. I vowed that I would honor Ethel's request and not make any announcement that might fall into the wrong hands or be picked up by the press. A promise made must be kept.

Later that evening, my daughter wrote a touching tribute. She said she was extremely sad because she realized that when my father died, I viewed Dick as an extension of my father. "He was such a good friend to you, to us. I hope Major Winters is reuniting with his good buddy Nixon up in heaven right now, sharing their old glory stories." How very perceptive! In a sense, Dick's death meant more than a loss of a close personal friend. It also represented the loss of the most visible representation to our nation's glorious past. For fifteen years, my life had literally revolved around my association with "the Greatest Generation." Now all whom I had befriended were gone. I felt as empty as when my own father passed two years earlier. Perhaps my daughter was correct when she had made an analogy between Dick and Dad. To me, Dick Winters embodied the best that was in us. My thoughts returned to a course I once taught at West Point on the Vietnam War. I used Phil Caputo's *A Rumor of War* as a textbook, and I had once heard Caputo speak about the death of a close friend with whom he had trained at Quantico, Virginia. Caputo eulogized his friend in print and said, "You were a part of us, and a part of us died with you, the small part that was still young, that had not yet grown cynical, grown bitter and old with death." As Caputo remembered Walter Levy, so I remembered Dick Winters. I loved Dick Winters for what he was, for what he stood for, and for what he shared with me.

The death of a public figure is newsworthy, and I realized that it was only a matter of time before Dick's passing would become part of the public record. I intended to keep up the charade as long as possible, but within two days, I received a call from the spouse of one of Dick's friends, asking me to verify the rumor that my friend had passed "if I were at liberty to say." I responded and merely said that the family would notify everyone at the proper time.

The following day, Tim Gray, who had organized the project to erect a statue representing America's junior leaders outside Brecourt Manor, called me and said he had received confirmation that Dick had died. Gray had sent flowers to Dick and Ethel at the assisted living complex, thanking them for letting him participate in a special project involving a monument in Normandy that was to be dedicated on the anniversary of D-Day. The facility returned the flowers and informed the florist that Dick had passed on January 2.

Other sources were beginning to pick up the story. A neighbor had spoken to a family member, and he had unwittingly confirmed the report of Dick's passing to a local reporter. A family doctor also verified Dick's demise. Word was definitely getting out. That Ethel had been partially successful in keeping the event from the regional and national news was incredible. Within a week of Dick's death, his passing was the worst kept secret in Southern

Pennsylvania. The news appeared on the Internet on January 8. And on January 10, the *Harrisburg Patriot News'* lead article announced the passing of Dick Winters.

Within days, the national news media picked up the story. NBC news anchor Brian Williams delivered a beautiful tribute during the evening broadcast on January 11. The *Washington Post* announced the passing of "a decorated Army officer whose courageous leadership through some of the fiercest combat of World War II was featured in the best-selling book and HBO mini-series 'Band of Brothers.'" The January 24, 2011, issue of *Time* magazine lamented the passing of the "beloved and humble" commander of Easy Company, whose soldiers were present for some of World War II's most climactic battles.

My friend Dick Winters was laid to rest in his family plot in bucolic Bergstrasse Evangelical Lutheran Cemetery in Ephrata, Pennsylvania, the Saturday following his death. He was a man who shunned the spotlight, and the interment was a very private exit for a very public hero. It was the way Dick would have wanted it to be—no fanfare, no honor guard, no reporters—just family members. He deserved such a peaceful start for his final journey. Dick had never sought publicity; it had been thrust upon him. His marker reads simply:

RICHARD D. WINTERS
WW II 101st Airborne
1918–2011

That same day, Ethel called and released me from my vow of silence. She said the burial was a beautiful ceremony—very private, with thirteen family members in attendance. The memorial service would be scheduled in mid-March, on a Saturday afternoon.

Not surprisingly, the Bergstrasse Evangelical Lutheran Cemetery has become a mecca for hundreds and then thousands of ordinary visitors wishing to pay tribute to an extraordinary hero who had touched their lives. The steady stream of visitors led to a torrent, and Lyman Hainley, the cemetery's superintendent, decided to build a small display case for the hundreds of mementoes left behind by the admiring public. Bergstrasse Cemetery also witnessed a renewed interest in other military veterans who were interred there, as evidenced by an increasing number of American flags over their graves. In death, Dick Winters continued to inspire the current generation long after his departure from this world.

The outpouring of grief following Dick's death was absolutely incredible. The "official Dick Winters website," official in name only since Dick never sanctioned it, recorded more than seventeen thousand hits in a matter of hours. MSN.com posted a photo-log of Dick on the front page. Heartfelt accolades and tributes arrived from producer Steven Spielberg, actors Tom Hanks and Damian Lewis, and General David H. Petraeus. Hanks's written statement was particularly poignant: "When the world needed heroes, he served in a company of heroes. In a historic time, he was both a humble witness and an honorable warrior. In the decades since, he cherished the peace he had earned with humility and integrity." Damian Lewis wrote, "It's a sad day today. Major Richard Winters, without question one of the great heroes of World War II, has died. His story, and those of the men of Easy Company came to prominence through the extraordinary HBO series 'Band of

Brothers.' I was honored to have played, no, represent him on the screen. He was unstinting in his support of the project and of me. He welcomed me to his house in Hershey, introduced me to his loving wife, Ethel, and constantly exhorted me to 'Hang Tough!' He has died quietly, in private, without fanfare, with the same modesty that he lived his life as one of the most celebrated soldiers of his generation. I will miss him, and I thank him. Currahee!"

Writing from Kabul, Afghanistan, Petraeus penned a moving tribute, expressing his deepest sympathies to Ethel upon learning of the death of her husband. Said Petraeus, "Those of us who wear the uniform today are proud inheritors of the tradition of courage, skill, and sacrifice that he helped establish during D-Day, Operation Market Garden, the Battle of the Bulge, and a host of other critical battles. We stand on the shoulders of those who came before us—and because of leaders like your husband, we stand very tall indeed."

Similar accolades followed from around the world. The city council of the Municipality of Eindhoven, Holland, expressed their sympathy as well. Writing on behalf of the mayor, the city's managing director said, "On behalf of the Municipality of Eindhoven and its citizens, we offer you our deepest condolences with the death of Dick Winters. As a young American officer he was at the head of the E Company, 506th PIR, 101st Airborne that liberated Eindhoven in 1944. We are glad that we were able to express our gratitude to Mr. Winters by presenting him the highest decoration of our city: '*Ereteken van de stad Eindhoven.*'" The director reminded Ethel that "Dick Winters and all the other liberators will never be forgotten: Each year they will be remembered at the celebration of the liberation. . . . We hope good memories will conquer the sorrow of his death." Dick Winters was such a beloved figure.

Easy Company veterans also added to the chorus of ordinary Americans who remembered an extraordinary leader. Few of Dick's men were alive to bid their commander a final farewell. Most of E Company were long deceased, patiently awaiting their commander to lead them to new triumphs. You could almost hear a paratrooper say, "It's Lieutenant Winters this time, boys. Time to move out!" Those who remained alive voiced their sympathy. Said former platoon sergeant William Guarnere, who had lost a leg outside Bastogne, "Dick always said, 'Hang tough and follow me.' When he said, 'Let's go' he was right in the front. He was never in the back. A leader personified. He was the best commander we ever had. We'd have followed him anywhere." Edward "Babe" Heffron, who served alongside Winters at Bastogne and who helped liberate Hitler's Eagle's Nest, added, "He was one hell of a guy, one of the greatest soldiers I was ever under. He was a wonderful officer, a wonderful leader. He had what you needed, guts and brains. He took care of his men, that's very important." Popeye Winn added, "It seemed as if he always made the right decision. He was a real soldier. He was one of the best. It started with him doing the right thing. I don't know how he survived the war, but he did." Another Easy Company veteran concurred, noting, "Every one of us, we'd follow him to hell. That's the type of guy he was."

I personally received ten calls, including one from Eindhoven, the Netherlands, and at least eighty email expressions of condolences. The one I treasure most was sent by Lieutenant Colonel Jamie Fischer, whom I had asked to transport Dick to my retirement ceremony in 2001, months before the first episode of the miniseries was telecast. After thanking me for giving him the opportunity to meet Dick, Fischer wrote, "Midway on my drive to Hershey and in my constant state of insufficient sleep, I was wondering why this man was so important that I would spend my day crossing hundreds of miles just to transport a World War II veteran. My doubts were quickly allayed when this gentle man stepped into my minivan and we proceeded back to New York. We talked the entire four-hour trip about leadership. Since I truly did not realize who I had with me, there were no airs, no young officer enamored by a hero, just two experienced leaders sharing stories and perspectives." Fischer said that Dick helped him focus his own thoughts on his return to the operational force following his rotation from West Point. He concluded by stating, "I received invaluable mentoring from a man who did not know me from Adam, but realized that if Cole Kingseed trusted me to drive him, my passenger must have been very important to him."

Later that evening my daughter Maura echoed Fischer's comments and succinctly summarized Dick's appeal to the public. In her exact words, "This says a lot about the man Major Winters was. I think so many people respect him because he was obviously a hero, but he was also a face to a generation of heroes. I feel so lucky, as I know you do, to have shared in his life."

Over the next two months, preparations for the memorial service consumed my time. Ethel had planned everything in advance and she handled all the arrangements to perfection. The identity of the speakers was bound to create some ill feelings because everyone who knew Dick, or thought that they did, wanted to speak. Local politicians, well-meaning veterans' associations, and a number of neighbors clamored to participate in the upcoming service in a more public role. To her credit, Ethel held firm. "I'll need your help here, Cole," she said. "I want no politicians, no one seeking self-aggrandizement, just close family friends. I intend the memorial service to be a celebration of life, not a tribute to a fallen soldier." Ethel personally selected the speakers, knowing full well that some of her decisions might alienate some potential speakers who felt they were "entitled" to address the assembly. She was certainly correct. According to Ethel, my specific charge was to "serve as the front man, to coordinate the speakers, and to ward off outside interference from those who might attempt to exploit the situation." It proved a more formidable task than I anticipated.

By mid-March everything was in order.

CHAPTER XV

Requiem

Old soldiers never die, they just fade away.
—GENERAL DOUGLAS A. MACARTHUR

The site that Dick and Ethel had selected for the memorial service was the majestic Hershey Theatre, in Hershey, Pennsylvania. Milton Hershey had his architect, C. Emlen Urban, draw up the original plans for a community center and theater in 1915. Construction and financial obstacles delayed the groundbreaking until 1929. To build the theater, six hundred skilled workers, unemployed by the Great Depression, found work as part of Milton Hershey's "Great Building Campaign." In September 1933, the Hershey Theatre opened to rave reviews.

Entering the theater through the Grand Lobby, a visitor cannot help but notice the symbolism conveyed by the artistic motifs that convey the cultural legacy of classical Greece. The Greek god Apollo, the patron of music, poetry, and the arts, driving his horse-drawn chariot pulling the sun across the sky, greets every visitor to the lobby. Hershey Theatre's Apollo is shown with sun rays shining from under a cloud. Additional symbols of Apollo, such as swans, dolphins, and griffins, the half-bird/half-lion of mythology, adorn the theater's interior design.

Passing through the Grand Lobby, one enters the main auditorium, which transports the visitor to the grandeur that characterized Venice during its golden age. Mounted above the stage is St. Mark's winged lion, the symbol of Venice. The sides of the auditorium appear to be the outer walls of a Byzantine castle, complete with balconies on windowed towers. As Milton Hershey was fond of saying, "The more beautiful you make something which people can see and use, the more enjoyment they will get out of it." Such a setting seemed appropriate when on March 19, 2011, 1,904 well-wishers filled the magnificent auditorium and balcony to capacity to honor Dick Winters, long the town's most famous resident. An additional five hundred people viewed the service from another auditorium, at the Hershey School, via a live-television feed.

My wife Mary and I had arrived the preceding evening after paying our respects to the major at the small cemetery where he was interred in his birthplace of Ephrata. There I placed a new flag on his grave and said a silent prayer that I would measure up to his expectations for having asked me to serve as master of ceremonies at the memorial service. Arriving in Hershey that night, we joined Bob Hoffman, the major's closest friend, for dinner at a local restaurant. Bob was experiencing great difficulty dealing with Major Winters's passing, but I was sure he would rise to the occasion. Together we reminisced about the numerous lunches and the laughter that we had shared over the years.

The memorial service was set to commence at 2 P.M. on Saturday afternoon. Mary and I arrived early and quickly reconnoitered the auditorium and the stage. As arranged by Ethel Winters, her niece Midge Christopher, who served as the vocalist, and I took our seats behind the podium and waited as the guests filled the auditorium. Ten minutes before the service was scheduled to begin, four of the five speakers had arrived, but Erik Jendresen was missing. Dick and Ethel had personally selected Jendresen to serve as the initial speaker since he had written the "bible" for the HBO miniseries. Where was Jendresen? Fortunately, an usher arrived and informed me he was backstage. I hurried behind the curtain, and there was Jendresen talking to Tom Hanks.

Hanks had taken a day off from filming *Extremely Loud & Incredibly Close*, a movie set in New York City at the time of 9/11, based on a 2005 novel by Jonathan Safran Foer, to pay his respects to Winters and the Winters family. As he extended his hand following a brief introduction, I said, "Well, Tom, I'm glad to meet you, but I'm particularly glad to meet Mr. Jendresen." Tom Hanks enjoyed a long history with the major. On his initial meeting, Hanks discovered that Dick Winters enjoyed ice cream, so every Christmas afterward, two gallons of vanilla ice cream arrived at the Winters home. Now he remained backstage to preclude becoming the center of attention. No sooner did he enter the auditorium by a side door, than the veterans of Easy Company stood to greet him. Babe Heffron was first to see him and yelled, "Hey, Tom, great to see you. How the hell are you doing?"

It was now time for the service to begin, and with military precision, the program commenced with an organ prelude that featured "Requiem for a Soldier," the theme from *Band of*

Brothers, followed in sequence by "The White Cliffs of Dover," "We'll Meet Again," "Theme from *M*A*S*H*," "Wind Beneath My Wings," and "Unforgettable." I next rose to address the crowd. My remarks were recorded as follows:

"Good afternoon, ladies and gentlemen.

"On behalf of the Winters family, welcome to this memorial service celebrating the life of a truly remarkable man, Major Dick Winters. I am Colonel Cole Kingseed, and I was privileged to be Dick's coauthor of his wartime memoirs, *Beyond Band of Brothers*. We have a beautiful service this afternoon and I know that you will enjoy it.

"Before we begin the service, I want to do something that Dick always treasured. Will every veteran in the audience please stand? Thank you for your distinguished service to our great country. And a special thanks to the members of Easy Company who are here to honor their wartime commander.

"Most of us remember Dick from his wartime exploits as the commander of Easy Company, 506th PIR. But today is not a remembrance of the war. You can watch *Band of Brothers* or read his memoirs, *Beyond Band of Brothers*, for that. Today we celebrate what occurred after the war, one man's lifelong quest for the quiet and the peace for which every soldier yearns.

"At times like this, it is easy to slip into melancholy, reflecting upon a life well lived, the public acclaim associated with an award-winning book and miniseries about one's life, both the notoriety and adulation of a grateful public in search of heroes and heroines.

"Dick Winters was more than that. He was my friend and my brother. Next to my father, he was the greatest man I ever met. I would have gladly laid down my life for him. I did not choose to be his friend; he chose me and permitted me entrance into his inner circle. My life is enriched one hundred–fold because he did.

"This friendship sometimes got me into trouble. You see, Dick Winters was not only my friend; he was my best friend. Normally, a man selects his spouse to be his dearest friend. Last year, my wife Mary told me that I was her best friend. I thanked her profusely, but I knew the next question that was coming. Mary then inquired if she were my best friend. Believing that honesty was the best policy and at the risk of sleeping alone that night, I responded, 'Mary, you are my best female friend. Dick Winters is my best friend.' You can imagine how that went over! I shared that story with Dick during our last visit, in late October. He grinned, laughed, and looked Mary straight in the eye and said, 'Thanks for sharing that.'

"So where do we begin this afternoon?

"In a recent commemoration of the centennial birth of Ronald Reagan, daughter Patti Davis reflected glowingly of her father, writing, 'He was not a perfect man . . . but he tried to reach higher, to understand what God wanted of him. He was a unique person who carved out a unique place in history.'

"So let it be with Major Winters. Rather than mourn for him, let us celebrate his wonderful life. So please join me for an hour and a half of unabashed nostalgia as we remember Dick Winters. And on this occasion, we salute the man, not the rank."

Midge Christopher followed my opening remarks with a beautiful rendition of "On Eagle's Wings." Local clergyman John Nagy, a personal friend of the Winters family, then delivered Bible readings from 1 Corinthians and Psalm 23. Following another reading from Nagy's wife Joan, John then read the major's favorite passage from William Wadsworth Longfellow's poem "A Psalm of Life":

> Lives of great men all remind us
> We can make our lives sublime,
> And, departing, leave behind us
> Footprints on the sands of time.

I was personally pleased with the words and songs of faith, because I knew how that faith formed the basis of Dick's strength and the basis of his character.

Next up were five speakers who shared their personal reminiscences. First was Jendresen, who related that his friendship with Major Winters began with a phone call in 1998. Enthusiastically, he had explained that his name was Erik Jendresen and that he was working with Tom Hanks to write and produce *Band of Brothers*. His specific tasks at this early stage were to collect all the materials and to conduct the person-to-person interviews because Tom and Steven Spielberg and he were setting the bar at an almost unrealistic height to dramatize what happened in the European theater of operations.

"I see," Winters replied. "How do I know you are who you say you are?"

"And so," Jendresen continued, "from the first moment of our meeting, with his first words after 'hello,' he had me thinking on my feet."

Jendresen recounted a number of anecdotes that provided him the measure of Major Winters. In his words, "I did go to Hershey. I passed a gauntlet of tests from both Ethel and Major Winters.

For the length, breadth, and scope of our relationship, which would evolve into one of the closest and most profound friendships of my experience, I could never find the wherewithal to call him 'Dick.' And he never once called me 'Erik.' From that first day in his general headquarters—his office at the top of the stairs—it was always Jendresen . . . and Winters."

Jendresen recalled that the major's first order of business— after Jendresen had taken a seat in a comfortable chair in the corner, behind which Winters had stashed the Corcoran jump boots that he had worn from Toccoa, Georgia, to Hitler's Eagle's Nest— *his first order of business* (Jendresen's italics) was to slide across his desk a letter from Shifty Powers's daughter regarding one of the few mistakes that Stephen Ambrose had made in his book, but which had caused Shifty a lot of grief and some amount of anguish. Winters's *first order of business* (Jendresen's italics) in discussing what would become a ten-hour miniseries about the men he commanded was to make sure that an accidental wrong was righted. "I think it was another test," Jendresen said. "He watched me closely as I read that letter. And later that afternoon, Winters entrusted me—gifted me—with five carefully bound binders containing all of his notes, thoughts, personal papers, and memories of his experience in World War II." As Jendresen remembered, the publication of Ambrose's *Band of Brothers* had acted as a catalyst and inspired the men of Easy Company, 506th Parachute Infantry Regiment, to reconnect, re-remember, and share even more of their memories with one another, and Winters became the nexus for much of that correspondence.

For the next six months and literally hundred hours on the phone, Winters and Jendresen worked seven days a week to get the full truth on paper. Episode by episode, draft by draft, fact-checked by Winters, tweaked by Tom Hanks. And so the 275-page opus became their collaboration—and, for Winters and Jendresen, a mutual six-month intensive therapy session. The net result was that Jendresen came to understand what it was about this man that helped win the war. He learned that Winters had had a simple yet profound insight at age twenty-four: that the most efficient and commonsense way to get through all that war was—from brutal training to Mickey Mouse bureaucratic nonsense, and through harm's way and all that one could not train for—was to pursue excellence in everything he did. "Dick Winters made it his personal quest to excel," said Jendresen, "whether it was in executing the perfect pushup or training himself to run the three miles up and down Currahee Mountain, this pursuit was his private tool, his solution. And it was that solo effort—that obsessive clarity and pure, determined, self-contained purpose—that his men observed and that caused them to follow when he said, simply, 'Follow me.' Not just through that hedgerow in Normandy and across that field in Holland under enemy fire, but follow my example, follow my commitment. And we'll get through this and we will succeed."

Following their initial six-month association, Jendresen came to understand how Winters had achieved the quality that Jendresen had identified in him but had not yet named. That night, Jendresen told his wife that Dick Winters was the most balanced man he had ever met. Balanced.

"He had to be," joked Jendresen. "This conservative Republican had married an FDR Democrat. Balanced. After the coalition of the willing invaded Iraq and the conservative voices of the United States were bemoaning France's resistance to joining the coalition forces, Winters was interviewed by the *Wall Street Journal* and he pointed out that when the Americans and allied forces liberated France in 1944, it was so that they would have the freedom to disagree with us."

Jendresen concluded his remarks with a simple tribute to the man who had redirected his life. "Dick Winters changed my life. What we shared over the course of the three intensive years that it took for *Band of Brothers* to evolve from bible to script to screen was, simply, extraordinary. And I will never forget—can never forget—the one constant . . . the single detail . . . the three words that I remember when I think of him. It was something that he said every time we spoke, every time we said good-bye. His way of signing off. After every phone call, every fact-checking, soul-searching, put-the-men-first session that we had. 'I'll talk to you in the morning,' I'd say. 'Call you around noon. I'll give you a ring and read to you what I've got . . . talk to you tomorrow . . .'

"His reply was always the same.

"'I'll be here.'

"Coming from Dick Winters, they were the most reassuring and comforting words any American—any man—could want to hear.

"'I'll be here.'

"And he will be. He'll be here . . . he'll be here . . ."

You could have heard a pin drop when Jendresen finished his remarks. But the best was yet to come. Three other speakers, all personal friends of Dick and Ethel Winters, added their memories, including Bill Jackson, the former editor of the *Hummelstown Sun* and Dick's friend for a quarter of a century, as well as a veteran of the U.S. Army's 1st Infantry Division; retired Air Force

Sergeant Major Herm Clemens, a decades-long friend who frequently accompanied the major around local military installations; and Dick Hoxworth, a familiar face in Pennsylvania's Susquehanna Valley and a News 8 and WGAL anchor for forty years. Each shared his story and each received warm applause from the seated assembly.

Jackson recounted that after fame found Dick Winters, he realized that Dick had never signed his copy of *Band of Brothers*. When Jackson took it to Dick's home and asked him to sign it, Dick jokingly advised him that it was a first edition, probably very valuable, so Dick initially kept it, handing Jackson back a paperback copy instead. Clemens called Dick "the epitome of everything good and decent in this world." He continued, "Heroes are remembered from time to time, but legends are remembered forever. Today, we salute a legend." Seeking to put Dick's place in history into proper perspective, Hoxworth stated emphatically, "In a day when people who are tall enough to dunk a basketball or athletic enough to score a touchdown and follow it up with a 'silly dance' are elevated to hero status, it's essential to remember there are true heroes" among us.

At the risk of alienating these engaging speakers, I unabashedly confess that the most touching tribute to Major Winters was given by his close personal friend Bob Hoffman. In the thirteen years that I stood at the major's side, I can safely say that there was no individual, outside his immediate family, whose friendship he valued more than Hoffman's. Dick had told me a decade ago that he had a special friend whom he wanted me to meet. That man is now my close friend, fellow veteran Bob Hoffman. In my humble opinion, Hoffman's eulogy deserves to be quoted in full.

"It was an abiding interest in the legacy of our World War II veterans, like my father, that brought Dick Winters into my life seventeen years ago, a time well before his *Band of Brothers* fame.

"A note to him went unanswered for several weeks, then one evening, the phone rang and I heard his ever so familiar voice for the first time. 'Hoffman,' he said, 'I knew who you were, but I didn't know what kind of guy you were, so I checked you out. Let's get together.' From that time on, I was Hoffman to him, he, Winters to me.

"Not given to casual friendships or causes, once engaged, he was so completely. He lived as Socrates advised, 'Be slow, slow to fall into friendship, but when in . . . continue firm and constant.'

"I had no idea that summer evening that those few steps to the phone would be the first in a journey of wonderful friendship and incredible adventure. The next decades were filled with trips to the Emmys; world premieres; visits with our president and Steve Ambrose; lectures to the FBI, military groups, and countless schools. And, of course, there was the front row seat in the making of *Band of Brothers*, the HBO series.

"But most special of all were the quiet times we spent talking in his den and favorite eating spots. It was on those occasions that the twinkle in his eye prefaced his observations of and advice about life. The same sincere interest and caring nature that characterized his relationship with those he led in war, was shared with his close friends in time of peace. Although, as I often chided him, his game face stare could sear a breach in the armor of a tank. That was not the gaze his friends ever saw.

"I will never forget the lunch when he said to me, 'Hoffman, I see you are chairing the United Way campaign again! I'd like to do something for you. Valor Studios would like me to autograph military prints. If you negotiate the arrangements, the United Way will get the proceeds.' That year a check in the name of Ethel and Dick Winters for fifty thousand dollars put the campaign over the two-million-dollar mark. To this day it is the most collected. In this, as in all things, he followed his instincts to do the right thing without regard to personal gain.

"Dick Winters's military leadership skills and tactical genius have been studied and praised by men far more experienced than this old captain of air intelligence could ever muster. But I can tell you today that his commitment and devotion to friends was every bit as impressive.

"And then there was the trip to the Emmys! Concern about his health nearly prevented his attendance. With others, I worked to make his involvement possible. He reached out to me to join Ethel and him on the journey for support. Arriving at the Philadelphia airport, he looked at me with that twinkle in his eye and said, 'Hoffman, if anyone in Hollywood calls you doctor, just go along with it.' As I raised my eyebrow, he was quick to add, 'Now, I didn't mislead anybody, but if they assume . . . well, it gets you to be with us.'

"When we arrived at the Peninsula Hotel, name cards and stationery announcing me as Dr. Robert Hoffman welcomed me! At a post-Emmy breakfast, Eric Jendresen laughed as he related that Tom Hanks had whispered to him that he was apparently the only one who didn't know Hoffman was an architect, not a cardiologist!

"I must confess I had breathed a sigh of relief when I found out that HBO had arranged for medical specialists to be in attendance at the E Company gathering, just in case any of the thirty-seven over-age-eighty veterans needed some assistance.

"Yes, as always, Winters made sure he had looked out for a friend. And his performance that weekend was wonderful.

"Dick Winters, my dear friend, you changed my life forever. Your strength of character, physical prowess, and leadership skills have endeared you to the world as the quintessential citizen soldier. Like the Roman Cincinnatus, you saw your duty, met the challenge, and returned home to find peace.

"And, as I shared with you often, I tell you now again, your mission to share the story of the American fighting man with generations younger than your own, has changed forever the legacy of your beloved Easy Company and all the veterans of every unit and every war they represent.

"In closing I recount a conversation we had several years ago. At war's end, while hunting in the Alps, Winters plucked an edelweiss flower from an Austrian mountain meadow. It was the beginning of a lifelong affection for this little white flower. He carried that edelweiss home and was proud to show it to me.

"My mother had also loved edelweiss flowers. I had designed a cemetery memorial for her, crowned by a beautifully engraved edelweiss. I shared this design with him and it made a deep impression. Last year, Winters informed me this special flower would also grace his marker. And so it is."

Before yielding the podium, Hoffman shared an excerpt from a poem that World War II veteran Harold Mohn had written to assist Bob to prepare his eulogy:

Edelweiss the mystic flower
Symbol of a soldier's power
High atop the mountain grows

Worn with pride it really shows
A man of steel and confidence
High morals and common sense . . .
Edelweiss your lovely scent
Yes, it must be heaven sent
I climbed so long to find you there
In the Alpine meadow so sunny and fair . . .
Edelweiss, yes I will save
Room for you atop my grave
You will keep me safe you see
Resting for eternity.

The major's favorite flower had always been the Alpine edel-weiss, a flower that grows high in the mountain regions of Austria, Bavaria, and Switzerland. How pleased he would have been to have heard Hoffman's remarks. And then on cue, the Hershey Theatre played the recorded version of "Edelweiss" from *The Sound of Music*. There was not a dry eye in the house as I returned to the podium to conclude the ceremony. I could not leave the stage without sharing a few favorite memories of my own.

In our many discussions in the upstairs office, Dick frequently said, "I'm thinking of the time when . . ." Now it was my turn. So as if Dick were sitting next to me, I said, "I'm thinking of the time when you, Ethel, and I first had dinner in Hershey, during the summer of 1999. After I turned left on Route 39 to return to West Point, Ethel turned to you and remarked, 'He's okay.' Dick then informed me that his files now included a folder labeled 'King-seed, Cole C., Colonel, U.S. Army' and it was up to me to make sure it was not a dead file.

"I'm thinking of the time when on a visit in August 2006, I

informed you that my only regret was not being able to join you in Europe on one of your visits to Brecourt Manor, where you led Easy Company on D-Day. You said, 'Is that right?' I then replied, 'But we have other memories.' And you responded, 'Yes, we do.'

"I'm thinking of the time when I told you that my fondest memory will always be that you have shared your memories with me, Dick. You and Ethel have opened your home to me and to my family on so many occasions. I hope in some small way I have repaid your many kindnesses. It has been my honor and the source of my greatest happiness that we have shared a decade of friendship and brotherhood. You truly are my dearest friend."

And finally,

"I'm thinking of the time when I reminisced in a letter in 2005 that our paths certainly could have crossed in 1978 when I first visited Hershey and how we might have passed within several yards of each other as I drove down Chocolate Avenue. In the same letter, I mentioned that 'Not a day goes by that I don't think of you. I don't know what the future holds for either of us, but I do know that when this old infantryman goes over the final hill, I expect to meet Dick Winters on the other side. And if I go first, I'll be waiting for you.'"

It seemed only fitting that Ethel Winters should have the final word, and she had spent a great deal of thought on exactly what she intended to say to express her gratitude to the thousands of people from all walks of life who had traveled so far to pay homage to her husband. Ethel had asked me to convey her sincere gratitude, and I stood at the podium for the last time to say:

Dick's wife, Ethel, asked me to say a few words for her today. Dick always loved this theater so much that it seemed a perfect place to remember him. Ethel finds it impossible to respond to all those who sent Mass cards and condolences.

"She wants you to know that they were greatly appreciated.

"She thanks you all so much for coming, and she apologizes for not being able to speak to each one of you today.

"Many thanks are also due for your continued friendship over the past several years and for respecting the family's privacy at such a difficult time.

"Finally, she wonders if those of you who have spoken to Dick on the phone ever noticed that he never said, 'Good-bye' at the end of the conversation. If Dick were here today, he would say, 'Thanks for coming. I appreciate your support. Don't forget to Hang Tough! See ya!'"

POSTSCRIPT

The memorial service left me emotionally drained. It took more than an hour for the theater to empty. The local television stations had covered the event extensively. Not surprisingly, the Easy Company veterans, particularly "Wild Bill" Guarnere, "Babe" Heffron, "Buck" Compton, and Sergeant "Buck" Taylor, attracted a lot of attention and requests for autographs. So did Hanks, who remembered Dick this way: "He was a great guy, a magnificent man, but very complicated. It's life-changing to meet a man like that. We had a lot of tests to pass, and if that meant being taken to the woodshed here in Hershey, we visited the woodshed at times." Hanks continued, "That visage. That look could pierce a tank."

I could not help but think that Dick would have been embarrassed with the flashing cameras and all the commotion surrounding the service. He was a proud man, but the celebrity status didn't suit him. He preferred the more mundane life, surrounded by his friends.

That evening Ethel hosted the Easy Company veterans and the speakers to a special dinner at Devon's Restaurant in Hershey. Tom Hanks, Bob Hoffman, Herm Clemens, and some of Dick's special friends were in attendance, as were Heffron, Compton, Taylor, and several other Easy Company veterans. Guarnere, who had family in town, was unable to join us. Hanks remained the perfect gentleman, posing for photographs with anyone who desired a picture. He constantly referred to me as "Colonel" and said how much he had enjoyed the service. "I have done this type of program before. It's never easy. You did a great job!"

Hanks then related an interesting story about a conversation that he had had with Dick shortly after the premiere of the HBO miniseries. When asked by Hanks what he thought of *Band of Brothers*, the major informed him, "I wished that it would have been more authentic. I was hoping for an 80 percent solution."

Hanks responded, "Look, Major, this is Hollywood. At the end of the day, we will be hailed as geniuses if we get this 12 percent right. We are going to shoot for 17 percent. And if we succeed, you need to be satisfied."

"Fair enough," replied Dick. And from that came genuine affection, tempered with responsibility to make the series as accurate as possible.

"The major was a complicated man," concluded Hanks.

Bob Hoffman, who had met Hanks at the Emmys, then escorted the actor around the room to introduce him to the forty guests whom Ethel had invited for dinner. The Winters family dined in an adjacent room. Hoffman also made a point of telling me how "very grateful" he was for my remarks. I, in turn, informed him that his eulogy was the most touching and how much Dick would have enjoyed listening to his remarks.

What a splendid evening it was!

And then no sooner than it had begun, the evening was over.

As I returned to the hotel, I thought about the person I was when I had first met Dick. Professionally, I was a highly successful army officer completing his terminal assignment, a dream assignment preparing young women and men to serve as guardians of the nation. Personally, my life was a shambles. Being a single parent, my world consisted of my two children and the close-knit community of West Point, New York. As disciplined as I was after a military career, I had trouble balancing the challenges of fatherhood and my pending retirement from the U.S. Army. Dick Winters helped me overcome those challenges. As my first marriage dissolved, Dick was always there, telling me to "Hang Tough! You'll get through it," he would say, "just Hang Tough!" Now that he was gone, I wished that I could tell him one more time, "Thanks for your friendship, thanks for sharing your twilight years with me. It has been an amazing journey, dear friend. You are and will always be my brother."

That evening I wondered if I had done a credible job with the memorial service. I thought about it the next morning as I returned to the cemetery at Ephrata. En route, I played my compact disc from the miniseries. Although never identified in the program, the theme from *Band of Brothers* is "Requiem for a Soldier." Its haunting score and lyrics begin with a lamentation for fallen soldiers. Reminiscent of the Gettysburg Address when President Abraham Lincoln so eloquently stated, "The world will little note nor long remember what we say here," "Requiem for a Soldier" proudly proclaims that warriors who have given their last full measure of their devotion "will live forever here in our memory."

The lyrics seemed even more appropriate as I stood once again at the foot of Dick's marker. I stood not so much to look, as to say something in finality to him, and perhaps to myself. As I paid my respects, my thoughts turned to an old cavalryman's ditty called "Fiddler's Green." Fiddler's Green is the mythical resting spot analogous to the Greek myth of the "Elysian Fields" where cavalry units memorialize their deceased before continuing their journey to the hereafter. And where is Fiddler's Green? According to a mariner's tale first printed in 1832, it lies "nine miles beyond the dwelling of his Satanic majesty." The cavalryman's version is slightly different. Fiddler's Green in cavalry lore lies midway down the trail to Hell, where dead souls camp and share their wartime memories.

I again envisioned those veterans of Easy Company lifting a toast to their commander who had finally made his last jump and had just arrived on the drop zone. First Sergeant Talbert was there, as were Captain Nixon, Colonel Sink, and that trooper whose name Dick had forgotten. So was Lieutenant Meehan, Easy Company's commanding officer on D-Day before Dick assumed command. Salve Matheson, who besides Dick had been the last surviving officer from Easy Company's initial contingent of paratroopers, was present as well. General Matheson had died on January 8, 2005. And also present were the faces of those paratroopers whose names history has long forgotten. In recalling Dick's words when I informed him that the publisher had accepted his memoirs and *Beyond Band of Brothers* would be released in February 2006, I whispered, "It is finished!"

Well, not quite. I still planned to fulfill my promise to record his conversations with his friends. Then and only then would *it* truly be finished.

★ ★ ★

That day has finally arrived. *Conversations with Major Dick Winters* was Dick's idea. So was telling his story by seasons since that is how he viewed his life. I was privileged to join him in the autumn of his life, the time when most men and women are more introspective, as they reflect upon the people and the events that made major impacts on their own lives. Dick urged me to record our conversations that went beyond those that appeared in *Beyond Band of Brothers*. He wanted to amplify the insights he gained when he reread his personal letters to DeEtta Almon and his wartime journals. Most importantly, Dick Winters wanted the world to know about his friends. He was not concerned if he would someday be forgotten; he didn't want his friends to be forgotten. "I won't live long enough to see the book published, but I want you to tell this story," he said. "It's that important to me. I know that you won't let me down." For better or worse, I tried to keep his essential points honest—freed from the emendations and penumbras of fallible memory. I trust that I have measured up to his expectations.

ACKNOWLEDGMENTS AND SOURCES

I would like to acknowledge the enormous help given to me in comprising this book. In a general sense, any author familiar with the story of the "Band of Brothers" remains indebted to Stephen E. Ambrose, and I am no exception. I first met Ambrose in 1994 when I attended a symposium in New Orleans on the fiftieth anniversary of D-Day. At the symposium I took the opportunity to introduce myself to a number of Ambrose's favorite veterans, including Major John Howard and Colonel Hans von Luck of Pegasus Bridge fame; Len "Bud" Lomell, who destroyed the guns at Pointe du Hoc; and Bob Slaughter, who landed at Omaha Beach. Through Ambrose, I later became acquainted with Captain Joe Dawson and Major Dick Winters, though they were not in attendance at the meeting in New Orleans. A year later, Ambrose was instrumental in the publication of my first book, on President Eisenhower and the Suez Crisis of 1956. I acknowledged my debt to Steve three years later, telling him that I hoped he was not offended when I stated I had copied his literary style. His answer was simply that he had no objections whatsoever because he had copied the style of his mentor William B. Hesseltine at the University of Wisconsin. Later Ambrose gave me some advice: "Take the word 'history' and drop the first two letters. What's remaining? You have the word 'story.' That's what I do, I tell stories, and I learned early that when you tell stories about soldiers, tell them in their own words." These stories about Dick Winters are told in that light.

As did Ambrose, World War II correspondent Ernie Pyle greatly influenced this work. I have read all of Pyle's dispatches, and Dick Winters and I often discussed how Pyle viewed combat. Pyle's *Here Is Your War, Brave Men,* and *Last Chapter* capture war from the perspective of the GI, the same way that the major saw things. In my opinion, Pyle's column "The Death of Captain Waskow" is the finest piece of combat journalism I have ever read. Given my own penchant for the infantry, it should not be surprising that I have quoted Ernie Pyle freely throughout this book. I regret that Pyle never spent time with the American airborne infantry. I know he would have liked what he saw. I guess even if you are Ernie Pyle, you can't cover everything. I can imagine the personal reward Pyle must have felt relating the saga of the American fighting men and women over the course of the conflict, because my telling the story of a single American soldier has been a rich experience.

On a more personal level, I owe an incalculable debt to Bob Hoffman, my close friend for more than fifteen years. As one of Dick Winters's intimate friends, Bob shared his memories of multiple visits to the Winters household and numerous trips with Major Winters. These excursions included accompanying the major to Los Angeles for the premiere of *Saving Private Ryan* and later for the Emmy Awards ceremony for *Band of Brothers.* Bob also shared his photographs and acted as my "sounding board" as I began compiling my own memories of a mutual friend whom we both admired. Also providing photographs was my dear friend Carol Webber, who generously gave of her time to assemble a special DVD for Dick that she titled "Moments in My Life."

I would also like to mention Colonel Kevin Farrell, U.S. Army (retired), who shared his own combat experiences in Iraq, providing me invaluable insight into the major's combat experience during World War II. Farrell not only offered constructive criticism that greatly enhanced the text, but he also prepared the text for publication. Kevin is a dear friend without whose assistance this manuscript might never have seen the light of day.

I owe special thanks to another historian, Professor Dennis Showalter of Colorado College. Showalter served two terms as the visiting professor of history at the U.S. Military Academy at West Point during my tenure as chief of military history. He remains a historian without equal and a mentor in the finest sense of the word. Aspiring and seasoned historians alike have greatly benefitted from Dennis's sage wisdom and firm guiding hand. It was through Dennis that I first learned of Lord Moran's *The Anatomy of Courage*, the classic Great War account of the psychological effects of war. As did Ambrose, Dennis insisted that a historian's first rule of thumb is to stick with the truth. Tell only what you can prove.

Three family members merit particular mention. From the first time that they met Major Winters, my daughter Maura and my son John have served as the principal motivating force behind my sharing my personal memories of the major with the public. After the release of *Beyond Band of Brothers: The War Memoirs of Major Dick Winters*, John and Maura continually inquired as to when I intended to publish my next book. When Dick Winters died in January 2011, they insisted that I owed it to Dick's memory to begin work. They were correct, but I needed time to reflect upon those memories and the man who had become so instrumental in my life. In addition to my children, I would be remiss without conveying my sincere gratitude to my beloved wife Mary, who retired from her career as a teacher to spend time with me, only to discover that my work and this book have consumed far too much of the years that we were supposed to dedicate to our retirement. Mary accompanied me on numerous visits to see Dick and Ethel Winters. She remains my staunchest supporter and my greatest source of inspiration.

Mostly, my heartfelt thanks belong to Dick and Ethel Winters, who for more than thirteen years opened their home and shared their memories. The conversations recorded here are the result of literally hundreds of hours of taped interviews, countless emails, and the personal correspondence of Major Winters. Though he did not live long enough to witness the publication of these memories, Dick's guiding hand is present throughout the manuscript.

INDEX

Index

Index

Index

Index

Index